CONFLICTING READINGS

PAUL B. ARMSTRONG

CONFLICTING READINGS

VARIETY AND VALIDITY
IN INTERPRETATION

THE UNIVERSITY OF NORTH CAROLINA PRESS

Chapel Hill and London

Library of Congress Cataloging-in-Publication Data
Armstrong, Paul B., 1949–
Conflicting readings : variety and validity in
interpretation / Paul B. Armstrong.
p.   cm.
Includes bibliographical references.
ISBN 0-8078-1895-X (alk. paper)
ISBN 0-8078-4279 (pbk. : alk. paper)
1. Reader-response criticism. 2. Criticism, Textual.
3. Books and reading. 4. Authors and readers.
5. Semiotics and literature. I. Title.
PN98.R38A76   1990
121'.68—dc20   89-37186
                                          CIP

An early version of chapter 1 appeared in *PMLA* 98 (1983): 341–52. Part
of chapter 2 was published in the *Journal of Aesthetics and Art Criticism* 44
(1986): 321–29. Versions of chapters 3 and 4 appeared in *Hartford Studies
in Literature* 16, nos. 2 and 3 (1984): 70–89, and 17, no. 2 (1985): 49–67.
Chapter 5 was published in *New Literary History* 19 (1988): 693–712.
Thanks are due to the editors for permission to reprint.

Permission has also been generously given to quote the poem
"In a Station of the Metro" from Ezra Pound, *Personae*. Copyright 1926
by Ezra Pound. Reprinted by permission of New Directions
Publishing Corporation and Faber and Faber, Ltd.

The paper in this book meets the guidelines for permanence and
durability of the Committee on Production Guidelines for
Book Longevity of the Council on Library Resources.

Manufactured in the United States of America
94 93 92 91 90   5 4 3 2 1

PAUL B. ARMSTRONG

CONFLICTING READINGS

VARIETY AND VALIDITY
IN INTERPRETATION

THE UNIVERSITY OF NORTH CAROLINA PRESS

Chapel Hill and London

Library of Congress Cataloging-in-Publication Data
Armstrong, Paul B., 1949–
Conflicting readings : variety and validity in
interpretation / Paul B. Armstrong.
p. cm.
Includes bibliographical references.
ISBN 0-8078-1895-X (alk. paper)
ISBN 0-8078-4279 (pbk. : alk. paper)
1. Reader-response criticism. 2. Criticism, Textual.
3. Books and reading. 4. Authors and readers.
5. Semiotics and literature. I. Title.
PN98.R38A76 1990
121'.68—dc20 89-37186
CIP

An early version of chapter 1 appeared in *PMLA* 98 (1983): 341–52. Part
of chapter 2 was published in the *Journal of Aesthetics and Art Criticism* 44
(1986): 321–29. Versions of chapters 3 and 4 appeared in *Hartford Studies
in Literature* 16, nos. 2 and 3 (1984): 70–89, and 17, no. 2 (1985): 49–67.
Chapter 5 was published in *New Literary History* 19 (1988): 693–712.
Thanks are due to the editors for permission to reprint.

Permission has also been generously given to quote the poem
"In a Station of the Metro" from Ezra Pound, *Personae*. Copyright 1926
by Ezra Pound. Reprinted by permission of New Directions
Publishing Corporation and Faber and Faber, Ltd.

The paper in this book meets the guidelines for permanence and
durability of the Committee on Production Guidelines for
Book Longevity of the Council on Library Resources.

Manufactured in the United States of America
94 93 92 91 90   5 4 3 2 1

For Tina, Tim, and Maggie

CONTENTS

Preface

Endless variety is possible in interpretation, but tests for validity can still judge some readings to be more plausible than others. Explaining this paradox and exploring its implications are the tasks I have set for myself in this book. Conflicting readings can occur because interpreters with opposing presuppositions about language, literature, and life can generate irreconcilable hypotheses about the meaning of a text. The role of belief in understanding makes disagreement inevitable in interpretation. But not all beliefs work equally well, and an interpreter's hypotheses about a text are accountable to various criteria for correctness. The basic presuppositions that interpreters hold must also demonstrate their effectiveness and are not beyond reasoned debate and critical examination. Literary criticism is a rational enterprise. Interpreters can defend their assumptions and their readings with coherent arguments, and they can present good reasons to justify themselves when they decide to alter their views (or when they refuse to). But the same reasons will not seem equally compelling to members of opposing communities of belief if they hold incommensurable assumptions about the matters at stake. Irreconcilable conflict is possible in interpretation, but understanding is still subject to various constraints and tests, even if these cannot conclusively settle all disagreements about how best to construe a text.

The first chapter attempts to explain the epistemology of this paradoxical state of affairs. It explains how the possibility of "strong disagreement" between readings results from the workings of belief in understanding, and it then shows how various tests for validity prevent the circular dependence of what we find in a text on what we expect and assume from becoming vicious, self-enclosed, and unaccountable. The second chapter explores the ontological consequences of this epistemology and calls for a re-conceptualization of the mode of existence of literary works. Regarding a work as an autonomous entity does not do justice to its potential multiplicity and mutability, but conceiving of texts as radically dependent on interpretation cannot account for such experiences as surprise and resistance in understanding, which suggest that a reading is an interpretation of something other than itself. In order to explain both the variability and the otherness of texts, I propose that we think of a work as "heteronomous" to its interpreters—paradoxically both dependent and independent, capable of taking on different shapes according to opposing hypotheses about how to configure it, but always transcending any particular interpreter's beliefs about it.

These problems are not limited to literary criticism. Chapter 3 calls into question the assumption that conflicting readings and interpretive uncertainty are unique to the humanities as opposed to the more rigorous, progressive, and uniform epistemological procedures of the sciences. The same processes of understanding and tests for validity are at work in both realms, I argue. Their differences are those of different epistemological communities with different assumptions and aims, but understanding in both literary criticism and science is an inherently ambiguous matter of experimenting with always contestable hypotheses and making always debatable decisions about what it seems better to believe.

One of my points in this chapter is that metaphor is crucial to understanding and communication in the sciences as well as the humanities. The fourth chapter takes this point further and explores the pervasive role of figures in the creation and construal of meaning. Metaphor is an especially important topic for a theory of interpretive conflict because the invention of new figures can contribute to the discovery of new ways of seeing. I try to show how the semantic innovations of metaphor can challenge and change prevailing interpretive conventions by manipulating habitual assumptions about how to build consistency. New, perhaps initially bewildering metaphors can multiply our ways of making sense by proposing new patterns for forging coherence, and their acceptability is subject to the same constraints and tests that govern other areas of understanding.

Chapter 5 demonstrates my argument about interpretive conflict and validity in a particular case of opposing readings, the notorious disputes about Henry James's novella *The Turn of the Screw.* My account of the reception of this controversial work is also an attempt to refute the claim of some critics, impatient with the inability of epistemology to guarantee determinate readings, that a return to history provides a way to bypass undecidable interpretive disagreements. Rather than offering a neutral ground to end hermeneutic disputes, history itself is an essentially contested area that can be emplotted differently by interpreters with opposing assumptions. My reading of the embattled reception of *The Turn of the Screw* uses history to help explain how such conflicts operate and tries to show, among other things, that disagreements about how to configure a text have the same epistemological structure as disputes about how to emplot a narrative of the past.

Disagreements about how to interpret texts are frequently paralleled by disputes about how to judge their worth. The sixth chapter attempts to demonstrate that evaluations, like interpretations, are inherently multifarious and disputable but also limited and testable. Judgment, like understanding, depends on a prior act of categorization, which establishes how the entity under consideration will be viewed. Guesses about something's kind are always subject to dispute, and readers with conflicting beliefs about literature and life may prefer opposing configurations. But typological hypotheses are not purely arbitrary, and some work better than others. An evaluation is always a judgment of something other than the evaluator, something that tests the assumptions and interests according to which it is judged.

Disputes about what to believe and value have a political dimension because they are conflicts about the distribution of power. The final chapter explores the role of power in interpretation both in the relation between interpreter and text and in the battles between opposing interpretive communities. Power is both productive and disruptive, essential to constructive work of all kinds (including the act of configuring textual meaning), but potentially destructive and distorting when force constricts free exploration and exchange. The paradox of hermeneutic power, I argue, is that it is in the self-interest of interpretive authority to limit itself in order to avoid the potentially self-undermining rigidity and narrowness of vicious hermeneutic circularity. The best interests of interpretation are served by democracy.

This book attempts to describe the field of conflicting interpretations but does not itself take a stand within it. My theory of interpretive conflict seeks to explain why interpreters with opposing presuppositions about language and human being may construe texts differently, but this theory does not endorse any particular set of assumptions or hermeneutic practices. I do not claim that my theory is neutral. Although I hope my arguments are reasonable, I do not presume to occupy a transcendent position of absolutely authoritative Reason. Throughout this book, as will be seen, I explain why I agree or disagree with different theorists about how understanding works, what sort of entity a literary work is, what criteria for validity an interpreter may invoke, and so on. I do claim, however, that my theory of conflicting readings allows for (indeed, requires) a variety of not necessarily compatible, equally defensible choices about the assumptions and aims interpreters should embrace. My theory does not prescribe for the reader which presuppositions to adopt among the many alternatives available. It hopes instead to help the reader choose more deliberately and self-consciously how to enter the arena of interpretive conflict by offering an explanation of how hermeneutic disagreement works. The choice of interpretive assumptions and aims remains the reader's own. My argument is that this choice is always a leap of faith, which logic alone cannot dictate and which can never be completely and conclusively justified.

An inescapable paradox of my project is that the argument I am making about the role of belief in understanding is itself a set of interpretive hypotheses based on presuppositions of my own about literature, language, and life. My own theory of interpretive conflict and validity is inherently contestable, as are all hermeneutic constructions, but it attempts to justify and win assent for its claims by appealing to the same criteria (inclusiveness, effectiveness, and intersubjectivity) that it contends govern all modes of understanding. My assumptions about the epistemology of interpretation do not, however, require anyone who agrees with me to choose the presuppositions I have elected to embrace in my previous books of practical criticism. In those works, as a practicing critic within the field of interpretive disagreement, I have chosen to stand alongside the phenomenologists.[1] According to the theory of interpretation I develop in the following pages, my own choice of presuppositions and interpretive practices in these other books is no less contested and no more intrinsically justifiable than the choices other critics make in deciding where to stand in the field of conflicting interpretations. In my other books I am a participant in that conflict. In this book I attempt to describe how that conflict operates.

The position that this book seeks to occupy is a middle ground between the extremes of absolutism and uncontrolled relativism. Such moderation has not been recently fashionable. Many theorists prefer to take extreme positions in the apparent conviction that such is the bolder, more difficult course. Moderation is seen as wishy-washy, an easy way out of hard dilemmas, a failure in rigor or courage. My reason for rejecting extremes, however, is that they are too simplistic to do justice to the complexities and dilemmas of our daily practice as interpreters. The middle ground I am trying to describe and defend is full of paradoxes that the simplifying logic of extremism does not adequately account for. Trying to explain them coherently, doing justice to their irreducible ambiguity without lapsing into self-contradiction, is neither safe nor easy. But it is what we need, I think, to understand the field of conflicting readings in which we as interpreters pursue our various interests and aims.

I have received considerable help while writing this book. I am particularly grateful to the many students with whom I have tested my ideas in courses on the theory of interpretation at the University of Virginia, Georgia Institute of Technology, the Free University of Berlin, and the University of Oregon. Their persistent, probing questions when my formulations were vague or faulty have helped me better understand the arguments I was trying to make, and all that I have learned from our discussions has confirmed my faith in the value of productive conflict. I am also grateful to the many colleagues and friends who have read and commented on all or part of this book. Evelyne Keitel has been, as always, a generous, rigorous reader of my work and an unfailing source of encouragement. Wolfgang Iser gave to early drafts of key chapters an extremely acute analysis, which taught me much about what it might mean to think theoretically. Robert Grudin, Paul Hernadi, and Richard Stein read the entire manuscript at a very late stage and offered good advice. I also received much-appreciated suggestions about various chapters from Winfried Fluck, Darryl Gless, Ihab Hassan, Heinz Ickstadt, Kenneth Knoespel, Murray Krieger, David Langston, Austin Quigley, Jahan Ramazani, Suresh Raval, Louise Westling, and Robert Westman. The generous support of the Alexander von Humboldt Foundation made possible two extended stays at the University of Konstanz, during which I conceived of this book and made important progress on it.

   The dedication of this book expresses a little, but very little, of what I owe to my wife and children.

Eugene, Oregon   P. B. A.

CONFLICTING READINGS

1

Interpretive Conflict and Validity

Can an interpretation ever lay definitive claim to correctness? The answer to this question is paradoxical. On the one hand, irreconcilable readings can justify themselves with equal validity. Interpreters with good reasons for their views sometimes disagree so radically that no higher synthesis can overcome their differences. On the other hand, however, literary criticism is not a free-for-all, where anything goes. Some interpretations are clearly wrong, and literary critics with different allegiances can also often say with considerable certainty that one reading is superior to another, even when both readings are permissible. The paradox here is that literary understanding is both limitless and constrained—endlessly open to unresolvable interpretive conflicts, but also bounded inasmuch as legitimate readings can be distinguished from fallacious ones (even if critics will not always agree where to draw this line). Literary criticism is a pluralistic universe in which opposing interpretations compete inconclusively for dominance, but it is also a rigorous, rational enterprise governed by strict controls on validity.

The question of how to judge the truth of an interpretation has been debated for a long time, but it has been an especially heated point of dispute in recent literary theory. Sharp disagreement divides those who argue that interpretation is limitless from those who hold that the meaning of a work is singular and ultimately discoverable. Taking as their slogan Nietzsche's contention that there is no truth but only an array of interpretations, the radical relativists insist that any text allows innumerable readings. In its most extreme form, this argument asserts that all interpretations are necessarily misinterpretations—that no standards of legitimacy can be found in the text or outside it that would pronounce any reading to be the "right" one.[1] The anarchistic, nihilistic implications of this position are more disturbing than the often playful, puckish attitude of its adherents might suggest. The dangers of denying interpretive limits have prompted others to insist that meaning is determinate. The monists support their claims variously, with appeals to the author's intention, to norms in the work itself, or to plain old common sense.[2] But they are united by their opposition to a pluralistic view of interpretation that allows for different, equally "correct" readings.

The rigidity of the monistic position is as unacceptable, however, as the nihilism of the radical relativists. Neither standpoint can account for the paradox that characterizes the actual daily practice of literary studies—the paradox that critics can have legitimate disagreements about what a text means but that they are also able to say with justification that some readings are wrong, not simply different. Contemporary criticism needs a theory of limited pluralism to explain this paradox and to chart a middle way between the anarchists and the absolutists. This book attempts to develop such a theory.[3] In this chapter I analyze the epistemological reasons why interpretive disagreements occur and the mechanisms of validation by which they are regulated. My objectives are, first, to explain why permissible readings may differ and, second, to show that criteria for validity still act as constraints and regulate claims to legitimacy even when unresolvable conflicts divide interpretations.

The Conflict of Interpretations

In order to explain why legitimate readings can disagree, we must go back to the foundations of interpretation and examine the role of belief in understanding. The first premise of hermeneutics is that interpretation is basically circular. The classic formulation of the hermeneutic circle holds that we can comprehend the details of a work only by projecting a sense of the whole, just as, conversely, we can achieve a view of the whole only by working through its parts. All interpretation consequently requires acts of faith—beliefs that compose parts into a whole, hypotheses for understanding that we check, modify, and refine by moving back and forth between aspects of any state of affairs and our sense of its overall configuration. Hence Leo Spitzer's assertion that interpretation depends on an "inner click"—a "divination" of the relation between part and whole.[4] Hence too Wolfgang Iser's description of reading as a process of "consistency-building," an ongoing quest for patterns that establish coherence among the elements of a text.[5] From the title page on, we ceaselessly and silently use the indications of details to project hypotheses about the whole, conjectures that are at first vague and provisional. Then we employ these guesses to make sense of the work's parts—just as everything new we come across helps us to refine and amplify our overarching construct (or leads us to overturn it if anomalies persistently crop up and the parts refuse to fit).

This version of the hermeneutic circle suggests three important implications for the relation between theory and practice. First, because interpretation always requires guesswork, no rules can guarantee successful hypotheses in advance. Even the most sophisticated theorists and the most practiced critics have had the experience of staring blankly at the page, waiting for its configurations to suggest themselves. Beginning students may dream of one day becoming expert enough to comprehend a novel or a poem automatically—without the hesitancy, confusion, and uncertainty of experimenting with guesses—but as they become more experienced interpreters, they will find that exegesis cannot escape trial and error. This already suggests my second point: A theory of interpretation is not a machine for cranking out readings. The practitioner of any method must start anew and try out guesses every time he or she takes up a work. Experience teaches because past acts of interpretation give us practice in guessing, but different texts demand different hypotheses. Thirdly, and consequently, no theory of interpretation can guarantee persuasive readings. Even a method that has shown itself to be very promising in the hands of some interpreters can prove ineffective when used by others.

Heidegger reformulated the hermeneutic circle to bring out its inherent temporality. As he explains in *Being and Time,* understanding requires expectations. Heidegger argues that we can interpret something only if we have already grasped it in advance through a "fore-seeing" (*Vor-sicht*) that projects and delimits a range of meanings it might have. Our interpretations turn these possibilities into actualities. To interpret is thus to lay out (*aus-legen*) an anticipatory understanding that has cleared the way for fuller, more explicit, and more refined acts of construal.[6] Phrased in the traditional language of the hermeneutic circle, Heidegger's point is that our preliminary sense of the whole gives us a particular set of expectations, which then direct our attention and which the subsequent explication of details checks, modifies, and fills in. To project a hypothesis is to anticipate a possible future. The surprise we sometimes experience in reading illustrates Heidegger's argument. We would not be surprised if we did not have expectations, a prior understanding that turned out to be unreliable.[7]

Heidegger's notion of anticipatory understanding suggests that making sense of literature involves beliefs of a more fundamental kind than the hypotheses that align parts into wholes. Every interpretive approach has its own anticipatory understanding of literature, one that reflects its most basic presuppositions. Phenomenology already sees human being as an incarnate subjectivity directed toward its objects, and so it interprets works as constructs of consciousness which display a world. Structuralism conceives of human being in advance as a mind governed by a linguistic logic of binary oppositions, and so it construes myths and other texts as logical models which attempt to resolve contradictions. As Bultmann notes, "All understanding, like all interpretation, is . . . continually oriented by the manner of posing the question and by what it aims at [by its *Woraufhin*]. Consequently, it is never without presuppositions; that is to say, it is always directed by a prior understanding of the thing about which it interrogates the text."[8] The characteristic hypotheses that a method of interpretation projects are the practical embodiment of more basic beliefs about human being, the being of the object it interrogates, and the being of the world as a whole. Psychoanalysis, Marxism, phenomenology, structuralism—each has a different method of interpretation because each has a different metaphysics, a different set of convictions that makes up its point of departure and defines its position in the hermeneutic field. If an interpreter believes with Freud, for example, that human beings are sexual animals and that literary works are the disguised expression of repressed libidinal desires, he or she will arrange textual details into configurations different from those of a Marxist critic who believes that we are social, historical beings and that art reflects class interests. To embrace a type of interpretation is to make a leap of faith by accepting one set of presuppositions and rejecting others.

I have so far chosen as illustrations kinds of interpretation that were originally extraliterary, and I have done so because they demonstrate with special clarity my point that a method's practical hermeneutic hypotheses reflect deeper metaphysical convictions. But my argument holds as well for methods that seem purely literary—like, say, the New Criticism. Although the New Critics advocated close reading unhampered by preconceptions and for the most part eschewed philosophical speculation, sticking instead to the concrete requirements of explication, it is now generally acknowledged that their interpretive practice rested on a specific set of beliefs about the human world.[9]

When Cleanth Brooks contends, for example, that "the language of poetry is the language of paradox," he might seem to be making a purely literary statement summarizing the results of numerous exegeses.[10] But the poetics of *The Well Wrought Urn* is actually an elaboration of principles that T. S. Eliot laid down in his famous essay "The Metaphysical Poets," where he claimed that "a degree of heterogeneity of material compelled into unity by the operation of the poet's mind is omnipresent in poetry."[11] For Brooks, paradox is the poetic vehicle that molds disparate, often contradictory materials into oneness. But for Eliot, poetry's powers of integration have more than aesthetic significance: He invokes them to counter a general cultural crisis caused by the prevalence of fragmentation, dissociation, and unassimilated complexity in all spheres of life. Brooks's masterful analyses of poetic paradox, therefore, are not purely literary; they carry a hidden freight of ideological commitment to the extent that his allegiance to unity in multiplicity endorses Eliot's views about modernism. This state of affairs is unavoidable, however, because there is no interpretation without presuppositions about the being of the work and the world. If we seek to understand without preconceptions, we do not escape them. Instead, we reproduce them in our interpretations, but without recognizing them for what they are—our own assumptions, not independent facts in the text.[12]

This argument about the implicit metaphysics of the New Criticism shows that the relation of part and whole in interpretation does not necessarily entail the ideology of organicism. Interpreters can choose among a variety of competing assumptions about how details typically fit together in patterns, and the belief that works of art are distinguished by a harmonious unity in which all the elements complement and complete each other is only one sort of assumption about textual configurations. Other interpreters may prefer to assume that a pattern of internal contradiction and disjunction is customary (whether attributed, for example, to psychological conflicts between desire and repression or to linguistic oppositions that refuse final resolution). The circular relation between part and whole in interpretation means only that understanding requires the fitting together of pieces into patterns, a work of construction that is inherently paradoxical because the typological hypotheses guiding it mold the evidence that in turn confirms them.

A few words would perhaps be useful here near the outset in order to clarify what I mean by the somewhat controversial term "theory." I use the word in two related but different senses, and the context always makes clear which is in force. There are "global" theories and "local" theories. A global theory hopes to explain the foundations of literature or the basic dimensions of the act of interpretation as such. My proposals about the limits of pluralism are global in this sense. A local theory of interpretation is the articulation of the assumptions and habitual ways of operating that define a particular method of understanding. In this sense there are Marxist and psychoanalytic theories of interpretation correlated to their concrete critical practices. The border between these two meanings of the word is sometimes fuzzy, however, and it is necessarily so. Every local theory about how best to do the work of interpretation has global ramifications, which touch aesthetic, metaphysical, and epistemological issues. Conversely, global theoretical statements of the sort "The work of art is X" or "Interpretation is inherently Y" commonly endorse some kinds of criticism and condemn others. For example, Iser's *Act of Reading* is simultaneously a global and a local theory; it is a comprehensive description of the reading process, but it also makes a case for a certain mode of interpretive activity.

My theory of hermeneutic conflict attempts to maintain an impartial stance allowing for any number of critical procedures.

But obviously there is no such thing as neutrality, even at the global level, inasmuch as many different ways of organizing the field of literary studies are possible. My "impartial" theory contests the claims, for example, of both absolutism and relativism (although it would permit them to continue practicing their local brands of criticism). The global and the local are different levels of discourse, however, and the importance of distinguishing between them is that the global level can be useful for clarifying the issues at stake at the local level—just as local considerations explain the practical significance of alternatives debated at a global level.

The presuppositions of any interpretive method are both enabling and limiting. They give the interpreter a place to stand from which to construe the work—a specific position of observation without which knowing would be impossible. They also provide a set of expectations with which to pose questions to a work that would otherwise remain silent, and they give guidance and inspiration to the interpreter as he or she begins to make guesses. But presuppositions are at the same time limiting because, in opening up a work in a particular way, they close off other potential modes of access. Every interpretive approach reveals something only by disguising something else, which a competing method with different assumptions might disclose. Every hermeneutic standpoint has its own dialectic of blindness and insight—a ratio of disguise and disclosure which stems from its presuppositions. To accept a method of interpretation is to enter into a wager—to gamble, namely, that the insights made possible by its assumptions will offset the risks of blindness they entail.[13]

Conflicting modes of interpretation can be classified by what they aim at and how they take their aim. For example, Paul Ricoeur divides the hermeneutic field between what he calls "archaeological" methods (including psychoanalysis, Marxism, and structuralism) and "teleological" approaches (including phenomenology and the New Criticism).[14] Archaeological interpretation is a hermeneutics of unmasking. For approaches of this kind, meaning is never on the surface; rather, the surface is a disguise, a mask that must be demystified to uncover the meaning behind it. The rule for reading is suspicion. For teleological approaches, the rule is trust. Meaning is to be found not behind but beyond—in the goals, possibilities, and values that literary works and other cultural objects testify to or try to point toward. The appropriate interpretive attitude is therefore not suspicion but openness to revelations.

There are further divergences between rival hermeneutics according to the kind of *arche* (or origin) and *telos* (or end) that they attempt to disclose. Among the great modern practitioners of suspicious interpretation, Nietzsche unmasks texts and institutions to show the will to power they disguise, Freud unearths the regressive pull of infantile fixations and unconscious desires, and Marx demystifies the seeming independence of the cultural superstructure to uncover its origins in the economic base. Similarly, although phenomenology and the New Criticism both approach a work more to reveal its values than to suspect its deceptions, they differ radically in their understanding of the object of interpretation. For the New Critics, the literary work is a self-sufficient structure of norms that an interpretation may approximate but cannot fully realize. For phenomenology, the literary work is not so much an objective structure as a meeting of subjectivities—the consciousness of the reader bringing to life authorial acts of consciousness, which lie dormant in the marks preserving them.

Interpretations conflict with each other when they embody opposing presuppositions. To what extent, then—if at all—can their disagreements be resolved? We should distinguish first between "weak" and "strong" disagreements. Some disputes involve a squaring off of critics who operate within a shared body of assumptions (two Marxists, for example, or two phenomenologists). Their battles may be vociferous, but I call their disagreement weak because it is not a dispute about fundamental convictions.

Strong disagreements may begin with differences about how to construe a particular text, but they ultimately go back to divergences between the basic presuppositions underlying the opposing methods. For example, structuralism and Marxism differ in their approach to Greek tragedy, with Lévi-Strauss viewing *Oedipus* as an attempt to resolve a logical contradiction between two explanations of human reproduction and Marx regarding classical mythology as an effort to establish an imaginary mastery over nature when backward economic conditions prevent material control. But this disagreement between interpretive strategies reflects a more fundamental conflict of belief—a conflict between the Marxist's conviction that human beings are social creatures whose nature changes with their daily practice over history and across cultures and the structuralist's assumption that human beings are linguistic animals defined by their unchanging capacity to order the universe by binary oppositions (hence Lévi-Strauss's contention that all versions of the Oedipus story, from Sophocles to Freud, are variants of the same mythic structure because all center on the same contradiction).[15]

An eclectic response to hermeneutic conflict ignores the implications of strong disagreement. A critic who borrows freely from many different methods runs the risk of introducing self-contradictions into his or her basic operating assumptions. Some presuppositions, as the dispute between structuralism and Marxism shows, exclude each other, or, when they are not mutually exclusive, they may be more or less harmonious than other combinations. Another danger threatens even philosophically rigorous, methodologically self-conscious efforts to amalgamate opposing strategies. A weak, watered-down criticism may result. The most powerful approaches to interpretation often owe their depth of insight to the radical one-sidedness of their beliefs. For example, after describing the potential for reductionism in psychoanalytic criticism, Ricoeur nonetheless warns that "psychoanalysis cannot be reproached for [its] narrowness; it is its *raison d'être.*"[16]

Among contemporary theorists of hermeneutics, Ricoeur has in fact made the most rigorous, sustained attempt to achieve what he calls "a true arbitration among the absolutist claims" of opposing systems of interpretation. He seeks to show that the theory behind each method is justified by the particular area of human experience that it singles out as its special province. In his view, "Each hermeneutics discovers the aspect of existence which founds it as method." We can then reconcile opposing methods, he argues, by resolving their theories into a unified image of human being— that is, by showing how the different modes of existence they focus on belong to the "coherent figure of the being which we ourselves are."

Ricoeur's project suffers from several problems, however, which may explain why he describes his dream of reconciliation as a "promised land," which, "like Moses," the philosopher can only "glimpse . . . before dying."[17] Not only is it the case that different theories of interpretation give a defining role to a single aspect of human being (viewing us as primarily linguistic, psychological, or social animals), but it also happens that the same aspect of existence welcomes conflicting interpretations (witness the disagreement among Freud, Jung, Lacan, and Sartre over whether the unconscious is, in order, libidinal, archetypal, linguistic, or nonexistent). And even if a method elevates one aspect of existence to a privileged status, its assumptions about that area may have for some other area implications that are incompatible with the presuppositions of other hermeneutics. Structuralism's views about language and Marxism's beliefs about society, for example, lead to irreconcilable disagreement over whether human nature is fundamentally universal or radically historical. Furthermore, theories of interpretation sometimes resist confinement within the limited realms of relevance to which Ricoeur would restrict them. Consider, for example, Freud's prolific writings about politics, art, anthropology, and religion, in which he works out the implications for other fields of his psychological assumptions about the vicissitudes of the instincts. Such encyclopedic explanatory ambitions are only to be expected, inasmuch as any presuppositions about human being, even if made at first in a limited realm, have wide-ranging metaphysical ramifications.

Merleau-Ponty argues that "all . . . views are true provided that they are not isolated." He advises that "we must seek an understanding from all . . . angles simultaneously."[18] In criticizing Ricoeur's dream of hermeneutic unification, however, I have tried to show that some "truths" cannot be brought into agreement because they rest on irreconcilable presuppositions. Some methods of interpretation are, of course, more compatible than others. Indeed, an important project for a philosophy of interpretation would be to investigate the extent to which hermeneutics can converge because their presuppositions are reconcilable—and to identify the lines across which antagonists face each other without the possibility of merger. But a single "truth" about the meaning of a literary work cannot be achieved by reconciling opposing positions in the conflict of interpretations.

One frequently encountered rejoinder from the monists is that differing interpretations must have some degree of identity because they derive from the same text. John Reichert insists, for example, that "multiple interpretations do not multiply the number of things which they are interpretations of."[19] He is right, of course, but he is also wrong because he oversimplifies the mode of existence of the literary work. The being of a text is just as paradoxical as the structure of understanding. A text is not an independent object which remains the same regardless of how it is construed. The literary work is not autonomous but "heteronomous." While a work transcends any individual interpretation, it exists only in and through its concretizations—so much so that it will cease to exist in any meaningful sense if it is no longer read.[20] Different interpretations concretize the work differently, and its identity is the synthesis of these changing construals across history and over the field of conflicting modes of understanding—a synthesis that may not be complete (and usually is not), so that the "identity" of "a work" is typically a multiplicity correlated to the many possible ways of construing "it."

Wayne Booth makes a proposal that seems more modest than Reichert's: "It would no doubt be impossible to determine precisely how *much* we share in the texts we dispute about, but we surely could not go on disputing at all if a core of agreement did not exist."[21] The metaphor of a shared "core" is unfortunate, however, because it implies an autonomous essence of textual identity. We need not assume radical textual sameness, though, to explain the possibility of literary discussion. All we need in order to exchange views are points of comparison and contrast, overlap and divergence. The name of the text, for example, and substantial agreement about the register of characters, the basic elements of the plot, and the actual language are all that we require to debate two different conceptions of *Hamlet*. There are usually areas of agreement between even the most widely divergent interpretations, but these establish only the possibility of discussion. They are not conclusive evidence of the text's autonomous essence. They allow us to exchange views, but they are not the text's "core." I can recognize a novel or a poem in a botched student essay, for example, but that does not mean that the student and I fundamentally agree about the text's meaning or that we both see the "same" text.

Some who acknowledge the possibility of multiple interpretations consider it to be a distinguishing feature of art. The attempt to distinguish the being of art is notoriously difficult, however—not least because competing hermeneutics insist on incompatible definitions.[22] Interpretive disagreement is not restricted to aesthetics, though, and art is not unique in lending itself to a variety of readings. Disciplines can be classified, in fact, according to whether they tend toward monism or pluralism. Some fields (most of the natural sciences, for example) are characterized by a high degree of unanimity about permissible assumptions and desirable explanatory goals, but other disciplines (including, among others and in addition to literary studies, psychology, economics, and philosophy) are marked by basic disagreements about such matters which lead in turn to fundamental differences of interpretation. The inability to reconcile opposing interpretations is a basic fact of professional and pedagogical life in the humanities, but it is a problem with broader epistemological and institutional horizons.[23]

Validity and the Limits of Pluralism

If the differences between rival readings cannot always be resolved, then we are left with a number of troubling questions about validity. Must we resign ourselves to relativism—with all interpretations considered equal and with no grounds available for choosing among them? Are there no standards of correctness to distinguish between legitimate and mistaken readings? (My students' version of the issue here is, What entitles Paul Armstrong to put grades on our papers?) These questions restate the traditional philosophical concern that the hermeneutic circle might be a vicious one. A self-confirming circularity would seem to threaten both of the levels of belief in understanding that I have identified—not only the hypotheses that align parts into a coherent whole but also the presuppositions that define any hermeneutic standpoint. How can we avoid getting trapped in a vicious circle where our hypotheses about the whole are vindicated by evidence they themselves have shaped in making sense of the parts? If any type of interpretation can discover only what its presuppositions open up to its view, then how can we be sure that these beliefs are trustworthy?

     In answering these questions, I will try to show that literary critics and other interpreters commonly invoke tests for validity which act as constraints on understanding and mark a boundary between permissible and illegitimate readings. But I will also demonstrate that the limits of these tests prevent them from establishing any single interpretation as the "right" one. I will argue that literary criticism is inherently pluralistic but that it is nonetheless what Stephen Toulmin calls "a rational enterprise," with standards and constraints built into its proceedings, and not a field of anarchistic free play.[24] The first test for the validity of a reading is inclusiveness. If understanding is a matter of fitting together parts into a whole, then that belief about their relations will be superior which can encompass the most elements in the configuration it projects. A part that refuses to fit is a falsifying anomaly. Critics and teachers invoke the standard of inclusiveness, for example, when they praise a reading for its "scope" and "depth" (or damn it for lacking them). The to-and-fro movement between a guess about the whole and the parts it seeks to make sense of need not become a vicious circle if we regard our hypotheses as at most provisional and remain open to indications that they need revision. According to the test of inclusiveness, a hypothesis becomes more secure as it demonstrates its ability to account for parts without encountering anomaly and to undergo refinements and extensions without being abandoned. The interpretive act may be "irrational" in the sense that it requires inspired guessing, but it is "rational" in the sense that our hypotheses must be able to withstand critical scrutiny.

Although an interpretation that is not inclusive is illegitimate, an inclusive reading is not necessarily the only "correct" one. The elements of a text can be brought into coherence in a variety of ways. Different interpretive methods based on different presuppositions can pass the test of inclusiveness with equal success. The absolutist E. D. Hirsch and the relativist Stanley Fish agree about very little, but they agree about this. Hirsch argues that the standard of inclusiveness "cannot, in fact, either reconcile different readings or choose between them. As a normative ideal, or principle of correctness, it is useless."[25] Hirsch exaggerates, however. The test of inclusiveness is indeed useful in that it can exclude bad guesses. There are limits to its effectiveness, though, because it cannot conclusively settle all conflicts between interpretations or put an end to "strong" disagreement. Fish claims that any interpretive framework can find a way of accounting for an apparent anomaly. Whenever someone confronts him with a counterexample, he explains, he looks "immediately for ways to demystify or deconstruct it" and to interpret it in a manner consistent with his presuppositions—and, he says modestly, "I always succeed."[26] Fish does not realize how close he is here to vicious circularity, but his boast shows that the test of inclusiveness cannot produce a single, definitive interpretation.

A second test—intersubjectivity—can supplement and strengthen the standard of inclusiveness. But it too is of limited effectiveness. Because of the integral role that belief plays in understanding, there is considerable hermeneutic significance to the lines from Novalis that Conrad chose as the epigraph for *Lord Jim*: "It is certain my conviction gains infinitely, the moment another soul will believe in it."[27] Inasmuch as interpretation requires us to project beliefs, our reading becomes more credible if others assent to it or at least regard it as reasonable. Conversely, the disagreement of others may be a signal that our interpretation is invalid because unshareable. As Charles Sanders Peirce points out, "Unless we make ourselves hermits, we shall necessarily influence each other's opinions; so that the problem becomes how to fix belief, not in the individual merely, but in the community."[28]

However, a serious weakness in the test of communal agreement results from the need to persuade others to assent to our convictions, be they our hypotheses about the meaning of a text or our assumptions about the best way to understand literature. Intersubjective validation necessarily entails the use of rhetoric. As an act of power designed to move others in a certain direction, rhetoric is open to abuses that may undermine the fair application of credibility as a test for legitimacy. In a modern restatement of the classical concern about the potential distortions of rhetoric, Hans Robert Jauss distinguishes between *Überzeugen* and *Überreden*—the genuine work of convincing others that one's reasons and beliefs deserve credence, as opposed to the employment of tactics to overpower others and trick them into granting assent.[29] The line between *Überzeugen* and *Überreden* is often hard to draw, but it stands as a warning that the agreement of others does not always prove validity.

If the ability to win assent suggests that a belief is legitimate, then complete and universal agreement about an interpretation would be the ultimate indication that it is correct. Such, in any case, is Spitzer's reasoning when he argues that the proper goal of literary criticism is a *"consensus omnium"*—a state of perfect intersubjectivity, with all minds at one about the meaning of a work.[30] This ideal is not finally attainable, however, because conflict between irreconcilable methods prevents unanimity. "Strong" disagreement about the fundamental presuppositions that should guide understanding stands in the way of universal consensus.

This impasse introduces some interesting complications to the test of intersubjective agreement, but it does not completely eliminate the usefulness of this criterion. Although a majority vote by itself does not decisively prove or disprove the reasonableness of a presupposition, the ability of a set of assumptions to rally a community of believers to its side is a test of its probable worth. Conversely, assumptions that cannot win endorsement probably deserve to die. Within a community of believers, the faithful accept, reject, and rank interpretations (psychoanalytic critics, for example, pass judgment on one another's work on the basis of how well each puts their shared assumptions into practice). Across the boundaries between communities, combatants attempt to prove the merits of their beliefs by winning converts. Furthermore, to recognize the other as a worthy opponent (as Marxism does, for example, in entering into a serious debate with phenomenology) is to acknowledge the credibility of his or her position. Monistic agreement about the truth does not result, then, from this second test for legitimacy; but, once again, accepting pluralism does not mean abandoning all standards and procedures for validation.

A third test is efficacy—the evaluation of a hypothesis or a presupposition on pragmatic grounds to see whether or not it has the power to lead to new discoveries and continued comprehension. In one sense, this test simply restates diachronically what the test of inclusiveness describes synchronically. Doubts should arise about the efficacy of a hypothesis if repeated anomalies interrupt the progress of interpretation, and such blockages suggest that a guess is not adequately inclusive. In another sense, though, the test of efficacy introduces something new and important because it extends as well to the most fundamental presuppositions of an interpretive method. William James argues that "we have the right to believe at our own risk" any assumption "that is live enough to tempt our will."[31] But he also warns that the actions ensuing from any set of convictions invariably have consequences, and these may rebound to cast doubt on what we believe. The presuppositions on which any hermeneutic takes its stand are not immune from practical testing. They must continually justify themselves by their efficacy. If they repeatedly fail to lead to persuasive, inclusive readings, friends as well as foes may conclude that the problem lies not with the limited skills of the method's adherents but with its assumptions. We put our presuppositions into play when we follow their guidance in interpreting a work, but we also thereby put them at risk, for our encounter with a text may defy our expectations and challenge the assumptions with which we began.

The importance of holding ourselves open to experiences that may prove our presuppositions ineffective is the reason why Peirce warns against the premature, dogmatic fixation of belief. He describes three roads to dogmatism which deserve attention because they provide a negative counterpart to the three positive tests for correctness—a set of thou-shalt-nots to accompany the interpreter's affirmative obligations in the pursuit of legitimate readings. But each of Peirce's warnings also needs to be qualified in ways that will shed further light, I think, on the relation between belief and validity.

Peirce warns first against what he calls "the method of tenacity"—"a steady and immovable faith" which holds stubbornly to its convictions in spite of any and all evidence against them.[32] This method runs the risk of solipsism by disregarding dissent from the community, and it courts a self-confirming, vicious circularity by blinding itself to potentially falsifying anomalies. But Peirce's warning must be modified because interpreters must hold to their beliefs with a certain amount of tenacity if they wish to avoid abandoning a promising hypothesis prematurely, without giving it a fair chance by struggling to solve the problems it raises. Similarly, in arguing with opposing readings and rival interpretive methods, critics must defend their hypotheses and assumptions with a degree of steadfast persistence in order to assure them of a just hearing. Interpretation requires a delicate balancing act between excessive stubbornness and overly hasty capitulation.

Peirce's warning against "the method of authority" needs similar amendment. According to Peirce, this method settles opinion by appealing to institutional sanction—to what the leaders of the community and its accepted ways of understanding allow to be true. The danger here is a tyrannical communal solipsism, which makes itself immune to the challenge of dissent and denies opposing views a fair test of their merits. But once again, authority has benefits that Peirce overlooks. In matters of interpretation, not all practitioners are equal. Some views are legitimately presumed to have a greater claim to validity because of the past performance or the specialized training of those who hold them. Teachers have the authority to grade student papers, for example, because they have successfully passed through an apprenticeship (taking oral exams, writing a dissertation) that has qualified them to receive the rights and powers of professional responsibility. This claim to authority must continue to prove itself in the classroom and in various professional forums, or else one's students and colleagues may deny it. Similarly, the institutional authority of leading members of a profession is a provisional mandate which they receive (and can forfeit) because of their intellectual authority in the field.[33]

The match between institutional authority and intellectual justification is not always perfect, but institutional sanction does not have the exclusively deleterious effect that Peirce assigns to it. Although it may discourage potentially promising but renegade innovations, its conservative force also prevents an excessively rapid overthrow of methods of understanding that have established their worth by their efficacy and their success in winning adherents. Authority may rigidify into dogmatic tyranny, but it wards off the anarchy of perpetual revolution.

Finally, Peirce's strictures against "the a priori method" also provide a useful warning that overstates the case. This method defends its fundamental assumptions by arguing that they are "agreeable to reason." Its standard of judgment is not "that which agrees with experience, but that which we find ourselves inclined to believe." Peirce protests that such a procedure removes belief from the testing ground altogether, allows the interpreter uncontrolled license, and reduces inquiry to a matter of "taste" and "fashion." The dilemma here, however, is that there is something a priori about the act of accepting any set of presuppositions as one's hermeneutic point of departure. In deciding where to place our allegiances as critics, we must choose among a variety of equally defensible alternatives. Clearheaded thinking or an appeal to com-

mon sense will not by itself show us the one right road to take.
Although the presuppositions and the results of any method must
prove their worth in the ways I have described, the choice of a
hermeneutic standpoint is inherently somewhat arbitrary. A different decision could always be justified with equal cogency.
By calling one's choice of hermeneutic allegiance "arbitrary," I
do not mean that it does not matter. I mean only that since it is a
choice we always have alternatives. It is obviously a deeply significant choice because of the wide-ranging epistemological and metaphysical implications that follow from it. In choosing a hermeneutic
standpoint, we decide how we are going to conduct ourselves, with
what kinds of objects and aims, in what sort of critical universe.
Even the monist Hirsch concedes that "the choice of an interpretive
norm is not required by the 'nature of the text,' but, being a choice,
belongs to the domain of ethics"; he insists, however, that "unless
there is a powerful overriding value in disregarding an author's intention (i.e., original meaning), we who interpret as a vocation
should not disregard it."[34] The difficulty that Hirsch wrongly mini-
mizes, though, is that "powerful overriding values" are always at
stake in the decision between opposing strategies of interpretation.
Indeed, by retreating to the ground of ethics, Hirsch must allow the
legitimacy of a choice he would prefer to condemn. Poststructuralist
critics often invoke the value of liberty in attacking the notion of a
controlling author as a debilitating restriction on the text's capacity
for signification.[35] Liberty is certainly a "powerful" ethical value
and, indeed, an "overriding" one in the eyes of many.
Ultimate ethical disputes of this kind always arise when one
reaches the fundamental principles that are in question in cases of
"strong" hermeneutic disagreement. The choice of the values one
will defend and pursue as an interpreter is always based on an
"ought" rather than an "is"—or, more precisely, it decides what one
will assume "is" the status of literary works and the human world
on the basis of what "ought" to be believed about them. Every
hermeneutic standpoint has an a priori foundation because it rests
on an ethical decision about what it is better to believe—whether,
for example, human beings are essentially historical agents or instruments of a universal logic (to recall one last time the debate
between Marxism and structuralism).
Literary criticism is a "rational enterprise," however, not only

because tests for validity act as constraints on its proceedings but also because our critical commitments can be analyzed and debated. If every method discloses some things at the cost of disguising others, then the merits and risks of its hermeneutic "wager" can be examined and discussed. A critic may prefer some kinds of insight and may find some areas of blindness tolerable; once again, what ratio between the two to accept is a matter of choice, but not of unreasoned choice. Fish may be right that "one man's reason is another man's irrelevance."[36] But interpreters are accountable to the community for the consequences of their commitments, and some wagers stand up to critical public scrutiny better than others do. The beliefs that constitute the theory implicit in any method may be ethical a-prioris, but they must still attempt to justify themselves through public debate and philosophical reflection. Critics can and do argue, for example, about whether it is better to hold with the Freudians that human beings are primarily narcissistic, relentlessly seeking fulfillment of unconscious desires in defiance of the ego's feeble attempts to tame the pleasure principle to the exigencies of reality, or to agree with the phenomenologists that human beings are defined by consciousness and freedom, by an ability to transcend limits and to embrace possibilities open to their choice.

Gerald Graff complains, however, about the inconclusiveness of such arguments: "The notion that choices *determine* norms rather than *obey* them does away with the idea that there are certain norms that *ought* to be chosen by societies and thus precipitates a radical cultural relativism."[37] Graff's demand for criteria independent of human choices can never be met. The question of what people "ought" to believe can be decided only by discussion and argument within the community. Such exchanges do not lead to agreement about a single, indubitable truth. However, they do introduce testing and evaluation into the field and thereby rescue it from the anarchy of total relativism. Literary criticism is a heterogeneous enterprise, but there are limits to its pluralism.

2

The Multiple Existence of a Literary Work

A pluralistic epistemology of interpretation requires a multiple, variable ontology of the literary work. Once again, two untenably extreme positions mark the poles between which such an ontology must situate itself. On the one hand, some relativists hold that the work does not have an autonomous existence but instead depends completely on how it is interpreted. For them, an interpretation is not an attempt to grasp something beyond itself but is, rather, a potentially boundless act of creation.[1] They deny that any pregiven constraints can limit the variety of irreconcilable meanings, values, and forms that can be ascribed to a work. For many of these critics, denying the authority of the text enhances our power to mean.[2] On the other hand, what seems to some to offer invigorating liberty and variety seems to others to threaten anarchy and nihilism. Conservative critics defend the autonomy of the work to preserve constraints on interpretation. They describe the literary work not as an endlessly mutable construct but as a pregiven entity that prescribes a right reading.[3] For them, the work must have an independent existence if we are to have standards for ranking interpretations according to how well they approach it. In this view, reading becomes the duty to recognize what is in the text and to obey the instructions embedded there.

Neither of these positions does justice to the paradoxes and complexities of our actual daily practice as interpreters. Contrary to the notion that the existence of texts depends totally on what we make of them, we typically come across abundant and powerful evidence that they are somehow "there" beyond our understanding. We find that others before us have interpreted the work, for example, and we know that it will continue to be read after we finish with it. We also customarily encounter resistance as we try out interpretations. Not all of our hypotheses work equally well, and they frequently require amendments and refinements that would not be necessary if we alone were in charge.

Nevertheless, even if all of these experiences suggest that we should credit the text with at least some degree of autonomy, the assertion of its complete independence runs into difficulties as well. The claim of total autonomy cannot account adequately for the ability of a work to inspire opposed readings. We often have radical disagreements with other interpreters which cannot be reconciled by pointing to a core of meaning common to all construals. And even over the career of any single interpreter, the meaning of a work as he or she construes it can vary greatly. The history of repeated readings is not the progressive improvement in approximating the work's pregiven norms that the notion of textual autonomy would suggest. Interpreters typically return to a work not because they did not get it right the first time or because they want to repeat an earlier correct reading but because they feel they have not yet exhausted its capacity to be understood in new and perhaps unexpected ways.

In order to resolve these difficulties, it is necessary to regard the literary work as neither dependent on nor autonomous of interpretation but as paradoxically both at once. The technical term for this state of affairs is "heteronomy." A heteronomous conception of the text acknowledges the paradox that interpretation is neither a total imposition of meaning nor a purely passive reception of it. Understanding both fixes a text's meaning and lets it emerge. Although interpretations may construct irreconcilable works according to their different presuppositions, interests, and purposes, this making is also always a finding. New methods of understanding may recompose a work in unexpected ways, but literary works can also react on interpretive approaches and compel them to revise their assumptions. This reciprocal interaction between text and interpretation requires a theory of understanding that sees the act of construal as both constructive and receptive, both actively formative and also open to otherness.[4]

Before I go on to examine the notion of textual "heteronomy" in more detail, let me briefly explain my appeal in the preceding argument to what "we" as interpreters customarily find in our everyday encounters with texts. This sort of invocation of the common experience of literary critics does not presume a truth beyond interpretation. It is, rather, an appeal to intersubjectivity—a claim to have discovered aspects of the process of understanding that other interpreters will acknowledge. Such an assertion is implicit whenever I refer to what "we" as critics typically experience. Interpreters with radically different assumptions and procedures may recognize the phenomena that I describe as intersubjectively characteristic of understanding—although not everyone will recognize them, of course, inasmuch as the inability of the appeal to intersubjectivity to achieve universal consensus is one reason why irreconcilable hermeneutic conflict occurs. This holds true at both the "global" and the "local" levels. The point at which my "we" seems alien to my reader will mark the limits of intersubjectivity, and this boundary will vary according to the reader's assumptions and allegiances. The effectiveness and the limits of the test of intersubjectivity, as I described them in the last chapter, apply as much to my interpretation of interpretation as to any act of understanding.

One of the most important characteristics of a heteronomous text is that it can be heterogeneous. A heteronomous work need not be a uniform entity but can instead be conceived of as a field of different possible meanings, each correlated to a particular method of interpretation, meanings harmonizing with each other to a greater or lesser extent (or not at all). Semantic fields of this kind may have different degrees of internal coherence. But whether or not they can be unified, fields have boundaries. A field may be multiple and various and open to new developments, but its heterogeneity is limited because not everything belongs to it. When pluralists argue that any text may have a variety of meanings, monists often reply that a text cannot mean anything and everything without losing its identity. A heteronomous conception of the work as a heterogeneous, bounded field can satisfy both of these demands. It preserves the work's multiplicity without sacrificing its distinctness.

The notion of textual heteronomy that I am proposing rests on two opposite but correlated postulates. First, every interpretation is an interpretation *of* something. All understanding is directed toward a state of affairs other than itself, even if it never reaches the object it pursues. The claim of an interpretation to make sense of its object is based on both its relatedness to and its difference from what it construes. Secondly, and conversely, texts are nothing more than objects of actual or possible interpretations. Anyone who searches for the "text itself" will find a never-ending series of construals of it. The very being of a literary work can vary radically according to the assumptions that different methods of interpretation make about what a work "is." These postulates argue that a text is heteronomous to interpretation because, paradoxically, its existence depends on how it is read at the same time that it transcends any act of understanding directed toward it.

I will develop my conception of textual heteronomy by opposing it in turn to the alternative positions. I will first show that the notion of radical textual dependence ignores crucial aspects of the process of understanding that make it an engagement with otherness. But I will then argue that to claim total independence for the work is not only to assert more than any interpreter can know but also to restrict without justification the variety of not necessarily compatible shapes that a work can assume. The last section of the chapter will attempt to clarify positively and on its own terms the chief characteristics of a heteronomous work—its paradoxical combination of dependence on and otherness to interpretation, its potentially radical heterogeneity, and its limited identity.

Textual Dependence versus Grappling with Otherness

The claim that texts depend solely on interpretation cannot account for the experiences of otherness and constraint that typically characterize understanding. The adversities that interpreters commonly encounter when they try to make sense of a work suggest that their strategies of understanding are not the only source of an interpretation. Some of the constraints that an interpreter experiences can be attributed to the instructions and restrictions that define his or her interpretive method, and this is how defenders of textual dependence often try to account for interpretive resistances.[5] But not all constraint and adversity in interpretation can be explained in this manner, because no hermeneutic is absolutely coercive. Any procedure of interpretation is a set of possibilities for understanding that cannot decide by themselves how they should be actualized and that often permit very different applications. Any set of presuppositions can support a range of different practical hermeneutic hypotheses. To learn and accept the basic beliefs of psychoanalysis, Marxism, or deconstruction about human being, literature, and interpretation is not to know in advance what hypotheses to project in order to make the elements of a text cohere. Something other than our presuppositions is necessary to enable us to focus and limit our hypotheses, and this otherness is provided by the interpreter's struggle and play with resistances that are more amenable to some guesses than to others.

Advocates of textual dependence sometimes compare interpretation to a game in which the permissible moves are delimited in advance by various rules.[6] But a game is more paradoxical than this argument suggests, and so too is interpretation. The analogy of the game suggests, rather, that to say that we interpret by applying pregiven rules does not necessarily imply that we call all the shots, as we would if the text were totally dependent on our strategies for construing it. The rules of a game never prescribe all its moves beforehand (if they did, it would not be any fun), and players must often decide which of many possible moves will maximize their advantages.[7] These calculations assume that the player is grappling with an otherness that will assert its presence by rewarding some choices and penalizing others. There may be more than one winning move—more than a single legitimate interpretation— but winning moves are identifiable because there are also losing moves. The results are partly determined by the player's actions, but they are not totally in his or her hands.

Similarly, like participants in a game, interpreters must decide how best to apply their rules for reading to handle the situation they confront, even if their sense of what that situation is will depend on the game they are playing. They may even decide to modify the rules in light of unexpected developments (as can happen in a game if an event unforeseen by the rules occurs or if the rules turn out to have disadvantages all sides agree need to be remedied). As in games, where unpredictable occurrences provide a good deal of the interest, in interpretation much of the difficulty and excitement comes from the challenge of adapting our principles and procedures to situations they did not fully anticipate.

When we employ the rules that define our hermeneutic stand-point, we apply them to a heteronomous state of affairs that may change its shape according to the strategies we invoke but that also affects and restricts the way we impose them.

The role of belief in understanding can help to clarify these paradoxes of the interpretive process—how it entails both action and reaction, both imposition and response, both the creation of new meaning and the discovery of a constraining otherness. Our hypotheses about the relations between parts and wholes actively form the text because they shape its elements into meaningful configurations. The hermeneutic circle can turn vicious precisely because the evidence supporting any hypothesis is not simply given but has already been molded by it. But the reverse move of the circle—that is, the need to work through the parts to achieve a vision of the whole—allows the text to assert its otherness. Persistent, recalcitrant anomalies can signal the refusal of the text's parts to conform to the hypothesis and can lead the interpreter to revise or to reject it. Even though a reader's schemes for understanding shape the evidence that supports them, rampant and stubborn inconsistencies can persuade even the most ingenious, tenacious interpreter to reassess his or her schemes. Such anomalies and inconsistencies are signs of the otherness of the text.

The very structure of a hypothesis suggests that the text is both dependent on and independent of interpretation. A hypothesis is both constructive and receptive because it is a guess. A supposition about the relations between parts and wholes posits meaning even as it holds itself open to confirmation, correction, or rejection by future acts of construal. An interpretive hypothesis is a wager about how a text might best be made to cohere, and a bet is a risky venture because it can be lost as well as won. For these reasons, any hypothesis is provisional. A guess is also horizonal, by which I mean that it projects expectations about what lies beyond its grasp. The horizonality of a guess is its inherent incompleteness—its inability to confirm or to refute itself without further evidence. A hypothesis is an experiment that succeeds or fails according to whether or not its predictions come to pass (and a failed experiment can often be instructive in suggesting new hypotheses to test). Interpretive hypotheses are creative constructions of meaning that respond to otherness and in turn invite that otherness to confirm, amplify, and overturn them by the way it behaves in the future. The provisional, horizonal character of a hypothesis suggests that a key moment in understanding is the decision to change our minds. We prevent the hermeneutic circle from becoming vicious by holding open the possibility of abandoning our guesses if they repeatedly produce anomalies or if other interpreters refuse them. Stephen Toulmin has even suggested that "rationality" be defined not by adherence to logic but by the judiciousness exercised in deciding whether or not to replace one set of conceptions with another—a decision that cannot be made by appealing to principles because they themselves are frequently what must be decided.[8] The revisions an interpreter must undertake can vary from minor to major. Even when the experience of construing a text confirms our most deeply held assumptions about art and the world, we can make sense of it only by continually modifying and refining our hypotheses about its meaning. But repeated frustrations in the effort to generate coherent hypotheses about texts can call into question even our basic presuppositions and demand a radical reconsideration of our habitual procedures of understanding. The choice between alternative hypotheses may not always be conclusive, since the same text can welcome opposing suppositions about its meaning, but it is a "rational" choice nevertheless, because some hypotheses show themselves more effective than others in molding a text's parts into coherence and in winning the agreement of other interpreters.

The rationality of the interpretive enterprise is called into question by those who doubt that anyone ever need change his or her views. Fish argues, for example, that "we *always* know for certain what is true (because we are always in the grip of some belief or other)" and that all beliefs are equal because "theories always work and they will always produce exactly the results they predict."[9] Because hypotheses are provisional and horizontal, however, to hold a belief is *not* to know with unshakable certainty. As William James notes, a belief is a conjecture that, as such, is not entitled to the privileges of "the apodictic words *must be*" but must settle for the tentativeness of the "hypothetic words *may be*."[10] Claiming a belief indubitable is dangerous because it can turn the hermeneutic circle vicious by preventing the emergence of possibly falsifying anomalies.

I have analyzed in detail the provisionality and horizonality of hypotheses in order to clarify one of the major paradoxes of textual heteronomy—the paradox whereby I act on the text (by projecting beliefs about it) only to have it act on me (by encouraging or discouraging them). A similar reciprocal interaction between work and interpretation is implicit in the frequently heard argument, derived from Collingwood, that the questions we ask about a text predetermine the range and kind of answers we will find.[11] Different modes of interpretation see different texts because each method poses unique questions that require their own answers. But here again the text is not totally dependent on interpretation. A genuine question does not decide completely beforehand what its answer is—if it does, it is not a serious question but an assertion in disguise (what we call a "rhetorical" question in recognition that it is not really a question). An unproductive question will be either too prescriptive or too diffuse—so narrow that it leaves open no variability in how the text might respond or so broad that the text will answer in no particular way at all. Productive questions are both pointed and open—directing the attention down some channels rather than others, but allowing a range of possible answers that may lead to new questions in an ongoing exchange. A truly interrogative question, even one motivated by specific interests and purposes, does not prescribe one right answer in advance; instead, it can be answered in a variety of ways, some perhaps totally unexpected, and surprising responses can challenge and change the line of questioning. We may always find what we seek, but it may turn out that we did not know what we were looking for.

The notion of the text's radical dependence cannot explain why understanding may lead to growth and discovery. Norman Holland argues that "each of us will find in the literary work the kind of thing we characteristically wish or fear the most."[12] But if I mold every work to fit my own desires and defenses, no experience of reading could ever teach me anything. Learning requires some challenge to my habits and convictions that compels me to change them. Hence Gadamer's forceful claim that "only through negative instances do we acquire new experiences."[13] All discovery implies some negativity—a confrontation with something not already assimilated into my world—even if the encounter expands and refines my interpretive schemes instead of overturning them. Although all understanding is guided by preconceptions, not everything we anticipate is fulfilled. Quite to the contrary, surprise is important for the very reason that texts challenge our beliefs by frustrating the expectations they give rise to.

Surprise can educate because the emergence of something unexpected points out the limitations of our view and calls on us to enlarge or alter it by inventing new assumptions. Surprise may initially cause bewilderment, inasmuch as something outside of our categories can incapacitate our interpretive faculties. But bewilderment makes growth and discovery possible to the extent that confusion is the precondition for a change in one's orientation aimed at restoring the bearings one has momentarily lost.[14] We can understand the unfamiliar only by grafting it onto the familiar, but that does not mean that we are forever confined to what we already know.

One of the main forms of discovery that interpretation offers is exposure to worlds other than our own. Henry James reports, for example, that reading literature "makes it appear to us for the time that we have lived another life—that we have had a miraculous enlargement of experience."[15] But to deny the text its otherness would prevent us from understanding how this miracle can take place. To reduce reading to self-projection is to imply that we never escape the prison of our own identity and, worse, that our monads lack windows that might at least allow us to look out at the worlds we cannot reach. In reading as in all aspects of human existence, however, the relation between the self and others is paradoxically both solipsistic and intersubjective. In explaining the paradox of the alter ego, Merleau-Ponty argues that there is "a solipsism rooted in living experience and quite insurmountable," inasmuch as "I am necessarily destined never to experience the presence of another person to himself." Nevertheless, he explains, "My experience must in some way present me with other people, since otherwise I should have no occasion to speak of solitude, and could not begin to pronounce other people inaccessible."[16] Ironically, then, our very worries about solipsism are themselves proof against it. They show that others concern us and that we are somehow with them. We must have at least partial access to the other's world in order to feel anguish that it is ultimately unattainable.

Interpretation makes other worlds available to us not by defying the paradox of the alter ego but by taking advantage of it. When I interpret a text, I do not climb out of my skin or leave my own world completely behind. Rather, I articulate aspects of myself in order to open up the world of the other. That is, I project hypotheses that reflect my presuppositions, my past experiences, and conventions I have learned. But as I deploy hypotheses that embody aspects of my own world, another world emerges before me—a world whose otherness I recognize because never have my procedures for understanding been used in quite the same way and because I often need to revise them as I go along in order to keep my interpretation moving and to accommodate what it discloses (enlarging my acquaintance with languages, conventions, and values, for example, which otherwise seem anomalous or bewildering). Although I never leave my own world, I use its resources to implant an alien world within it.

At least two different outcomes may result. My world may expand by assimilating the previously foreign ways of meaning that have been revealed to it. Or the encounter of my world with an alien world within my own being can lead to the doubling of consciousness back on itself that constitutes self-consciousness. Understanding others can promote self-understanding by differentiating more explicitly and precisely than before the boundaries and characteristics of my world by confronting me with what I am not. Or, of course, we may experience an alternation between these movements of personal expansion and self-delineation. The work is both dependent on and independent of my understanding because the world my interpretation discloses is both within and beyond me, my own product and an alien presence.[17]

Although I may find that I alone am not totally in control of what happens when I read, the assumption that a constraining otherness is the object of interpretation need not diminish the interpreter's freedom. Limits and adversity do not deny freedom but provide it with a field of play, a sphere of work, an opportunity to exercise itself. Hirsch exaggerates in his claim that "when we construe another's meaning we are not free agents" but "are completely subservient to his will."[18] Interpretation demands freedom because the projection of hypotheses requires the possibility of choice. Not only do we choose which presuppositions to adopt as the precondition for interpreting, but the act of construal itself is an ongoing selection from an array of possibilities as we experiment with alternative hypotheses for making the text cohere. If we were not free, we could not understand.

But resistance is necessary to the very constitution of freedom because choosing is not the same as dreaming and interpreting a text is different from pure imagining. Choice is meaningful only when it is a selection from a bounded set of possibilities. Each of our choices, furthermore, sets limits on subsequent choices we might make. Limits grant freedom a situation, but then freedom asserts itself in turn by giving those limits meaning in deciding how to engage them. Translated into hermeneutic terms, the constraints encountered in any interpretive situation offer our powers of understanding the chance to exercise themselves, but we are still free as interpreters because it is up to us to decide what to make of the adversities we meet. In yet another paradox of interpretation, then, we choose how to constitute the limits of the text even as the text's limits constrain our choices. The multiplicity of a heteronomous text gives evidence of the freedom of interpretation, and its boundaries attest to the limits that make freedom meaningful.

Textual Autonomy versus Radical Heterogeneity

Although the work may not be reducible to its interpretations, the claim that textual norms have an autonomous existence promises more than it can deliver.[19] Implanting standards for correctness in the text begs rather than answers the question of validity. The obvious and frequently asked question about the claim of autonomy is this: Inasmuch as we have access to the text itself only through our experience of it, how can norms within it act as a check on the validity of the very experience through which we know them? Positing an autonomous work is an attempt to step outside the hermeneutic circle, but another circularity returns: How can we know whether or not we are interpreting correctly, since the norms that are supposed to decide legitimacy are available only through the act of construal?

The claim that norms are independent defies the limits of understanding. The tests for validity are all intrinsic to the act of interpretation, and they cannot always decide conclusively between alternative readings. Some monists argue that we identify an entity seen from different perspectives by grasping a " 'structure of determination' in the object which makes the act of cognition not an act of arbitrary invention . . . but the recognition of some norms imposed on us by reality."[20] This "structure of determination" is a product of interpretation, however, rather than something outside it. We grasp an object's seemingly invariant properties by projecting hypotheses about them based on how our perspectives have so far combined, complementing and completing each other. As Merleau-Ponty argues, we assume that objects are stable and determinate because "perspectives blend, perceptions confirm each other."[21] The inclusiveness and efficacy of our assumptions about how parts combine into wholes give us evidence that our interpretations are not arbitrary, purely imaginative creations. Also, if my perceptions harmonize with what another sees from a different standpoint, my belief in their "reality" may further increase. But my assumption that some otherness is pressing upon me results from the interaction of hypotheses I myself produce.

What, however, if perspectives refuse to blend? This may signal the incorrectness of some of them because, as I have argued, incongruity is one way otherness may call on us to revise our hypotheses. But incongruity can be an ambiguous signal. Perspectives may fail to cohere not because of an anomaly attributable to the object but because of a conflict between opposing methods of understanding. Disagreement about what the object is may emanate not from the text itself but from opposing assumptions about what the proper goals and procedures of interpretation should be—assumptions based in turn on opposing presuppositions about the world, human beings, and other fundamental matters. It may not be possible to decide whether textual otherness or incompatible presuppositions are responsible for a divergence of perspectives because our sense of what a text is can vary widely according to what we believe.

The monist replies, however, that "different points of view are by no means equally right. It will always be possible to determine which point of view grasps the subject most thoroughly and deeply."[22] Adjudicating between opposing interpretations is more difficult than this claim suggests, though, because different methods of understanding may operate with different notions of "thoroughness" and "depth." For example, an exhaustive Marxian analysis of a work's involvement in the ideological structures and class conflicts of its time may seem incomplete and superficial to a formalist critic who asks how a work takes up existing stylistic conventions in order to renew them or innovate against them (and, of course, the reverse is also true). A Freudian critic may claim to have revealed a text's depths by uncovering how it appeals to repressed desires in our unconscious thanks to disguises at the level of its formal features, disguises that put our censoring faculties off guard. A Jungian critic, however, will find radically different but equally unconscious depths—not libidinal impulses, which can be disruptive if they are not held in check, but healing and redeeming forces of the collective psyche, which seek to correct the imbalances and one-sidedness of consciousness. Methods of understanding based on radically opposite presuppositions can come up with equally inclusive, effective hypotheses about a text's meaning—guesses that embody different criteria for judging a reading "thorough" and "deep." An appeal to intersubjectivity cannot decide the issue because different interpreters can call on their different communities for support.

Although the need to struggle with resistances gives evidence of the otherness of the text, the adversities that interpreters encounter will vary according to the assumptions and procedures with which they approach it. Resistance commonly takes the form of anomalies that defy the patterns in which we attempt to make the work's elements cohere. But the anomalies that arise depend on the hypotheses that the interpreter wagers. The inconsistencies and difficulties with which an interpreter struggles are resistances and challenges to the particular hypotheses he or she has deployed. Different interpreters may recognize that they are dealing with the same text because similar anomalies typically beset all or most attempts to interpret it—anomalies that have historically taken on the status of the "nub" of interpretation in that work. But some anomalies are unique to the particular method of understanding employed. They would not appear if a specific set of assumptions had not been made—assumptions that create unique opportunities but also special obstacles for interpretation.

Interpreters will not find the same norms in a work if they have different definitions of art. Different conceptions of aesthetic structure imply different instructions for how to put the work together. For example, the phenomenological theorist Roman Ingarden understands the literary work as a stratified structure whose various levels coalesce and reinforce each other over the course of a concretization in order to create a "polyphonic harmony of value qualities."[23] Readers following Ingarden's model would tend to suppress disjunctions and disruptions or to regard these as disturbances to the harmony they seek—anomalies that they should if possible overcome by discovering hidden parallels or subtle continuities that they may then value all the more highly because they are not obvious. By contrast, what these readers regard as anomalous would fit quite well into the scheme of an interpreter who regards interruption and discontinuity as primary aesthetic values. For example, the Russian formalist Victor Shklovsky defines the purpose of art as dehabitualization. He argues that "the technique of art is to make objects 'unfamiliar,' to make forms difficult, to increase the difficulty and length of perception," in opposition to the tendency of everyday understanding to reduce objects to insignificance by taking them for granted.[24] For readers who value defamiliarization, disjunctions are important because they destabilize our assurances about the world, whereas harmonies tend to reinforce established habits of making it cohere. Shklovsky's reader would consequently seek out the disruptions that Ingarden's reader would try to avoid.

The extent to which Ingarden's and Shklovsky's readers would find some works more amenable to and others more recalcitrant to their models suggests that texts are not totally malleable. Different definitions of art consequently create different canons with different rankings. But opposing methods can also rank the same works highly in their different canons, and they can assimilate these texts only by recognizing in them different structures of norms. The Shakespearean play that seems harmonious and unified to Ingarden will seem disjunctive and estranging to Shklovsky. To say that textual norms determine readings is to underestimate the degree to which different assumptions about art can lead to the discovery of different norms.

Each epistemology of interpretation has its own ontology of art, and the radical divergences that can arise in defining the being of the literary work make it ultimately impossible to reconcile all opposing readings. The ontological variability of literature calls into question the explanations that defenders of textual autonomy offer for disagreements between readings. If the standards for adjudicating how a text should be read are assumed to reside in the text itself, then the differences between interpretations must result from how well or poorly each grasps the work's norms or which portion of them each may actualize. But all conflicts between legitimate readings should be reconcilable in one of two ways: either by discovering their hidden harmony or by adding them up to complete each other's deficiencies. The problem with this view, however, is that opposing interpretations can posit different kinds of objects that cannot be reconciled through harmonization or addition.

Competing readings cannot be regarded as partial views that collectively complete each other if they are based on different notions of the being of art which refuse to coalesce. We cannot view opposing interpretations as incomplete components of a larger, more encompassing whole if each makes a different claim about wholeness which leads in turn to different standards of completeness. For example, phenomenology's conception of a work as an interplay of consciousnesses cannot be harmonized with structuralism's claim that a novel or a poem is an impersonal hierarchy of internal oppositions. Marxism's view of a work as a representation of political, economic conflicts is ultimately incompatible with the formalist's assumption that literature is a self-contained experiment with language. Fundamental ontological disagreements like these frustrate the strategy of reducing away extraneous matter in order to reveal the selfsame text beneath its different actualizations. Such a core will not exist if opposing readings attribute different modes of being to literature.

I am not arguing that opposed readings are not interpretations of the "same" text. I am trying to point out, however, that monistic assertions of the text's underlying "sameness" rest on an overly simplistic notion of identity. Consider a classic example of hermeneutic conflict: Do Mark Schorer and Samuel Hynes interpret the "same" work when they disagree about the narrator of *The Good Soldier,* one seeing a self-deceived fool who is passionless, ineffectual, and dishonest, the other seeing an innocent, all-too-trusting character who gradually overcomes his naïveté and is capable of genuine love?[25] The answer is paradoxically both no and yes: no, because they disagree about the very being of the character and their views cannot be reconciled either by harmonizing them or by reducing them to a shared essence; but yes, because their descriptions of the narrator do overlap at some points (both agree, for example, that he is an American from Philadelphia and that he was married to a woman who cheated on him) and there are enough convergences so that we do not think one critic is really talking about *Heart of Darkness* or *The Golden Bowl.*

The text they both see is the "same" not in the sense that an identical core of meaning underlies their readings or that their readings are ultimately compatible but only in the sense that there are enough similarities amid the two readings' differences for us to recognize that these critics are offering alternative interpretations of a single text and are not discussing two different novels. Rather than risk confusion, however, by claiming that they understand the "same" text, we should say that *The Good Soldier* is a heteronomous object that allows both of these opposed readings but cannot be reduced to either of them. Instead of looking for the "same" text beneath competing interpretations, we should instead regard a text as a more or less heterogeneous collection of possible modes of being—a field that is heteronomous to its various elements inasmuch as it goes beyond them even as it arises from them.

The overlaps and convergences that allow us to associate conflicting interpretations with a single work do not constitute the text's essence or core. This is the error of Booth's distinction between "data" and "danda." Beginning with the observation that "an astonishing agreement" exists "about what we might call the text's central preoccupations," Booth distinguishes between what seems "there," given, and indisputable "to all or most inquirers" ("data") and what is "accessible only to those who work within one particular theory" ("danda").[26] Although points of agreement between opposing interpretations do help to adjudicate validity and to facilitate critical exchange, Booth's distinction suggests a monistic conception of the text. The relation of data to danda implies a central stable core surrounded by more or less extraneous trappings (the very term "danda" seems frivolous and trivial as opposed to the tough-minded "data"). Only apparently a pluralistic theory, Booth's two-part model runs into difficulties similar to those that plague textual autonomy. Just as a single core-text cannot underlie opposing interpretations if they disagree about the very being of literature, so the "data" will not exactly coincide if different methods disagree about what a "fact" is. The areas of seeming overlap or convergence, which suggest that opposed interpretations are concerned with the "same" text, may be difficult to define in a way that all parties will agree to because they may dispute what counts as a significant entity or relationship.

Furthermore, some appearances of agreement may be misleading. Because the meaning of any element of the text depends on the place we assign it in the whole configuration, a part taken out of one arrangement and placed in another can change its meaning radically. A list of "facts" about which all interpreters presumably agree runs the risk of ignoring that the way any entry is understood can vary widely according to how and where it is located in what kind of whole. Although the possibility of identifying similarities in opposed readings enables us to relate them to a single work, the impossibility of translating these convergences into exact, one-to-one correspondences prevents us from regarding them as elements of a stable, homogeneous entity that is *the* text.

The mutually constituting relation between parts and wholes similarly casts doubt on Booth's distinction between "understanding" and "overstanding"—between doing justice to the "Questions and Responses Insisted Upon by the Text" (capitalized as a sign of their authority) and "impos[ing] the critic's character and interests upon a text."[27] Booth defends the propriety of overstanding but argues that understanding should come first. If interpretation entails the projection of hypotheses based on more basic presuppositions, however, then Booth's two stages cannot be separated. Interpreters cannot first respect the text's limits and then bring their own assumptions and concerns to bear because they must generate hypotheses to make the text take shape, and these will reflect their presuppositions about the kind of object they are dealing with and the goals understanding should pursue. Understanding and overstanding cannot be divided because the work's own demands emerge only in response to the questions the interpreter asks and will vary with different modes of inquiry.

I have chosen the metaphor of a "field" to describe textual heteronomy because it avoids the monistic implications of a "core." Although a field is bounded at the edges, it is not necessarily unified at the center. Objects at different points within the field may have very little in common even though they have a legitimate claim to a place within its borders. Some parts of the field may be more densely populated than others. But no position within it is necessarily privileged. Each position has its own characteristic advantages and disadvantages. Such a semantic field is constituted by the many different readings it includes but is not reducible to any one of them and transcends them all. Multiple, changing, but bounded, it is heteronomous to the conflict of interpretations.

The Characteristics of Textual Heteronomy

Conceiving of the text as a heterogeneous but limited semantic field offers an ontology complementary to the epistemology of interpretation. The work's ontology is variable because of the many different presuppositions about the being of literature which may guide interpretation, but the work's identity is bounded because not all hypotheses work equally well. The notion of textual heteronomy is necessary to account coherently for both the malleable variability and the resisting otherness of a literary work.

A heteronomous text is both determinate and open-ended. At any given moment in its history, a work's range of permissible meanings is limited. Its identity is correlated to a finite set of ways in which it is actively interpreted. The work's critical heritage belongs to its contemporary meaning but is also distinct from it in the same way as anyone's past experience is both joined to and yet separated from the present moment through its "retentional" horizon (to borrow Husserl's term).[28] But a work's semantic potential cannot be completely described or be said even to exist in determinate form until its history of reception has come to a close (the future that hovers vaguely ahead of it across the "protentional" horizon of the present). As Jauss has suggested, a particularly interesting case of potential meaning is provided by innovative works that cannot be understood at their time of production because they require conventions and procedures of interpretation the community only later develops. But such texts also suggest that Jauss is somewhat misleading in describing a work's historically actualized "potential for meaning" as "*embedded in* a work."[29] This potential can be specified only after the fact. The work itself cannot determine or foresee how later generations will perceive and respond to its demands. Reading Joseph Conrad or James Joyce may help us to understand Flaubert's use of irony and point of view, but *Madame Bovary* does not contain within itself *Lord Jim* and *Ulysses* and could not have predicted them, nor can it foresee how reading them might change the way it is understood. We discover the work's potential by experimenting with different ways of reading it, and the boundaries of these discoveries are not given in advance.

A work's meaning is relative to the time of interpretation, but it is not simply equivalent to present relevance. Historical distance does not collapse entirely in interpretation. For example, the anomalies that signal a text's resistance to our guesses frequently testify to its temporal remoteness—a pastness that requires us to adjust our assumptions and expand our horizons in order to assimilate seemingly bewildering, incongruous elements. The adversity that understanding encounters can challenge our historical imaginations, and this challenge can be a source of the pleasure and instruction on which our continued interest in a work depends. But as I have argued, the anomalies interpreters meet will vary according to the hypotheses they project, and their guesses may reflect assumptions unique to the interpreter's temporal standpoint. Even the way the text offers itself as "past," then, may differ with changes in contemporary habits of understanding. The pastness of the text is not a stable, fixed quality but varies in relation to the present of interpretation. Texts consequently endure not by presenting the same timeless face to generation after generation but by undergoing continual reinterpretation motivated by the shifting horizon between past and present. Preservation requires a heteronomous text—a text that endures in and through a changing history of interpretation, a text that is open to variations according to how it is understood but also transcends any particular moment in its critical heritage.

Because of its historical variability, a heteronomous text cannot be limited to the meanings its author may have originally intended to convey. Authorial intention is notoriously difficult to determine, not least because the notions "author" and "intention" are essentially contested concepts that opposing methods of interpretation can construe quite differently. Even if we could discover what authors had in mind, however, limiting interpretation to resurrecting their original meaning would not necessarily serve their interests and purposes. The only intention we might assign with any certainty to most authors is the wish that their work survive. But it will do so only if it demonstrates the capacity to provide enlightenment and pleasure to future generations of readers who will adopt a variety of new, unpredictable approaches to it. As Gadamer points out, later generations will "understand in a different way, if [they] understand at all."[30] If authors were to realize this, they could *intend* that their original meaning be transcended so that their work might be preserved. Even Hirsch, the defender of authorial intention, acknowledges that "for some genres of texts the author submits to the convention that his willed implications must go far beyond what he explicitly knows." Although Hirsch is referring here to legal texts, it is not clear why the same convention should not hold for literature.[31] An author can communicate with future generations only if the work goes beyond his or her original intentions. A work paradoxically (and heteronomously) depends on those intentions to bring it into being even as it transcends them by surviving after they are gone, perhaps even irrecoverable.

The notion of textual heteronomy also helps to explain why readers with different interpretations can nevertheless communicate. The argument that a work's meaning can vary widely often encounters the objection that such instability would make communication about it impossible. We can talk productively, this objection claims, only if we share an understanding of what it is we are discussing. Hirsch phrases this position most provocatively when he argues that all who disagree with his assertion that meaning is determinate are guilty of a self-contradiction because they must have grasped his meaning determinately in order to judge it incorrect. Determinacy, Hirsch argues, "is the minimum requirement for shareability."[32] As Iser notes, however, "Indeterminacy is a prerequisite for dyadic interaction"; after all, he argues, "One only communicates that which is *not* already shared by sender and receiver."[33] Hirsch has transformed a goal of communication into its precondition. If we already determinately understood each other or the object we are discussing, we would have less reason to talk (and indeed, when interlocutors say they disagree with me, I assume they have *not* understood my meaning and consequently try to give a fuller, clearer explanation of it). What the speaker and hearer do not have in common is just as important as what they share for making communication possible and necessary. Prior agreement about the object is not necessary for exchange but may instead make it superfluous.

Interpreters who understand a text differently can communicate as long as their readings have enough overlap and resemblance to make comparison possible—and enough dissonance and disjunction to make it seem useful and important. Either total agreement or blind antagonism will kill critical debate—an exchange usually characterized by both mutual misunderstanding and shared comprehension in shifting, variable combinations. Rather than making communication impossible, viewing the text as a heterogeneous ensemble of readings (some more similar, others more remote) explains why critical exchange takes place, why some interpreters have more to discuss than others do (either because their agreements offer important points of confirmation or because their disagreements provide a provocative challenge), and why communication sometimes never gets started or soon breaks down.

Interpreters derive different benefits from conversations within and across the boundaries of their interpretive community. Fish suggests too solipsistic a view of communal relations, however, when he claims that "you will agree with me (that is, understand) only if you already agree with me."[34] Although interpreters with mutually exclusive presuppositions may never persuade each other to see things the same way, they can still converse and profit from the exchange. Even within a community of like-minded interpreters, there must be some differences of opinion for discussion to result in the refinement, correction, or extension of the assumptions they hold in common. Conversations with members of opposing communities can compel us to reassess and revise our beliefs by presenting challenging questions from surprising perspectives or by giving examples of other kinds of competence that we may openly admire or secretly envy. Debates between opposing interpretive schools do not usually result in consensus, victory for one side, or the conversion of the other. But even when such encounters do not lead either party to modify its assumptions, benefits can accrue to both sides—sharper recognition, for example, of each community's central commitments, what they imply, and why they prevent agreement with some other perspectives. In addition to promoting the self-consciousness of the participants, such debates also help to preserve the literary work by testifying to its power to mean.

A heteronomous work is both bounded and internally diverse because it is an intersubjective construct. Not only the relations but also the disjunctions among its elements testify to the paradoxes of intersubjectivity. Just as I am "with" other people inasmuch as I sense that we occupy the same world despite the divergences between our perspectives, so the most distant points within a work's semantic field still belong together. Conflicting interpretations of a text are still related enough that we can recognize them as belonging to the same critical heritage, the same history of reception, the same ongoing dialogue about how to construe it. Illegitimate interpretations are pronounced private and unshareable by being barred from entering this dialogue as serious interlocutors with a claim to be heard, which others can recognize even if they are not persuaded by it. But just as I can never see the world as another perceives it, so the conflicting views in the debate about a text remain irreducible and somewhat opaque to each other. If a work's semantic field can never be perfectly, finally unified, one reason is that complete intersubjective transparency can never be achieved.

A heteronomous text contains many incompatible readings within its boundaries, but this is not the same as eclecticism. No single interpreter can simultaneously combine all the different ways in which a work may be legitimately construed. Mergers between conflicting interpretive standpoints can sometimes occur and may indeed productively counterbalance each method's deficiencies. But when basic disagreements about what to assume about literature, meaning, and human being divide interpretive approaches, an eclectic combination of them may create more difficulties than it resolves. Amalgamating opposing methods may introduce self-contradictions into the interpreter's assumptions and thereby prevent him or her from generating self-consistent hypotheses about a work. Anomalies may arise, for example, which testify not to the otherness of the work but to inconsistencies in the interpreter's own presuppositions (although one may not be able to see this difference until an eagle-eyed colleague or reviewer points it out). Or eclectic interpreters may find themselves at an impasse because their contradictory assumptions suggest contradictory hypotheses without providing criteria for choosing between them. Even when such mergers are productive, however, the result is a new position within the field of conflicting interpretations and not an end to disagreement. Eclecticism does not provide a backdoor route to omniscience. The work still transcends the most eclectic interpretation of it.

The main characteristic of a heteronomous text is that it is both limited and potentially inexhaustible. Its semantic field is bounded because a work does not welcome any and all interpretive hypotheses. Some guesses about a text's meaning meet more resistance and generate more anomalies than others do. But a work is nevertheless unpredictably variable because many different, incompatible hypotheses can make its parts cohere by invoking different notions of consistency and completeness.

Is a heterogeneous, changeable field sufficiently distinct to have an identity? Not according to Hirsch, who complains that "an inexhaustible array of possibilities . . . is nothing in particular at all," whereas "a determinate entity is what it is and is not another thing."[35] A field has boundaries, however, which identify it as itself and not something else, even if we cannot account for everything that might occur within it—or for how its boundaries might change. Even Hirsch admits that "the broad genre is a loose family group."[36] We may not be able to give a unified, comprehensive definition of the "novel," for example, but we can still tell it apart from the "lyric" in most cases. We do not require determinacy in order to distinguish identity, then, and identity may be variable and open to change. By the same token, even though we cannot assign a single, authoritative meaning to an especially heterogeneous work like *The Turn of the Screw,* we can still differentiate it from another equally volatile work like *Lord Jim.* All interpreters may not agree where and how to draw these lines, but a dispute about the boundary between two fields does not prevent us from recognizing that they are different. A text is a variable entity that may undergo ever-unexpected transformations, but each text's multiplicity is uniquely its own. Paradoxical in its mode of existence, a literary work is both one and many.

Understanding and Truth in the Two Cultures

Are the processes by which we make sense of a novel or a poem unique to literary interpretation, or are they common to other areas of understanding as well? I have frequently spoken as if literary understanding shares the same basic characteristics of all knowledge and perception, but this is not a claim to which everyone would immediately accede. The best way to substantiate it is perhaps to compare the activity of interpreting texts to the pursuit of knowledge in the natural sciences, the mode of inquiry seemingly most remote from humanistic understanding. The conventional wisdom in both the humanities and the natural sciences has long held that the two fields have incommensurable methods of understanding and radically different standards of truth.

For example, literary understanding is widely considered to be intuitive and subjective, with the implication that its findings can never be conclusively proved. By contrast, science is regarded as empirical and objective, with indubitable procedures of verification. Progress is consequently possible in the sciences, it is said, but not in the humanities. Scientists are thought to pay for this privilege, however, by submitting themselves to a rigid methodological lockstep that prohibits individual expression, whereas the humanities allow conflicting points of view and creative eccentricity. Similarly, literary criticism is presumed to encourage an inventive, metaphorical use of language analogous to its objects of study, whereas the sciences are said to employ a transparently referential, unambiguous notation. This dualism has been challenged in some quarters, but it is still deeply ingrained in the temperament, worldview, and self-understanding of members of both of the so-called two cultures.[1]

Is this series of oppositions an accurate depiction of the epistemological conditions governing the two fields? Or is the traditional polarization of the humanities and the sciences based in some measure on superstition? Are the methods of understanding and procedures of validation that they use fundamentally different, or do they employ the same interpretive operations for different purposes?

The classic formulation of the opposition between the humanities and the natural sciences is Wilhelm Dilthey's contrast between the *Geisteswissenschaften* and the *Naturwissenschaften*. Although Dilthey acknowledges that "the elementary logical operations which occur in the sciences and the human studies are, of course, the same" (he has in mind "induction, analysis, construction, and comparison"), he claims that "the methods of studying mental life, history, and society differ greatly from those used to acquire knowledge of nature." The natural sciences "deal with facts which present themselves to consciousness as external and separate phenomena," and scientists seek to uncover "connections within nature through inferences" and "hypotheses." Science projects theories about states of affairs in the external world, independent of the mind, in order to determine their logical order and causal relations. By contrast, the humanities entail "re-creating and re-living" a past mental state through "empathy." "Here life grasps life," Dilthey argues, through a "special, personal inspiration" that makes possible "a rediscovery of the I in the Thou"—an intimate, internal experience of the connection between one's own consciousness and the world of another.

Perhaps surprisingly, Dilthey argues that the humanities enjoy greater certainty about their knowledge than the sciences do because, in his view, empathic intuition is based on direct inner contact of like with like (one mind assimilating another mind to itself). In the sciences, the mind seeks to make sense of an alien reality, which it knows merely through appearances and which it can explain only through such indirect instruments as hypotheses and inferences. In humanistic understanding, according to Dilthey, empathy puts spirit in touch with spirit.[2]

Dilthey's separation of the *Geisteswissenschaften* and the *Natur-wissenschaften*, I will argue, is not tenable on epistemological grounds. The procedures of interpretation and validation that I have described in the previous chapters cover both realms, and this convergence should call into question the conventional wisdom that they are incommensurable. The humanities and the sciences are not separated by an unbridgeable epistemological divide. Literary criticism is not a private intuition of the spirit; it is, rather, a public enterprise of testing collectively held assumptions about literature, language, and human being. Science is not a mirror of nature, a reflection of external fact; it is, rather, a social and historical process of testing and modifying theories, which may become more secure as they withstand repeated challenges but which always remain provisional. Understanding in both fields is experimental, not empathic or empirical. The differences between them are local and particular, not general and absolute. Humanists and scientists interpret different things and make different assumptions, but they understand in the same way. They belong to different communities of belief, but they are all citizens of a pluralistic universe governed by the same hermeneutic laws.

Hypotheses in Science and Literary Criticism

Dilthey's description of the natural sciences is partially correct. He is right that the sciences operate with inferences and hypotheses, but his apologetic attitude toward their indirectness implies a misleading dualistic structure of knowledge. According to this view, hypotheses are, unfortunately, the only way in which external facts can present themselves to consciousness. The ideal way would be directly, without intermediaries, which necessarily misrepresent what they stand for. This dualism of fact and appearance recalls Francis Bacon's famous complaint that "the human understanding is like a false mirror, which, receiving rays irregularly, distorts and discolors the nature of things by mingling its own nature with it."[3] For Bacon, true knowledge would be achieved if the mirror would reflect purely and transparently. The duty of scientists is therefore to purge themselves of distorting preconceptions and ideas rather than to pursue pregiven interests and theories. Isaac Newton similarly warns that "whatever is not deduced from the phenomena is to be called an hypothesis; and hypotheses, whether metaphysical or physical, whether of occult qualities or mechanical, have no place in experimental philosophy."[4] Because hypotheses embody the experience, beliefs, and concerns of the scientist, they distort the mirror and prevent it from colorlessly reflecting the external world. Dilthey's skepticism about the deficiencies of hypotheses is a legacy from the reflective epistemology of classical empiricism.

Hypotheses are necessary and productive instruments for knowing, however, because the mind is not a mirror. Contemporary philosophy of science is a field filled with controversy, but one claim that is accepted almost unanimously is that scientists know by testing hypotheses. Although Karl Popper shares Bacon's and Newton's belief "in 'absolute' or 'objective' truth," he recognizes that "we approach everything in the light of a preconceived theory"—and that this is not a weakness we should minimize or lament.[5] As Popper explains, "The belief that we can start with pure observations alone, without anything in the nature of a theory, is absurd. . . . Observation is always selective. It needs a chosen object, a definite task, an interest, a point of view, a problem. . . . Objects can be classified, and can become similar or dissimilar, *only* in this way—by being related to needs and interests."[6] This passage suggests that theories and hypotheses are inextricably implicated in observation in several ways. Popper describes a theory as a pregiven scheme that cuts up the world according to one pattern and not another. It consequently directs the observer's attention down some paths and deflects it from areas a different theory might point toward. We can see something only by perceiving it in relation to a scheme of possible similarities and differences, and this scheme is a product of the observer's past experiences, interests, and assumptions. Like Heidegger, Popper argues that what we understand depends on what we expect to discover. An observational hypothesis is not simply a presentation of what is indubitably "there" or "given." It is, rather, a wager—a supposition that awaits confirmation, modification, or disproof. The spatial image of the mind as a mirror of the external world should give way to a temporal notion of understanding as a process of projecting and testing expectations.

Hypotheses are necessary not only for scientific observation but also for literary understanding. I have argued that this is the case for interpretation in general, but now let us consider the specific form of understanding Dilthey ascribes to the humanities—empathy—and let us do so by examining a critic who describes himself as a descendant of Schleiermacher and Dilthey in the German hermeneutic tradition. Echoing Dilthey's declaration of the goal that humanistic knowledge should pursue, Leo Spitzer argues that "the reader must seek to place himself in the creative center of the artist himself—and re-create the artistic organism." Spitzer pursues this aim not by immediate, intuitive identification, however, but by projecting hypotheses about the relation between "certain outward details" of the artist's corpus and "the inner center" from which they seem to radiate. As Spitzer explains, he must resort to hypotheses because literary understanding "is reached not only by the gradual progression from one detail to another detail, but by the anticipation or divination of the whole. . . . 'The detail can be understood only by the whole and any explanation of detail presupposes the understanding of the whole.' "[7]

Spitzer quotes Schleiermacher's formulation of the hermeneutic circle—the circle whereby, as I have explained before, we can understand the parts of any state of affairs only by projecting a sense of the totality to which they belong, just as, conversely, we can understand the whole only by working through its elements. As I have argued, critics may see the details of works in relation to many different kinds of wholes (not only the artist's mental state but also, for example, the work's social setting or its intrinsic formal structure). But a sense of the relation between part and whole can be attained only by projecting hypotheses. Spitzer consequently argues that understanding begins with a moment of "divination," when a likely hypothesis about the work's configuration occurs to the interpreter—a guess that he or she then seeks to amplify and refine by making a series of back-and-forth movements between a text's details and the interpreter's sense of their overall pattern.

The example of Spitzer suggests that even a critic who wishes to recreate an artist's mental state must employ hypotheses. As an instance of hermeneutic circularity, the reconstruction of a writer's frame of mind requires inferences based on details from his or her writings—suppositions that in turn justify themselves by their ability to make sense of the writer's works. Dilthey's assertions about the certainty of empathy therefore seem questionable. Literary understanding is no more direct or immediate than scientific observation. In both fields the structure of knowledge is a tissue of assumptions, guesses, and wagers that are always provisional.

This much many scientists might concede, but many, if not most, would contend that their tests for truth are more rigorous than those in "softer" disciplines. One of the first things to be said in defense of the epistemological integrity of the humanities is that, even though literary understanding is based on guesswork, it is not irrational and uncontrolled. Spitzer acknowledges that "to understand a sentence, a work of art, or the inward form of an artistic mind involves . . . irrational moves" because no logical calculus can guarantee successful hypotheses, but he also argues that these "moves" must be controlled by reason.[8] Interpretation is an ongoing alternation between two phases—an "irrational" phase, in which the critic's imagination projects a guess about meaning, followed by a "rational" process of analyzing, criticizing, and evaluating the hypothesis.

The rationality of literary interpretation is guarded by the three tests for validity that I have analyzed—inclusiveness, efficacy, and intersubjectivity. To begin with, by going back and forth to check the fit between the work's details and his or her guess about the whole, the critic tests the inclusiveness of a hypothesis and may modify or refine it if recurrent inconsistencies call into question its scope and penetration. If a hypothesis gives critics a set of expectations about how their future experience with the work will unfold, then a series of surprises and anomalies can cause them to revise or reject it by casting doubt on its efficacy. In addition to the tests of inclusiveness and efficacy, there is also intersubjectivity—the ability of a hypothesis to win the assent of other interpreters. If no one agrees with them, interpreters may stubbornly persist, but increasing isolation may undermine their confidence in their beliefs. These tests cannot guarantee the truth of a hypothesis. But they do suggest that literary understanding can lay a claim to "rationality" to the extent that its hypotheses can produce coherence, demonstrate their usefulness, and develop a community of supporters.

According to some scientists and philosophers, however, a truly "scientific" theory must satisfy stricter criteria than these. Popper argues that "the criterion of the scientific status of a theory is its falsifiability, or refutability." Noting that "it is easy to obtain confirmations . . . for nearly every theory—if we look for confirmations"—he claims that a hypothesis is "scientific" only if it can be conclusively proved wrong: "A theory which is not refutable by any conceivable event is non-scientific."[9] The Popperian scientist should try to invent an experiment that would produce results incompatible with the theory he or she is testing. If they occur, we know for certain that the theory is wrong; if they do not, our confidence in it may increase (although we cannot be sure that someone will not eventually find means of disproving it). Psychoanalysis and Marxism are not scientific, Popper argues, because no single test could ever prove them wrong—they are always able to find some explanation that makes an apparent anomaly consistent with their schemes. Einstein's theory of gravitation impresses Popper more because it made a "risky prediction"—that is, a prediction that runs counter to what we might otherwise expect. Einstein speculated that stars near the sun would not seem to be in their proper places because their light beams would be pulled by solar gravitation. This daring hypothesis was borne out by Eddington's measurements, made during an eclipse. If the stars had been where the astronomical charts said they should be, Einstein's theory would have been falsified.

Is Popper's notion of falsification an accurate depiction of the actual practice of science? One of its shortcomings is that it assumes too clear and tidy a relation between a theory and its possible disproof, a relation that is often confused and messy. A sympathetic critic of psychoanalysis has recently argued, for example, that even a "hard" science like physics could not satisfy Popper's requirements because most scientific theories involve so many interrelated hypotheses that no single experiment could falsify all of them. A failure in the theory could indict an auxiliary hypothesis, not its central assumptions, but the experiment might not show unequivocally where the inadequacy lies.[10] Anomalous evidence may not decisively refute an entire hypothesis but only suggest that some of its details need adjustment. Or anomalies may indicate that the quality of the data and the accuracy of measurements are faulty.[11] In all of these cases, an inconsistency between the theory and the evidence may call not for abandoning the hypothesis but for modifying, refining, and amplifying it to make it more inclusive and effective.

For these and other reasons, Thomas Kuhn argues that very few, if any, scientific theories meet Popper's criteria: "No theory ever solves all the puzzles with which it is confronted at a given time; nor are the solutions already achieved often perfect. . . . If any and every failure to fit were ground for theory rejection, all theories ought to be rejected at all times."[12] Because no scientific theory can completely and conclusively answer every question put to it, scientists customarily regard recalcitrant evidence as a challenge to improve the power and coherence of their hypotheses— not necessarily as grounds for overturning them. Only if the cumulative weight of the difficulties a theory encounters makes adjustment a cumbersome process will the scientist find it expedient to develop a new hypothesis. The opinions of one's fellow scientists as to whether or not a theory is promising and the struggle to make it work worthwhile will also influence an investigator's decision about whether to abandon it or to carry on despite adversity. This decision is rarely, if ever, as automatic or clear-cut as Popper describes it. His test of falsifiability does not render irrelevant to science the tests of coherence, effectiveness, and intersubjectivity, which literary understanding must also pass. They are all criteria that scientists must invoke to help them decide how to proceed in a world of ambiguous choices.

Another problem with the doctrine of falsifiability is that scientists, like literary critics, often have firm biases and strong commitments, which they vigorously defend and actively seek to confirm. Scientists often have good reason for refusing to abandon a favored hypothesis that faces a potential refutation, even though this is a stubbornness Popper would frown on. For example, when asked how he would have reacted if Eddington's measurements had come out differently, Einstein replied: "Then I would have been sorry for [Eddington]—the theory *is* correct."[13] Such tenacity can degenerate into dogmatic narrow-mindedness, but a certain firmness and persistence are necessary in science in order to give a theory a fair chance to demonstrate its ability to overcome the various obstacles in its way. The problems that a theory must solve rarely take care of themselves without considerable toil and ingenuity on the part of the scientist. Tenacity is also required to defend and proclaim a theory's merits against the skepticism of authorities reluctant to part with firmly entrenched habits of understanding. It is well known, for example, that Darwin's theory of evolution met massive resistance from many of the best scientific minds of his day. No key falsification experiment has vindicated Darwin. Instead, his theory has gradually won acceptance because its inclusiveness and effectiveness as an instrument for understanding have replaced the original opposition with a community of support.[14]

No literary interpretation can ever be decisively falsified by a single experiment—but then this does not clearly demarcate literary study from scientific understanding. According to Popper, science "consists of bold conjectures, controlled by criticism."[15] But this is also a good description of literary understanding because, as I have tried to show, it too alternates between boldly making guesses and critically evaluating them. When anomalies frustrate our hypotheses, we critics behave very similarly to the scientists. All of us in both of Dilthey's worlds face the same difficulties, alternatives, and dangers as we try to decide whether to save a theory by modifying it or to throw it out and start over. Critics are also always able to find confirmations. They must worry, however, about the danger of the hermeneutic circle turning vicious—their hypothesis about the whole confirming itself with evidence that it itself has shaped. The anomalies and inconsistencies that a hypothesis may generate provide an important hedge against this danger, but they rarely indicate unambiguously whether a reading should be rejected or merely refined. No automatic calculus can decide this question indubitably in every case. In science as in literary criticism, tenacity in working through the problems a hypothesis encounters sometimes pays off—although persistence can sometimes lead to rigidity and isolation. Like scientists, critics can consult their fellow investigators to shore up their confidence or to take warning about possible mistakes—but again the results may be inconclusive, since the encouragement as well as the skepticism of others may simply reflect their own biases. The decision whether to struggle with a hypothesis or to abandon it is a risky and difficult one in both literary criticism and science because the criteria for validity in both fields can provide only limited guidance and assurance.

Univocity versus Multiplicity in Scientific Truth

If literary and scientific understanding cannot be demarcated on the grounds that each employs unique interpretive procedures, it might still be possible to find other criteria to distinguish absolutely and unequivocally between them. Do they, for example, have different conceptions of truth? If literary criticism is an inherently pluralistic enterprise in which competing interpretive frameworks pursue opposing "truths," it is widely believed that science is fundamentally monistic in its goal of disclosing the absolute "Truth" about nature. Max Planck professes the faith of many scientists when he claims that "the search for the absolute" is "the noblest and most worthwhile task of science."[16] This ideal contrasts sharply with the veritable conflict of interpretations prevailing in the humanities.

Dilthey's model of *Geisteswissenschaften* is too homogeneous. The empathetic disclosure of the author's lived world is not the only or even the primary mode of literary understanding. Dilthey describes interpretation as a revelatory process that opens the interpreter's consciousness to communion with a foreign but also kindred spirit. Many interpretive methods stress not revelation, however, but suspicion. For example, Freud, Marx, and Nietzsche, although in different ways, all practice hermeneutics of unmasking that would demystify what Dilthey trusts—calling into question the subject's self-understanding by uncovering the unconscious desires, hidden class interests, or secret will to power it disguises. Similarly, not all revelatory modes of understanding are based on empathy. For example, a formalist criticism may trust the text, not suspect its disguises, in order to disclose the values, resources, and powers of language. But formalism denies what Dilthey assumes—that consciousness is the home of meaning and the goal of interpretation. The formalist does not seek a communion with the author but, rather, undertakes an impersonal analysis of a work's invocation and variation of linguistic norms. In apparent opposition to the "search for the absolute" that characterizes science, this diversity of methods makes the "truth" about literature a pluralistic collection of irreconcilably competing "truths."

It is not at all clear, however, that truth in science is ultimately single rather than multiple. This is, indeed, one of the central points of dispute in the classic debate between Popper and Kuhn about the epistemology of science. According to Kuhn, the "truth" a scientist sees depends on the "paradigm" governing his or her perception. Kuhn's use of the term "paradigm" is somewhat slippery, as many have pointed out, but it seems to have two primary meanings. A paradigm is, first, the set of assumptions, definitions, and basic theories that constitute a scientific community's understanding of its field and guide its program of research. But Kuhn also refers to a paradigm as, secondly, the exemplary problem-solutions that provide the community with its models of how to pursue its commitments in practice.[17] Similarly, a school of literary interpretation is united not only by certain basic presuppositions and principles (of the kind outlined for the New Criticism, for example, by Wellek and Warren's *Theory of Literature*) but also by generally esteemed models of critical practice that give these assumptions exemplary application (the role played for the New Critics by Cleanth Brooks's elegant interpretations in *The Well Wrought Urn*). There are two basic definitions for the term "paradigm" because any community's interpretive framework has two dimensions: It is both a platform of shared theoretical assumptions and an implicit practical protocol of how to apply them.

According to Kuhn, the history of science is not a gradual approach to a single, fixed goal. It is, rather, a series of shifts in the paradigms governing research as the anomalies besetting a particular theory accumulate to such a degree that they call for a change in the scientific community's assumptions and goals. A paradigm shift can transform the scientist's very notion of what "truth" is and how to discover it—hence Kuhn's dramatic claim that "when paradigms change, the world itself changes with them."[18] From Ptolemaic to Copernican astronomy, from Newtonian to Einsteinian physics, from phlogiston theory to Lavoisier's chemistry of oxygen—such shifts transform the world in which a scientist operates. They alter the kind of entities one expects to find, the relations one assumes unite and divide them, and the program of research one must pursue in order to increase confidence in the community's theories and to illuminate areas they leave dark.

Kuhn is ultimately ambiguous, however, about exactly how much a scientist's world changes when paradigms shift. At times Kuhn suggests that the transformation entails a radical "conversion" to a new mode of perception totally at odds with old patterns of thought. But this surely goes too far. Although any scientific revolution worthy of the name does cause an epistemological rupture with the past, continuities in the community's assumptions, techniques, and goals persist after even the most radical alterations. Kuhn himself notes that one criterion for choosing a new paradigm is that it "must promise to preserve a relatively large part of the concrete problem-solving ability that has accrued to science through its predecessors."[19] If old ways of thinking endure after a new paradigm has been adopted, then the change cannot have been total and absolute.

Complete incommensurability is not necessary, however, in order for "truth" in science to be multiple. Overlaps and similarities may exist between different research programs even if they are not ultimately harmonious and cannot be merged under a single set of concepts. At any given moment in history, the many different scientific disciplines are different communities constituted by different paradigms that may be compatible in some areas but are not necessarily perfectly unifiable.

For example, even though particle physicists and microbiologists investigate the basic building blocks of nature, each community has its own understanding of what is fundamental (quarks as opposed to deoxyribonucleic acid). Each group has its own set of exemplary problem-solutions that it most admires and finds most useful, and each has particular instruments geared to disclose the kind of building block it considers most basic. A particle physicist would not gain much useful guidance from Watson and Crick's model of the double helix, but a microbiologist would not be much helped by a linear accelerator. Larry Laudan is correct, of course, when he says that "the various scientific disciplines and domains are never completely independent of one another."[20] As Laudan notes, for example, chemists borrow ideas about atomic structure from physicists, and biologists use chemical theories to analyze organic microstructures. But once again these areas of overlap do not make the disciplines they join homogeneous or homologous. Chemistry, physics, and biology constitute unique perspectives on nature which refuse to be totally absorbed into each other. Their resistance to complete mutual assimilation makes the "truth" of science not single but multiple. The long-cherished dream of a unified science is impossible.

Although Popper shares Kuhn's belief that observation must be guided by theories, this view of knowledge does not seem to him incompatible with a faith in science as an ever-closer approximation of the absolute. "I do admit that at any moment we are prisoners caught in the framework of our theories, our expectations, our past experiences, our language," Popper explains. But he also argues that "if we try, we can break out of our framework at any time. Admittedly, we shall find ourselves again in a framework, but it will be a better and roomier one; and we can at any moment break out of it again."[21] If understanding always depends on an underlying theoretical scheme, however, it is not self-evident that we can find neutral standards with which to judge one framework "better and roomier" than another. I have already shown, for example, that the test of falsification cannot always provide decisive disproof of a theory or conclusive vindication of its merits. Any other criteria we might invoke to evaluate a framework will themselves reflect the assumptions and goals of a framework. The standards of inclusiveness, efficacy, and intersubjectivity operate in all epistemologies, but they will be applied differently according to the values and interests of different research communities.

Kuhn points out a further problem in comparing the adequacy of competing frameworks. A new paradigm that removes an anomaly embarrassing to the old theory, he notes, is frequently unable to solve many other problems that the system it replaces handled gracefully.[22] The inclusiveness and efficacy of the emerging paradigm may therefore not be self-evident; indeed, they may be crucial points of contention. A new framework may be "better and roomier" than the old not in each and every respect but only in ways of pressing importance to the community that adopts it— although not necessarily to all researchers, since those who resist the change will argue that the old framework's deficiencies are less inconvenient than the questions left unanswered by its prospective replacement. In science as in the humanities, the tests of inclu-

siveness, efficacy, and intersubjectivity are useful but not conclusive in determining the merits of alternative ways of knowing.
Standards of better and worse do not exist in some absolute realm
apart from interpretive frameworks but themselves may change
when paradigms shift.

The very fact of the disagreement between Kuhn and Popper
shows that science cannot be cleanly demarcated from literary criticism on the grounds that one is monistic and the other pluralistic.
The dispute about the status of truth in science is strikingly similar
to the disagreement among literary theorists over whether criticism
is an irreducibly plural enterprise or an ultimately monistic pursuit
of the single true meaning of a work. My own view, as I have tried
to show, is that science and literary criticism are both pluralistic—
that "truth" in both fields is a multiplicity of "truths." Even if one
refuses to accept that argument, however, the point remains that
the notions of truth in the two fields cannot be radically incommensurable inasmuch as the sciences and the humanities both give rise
to the same debate about whether "truth" is one or many, absolute
or relative, fixed or ever changing. This very dispute shows that
the problem of "truth" is analogous in both realms—if only analo-
gously undecidable. Scientists may believe that they are pursuing
the absolute, but this is a conviction that the philosophy of science
cannot conclusively justify.

The disagreement about monism versus pluralism in science
raises the very literary problem of translation. A scientific paradigm is like a language in many important respects. Just as a
language consists of a series of conventionally stipulated semantic
entities and rules for their combination, so a scientific discipline's
operations consist of traditionally agreed-upon constituent elements and laws for relating them. The discipline's conventions
limit the kinds of expression the research community will understand and accept, but these restrictions also allow and indeed make
possible innovative utterances and creative discoveries. Linguistic
norms similarly both limit and facilitate original speech.[23] A scientific community's terms and rules for their use provide its members
with a shared sense of the world and allow them to communicate
about it and to refine or change it by modifying their vocabulary
and syntax.

Popper warns, however, that "it is just a dogma—a dangerous

dogma—that the different frameworks are like mutually untranslatable languages."[24] Popper's warning is motivated by the realization that the languages of the various scientific paradigms must be ultimately equivalent—the meanings of each expressible in the codes of the others—if their disclosures are ever to be synthesized into a single "Truth." Kuhn denies the possibility of perfect translation, however. In his view, "Words change their meanings or conditions of applicability in subtle ways" from one paradigm to another. Not only does the meaning of a term vary with its context, but more fundamentally, Kuhn argues, "Languages cut up the world in different ways, and we have no access to a neutral sub-linguistic means of reporting."[25]

A language makes knowing possible by deploying a system of differences in which comparisons and contrasts between objects can be recognized—relations that reveal what something "is" by setting it in opposition to what it is not. Identity is not, therefore, a simple given or an invariable positive term. It is, rather, a reflection of certain fundamental analogies at the basis of the system—analogies that construe the world "as" a particular configuration of actual and possible elements (and not as some other, alternative arrangement, which a different set of analogies would disclose). Understanding is a basically figurative process of seeing something *as* something. Two systems of differences superimposed on each other will probably not agree at every point. Similarly, the territories opened up by alternative analogies may not overlap or coalesce. Different sets of terms and rules for combining them may direct the observer's attention down paths that do not ultimately lead to the same point.[26]

Translation hopes for the same ideal state that the dream of unified science envisions—the ideal that, even if each framework for understanding disguises something as the cost of what it discloses, a synthesis of every method's particular kind of light might result in a grand, all-encompassing illumination. Different scientific paradigms can disagree, however, over what the basic units are and what procedures to apply to them. An atom of helium is a "molecule" to a chemist but not to a physicist, for example, because of their different definitions of the concept and rules for its use.[27] The point of this example is not that the atom of helium does not somehow exist beyond the scientists' different interpretations of it or that physics and chemistry are completely dissimilar; rather, the point is that the two disciplines cannot be translated into each other's terms here without forcing one field to alter its categories and syntax. Translation is invariably imperfect because it always encounters areas where languages are not homologous.

If different paradigms operate with incompletely compatible vocabularies and grammars because they define entities differently and search for different relations, translation may sacrifice what is unique to each rather than disclosing their common truth. The "as" underlying one paradigm may not be fully reconcilable with the "as" of another. Rather, the differences between scientific languages may give each its particular value as a mode of construal. Richard Rorty notes that "there is no such thing as the 'language of unified science.' We have not got a language which will serve as a permanent neutral matrix for formulating all good explanatory hypotheses, and we have not the foggiest notion of how to get one."[28] This lack may be not a temporary inconvenience but an irremediable consequence of the epistemology of language. A neutral, universal language of observation cannot be found because conflict between irreconcilable frameworks for understanding is as much a condition of the sciences as it is of the humanities.

The competition between incompletely unifiable frameworks does not make either the sciences or the humanities "irrational" or prevent us from distinguishing "truth" from "falsity." In a world of hermeneutic conflict, however, "truth" is neither absolute nor purely reflective of external fact. When a scientific community switches paradigms, for example, it can typically cite good reasons to justify the change. Recalcitrant, disturbing anomalies may have diminished the effectiveness of the old framework, and the new theory may seem to promise greater explanatory power in areas of generally acknowledged importance. But the community's reasons cannot base themselves on a priori logical principles, since the shift from one framework to another may change what counts as "logical" and "reasonable." Nor can the scientist simply claim that the new paradigm offers a better match with nature, because the choice of a framework is a decision about what to view "nature" *as*.

"Logic" and "nature" are not simple givens in the independent spheres of ideas and reality but may vary with the theoretical constructs guiding observation. Not irrational, however, the choice between such constructs is a pragmatic decision based on a critical assessment of their comparative ability to attain goals and satisfy interests the investigator considers valuable. Different choices are always possible, inasmuch as different investigators may place equal value on incompatible aims. But this choice is not solely an individual matter, because the interpreter's community will ultimately either ratify or condemn it. Nor is it purely whimsical, since it must justify itself by the consequences it leads to. "Logic" and "reality" are not the arbiters of "truth" and "falsity" in either the humanities or the sciences—but both are nevertheless rational enterprises which must justify their decisions with persuasive arguments and which bear responsibility for the consequences of their intellectual commitments.[29]

These complications suggest that the notion of scientific "progress" is more problematic than many literary critics or scientists realize. The claim that progress is possible in the natural sciences but not in the humanities is an oversimplification of the conditions governing knowledge in both fields. Because standards for judging the adequacy of an explanation may change with a shift in paradigm, scientific inquiry is not a continuous advance toward a single, absolute ideal of knowledge. After a radical shift in framework, a scientific community may nevertheless feel that "progress" has taken place. But this feeling reflects nothing more—or less—than its confidence that various benefits will accrue thanks to the change. A literary community may feel similar confidence that its interests have been well served when it discards an interpretive method plagued by anomalies and discontent and adopts new procedures that for various reasons may seem more promising. In both cases, any claim of "progress" simply reflects faith that the future will be better than the past, even though the standards for evaluating advancement may have shifted because the group has adopted a new research program with different assumptions, goals, and procedures.

Demonstrable advancement of knowledge may occur within a single, unified research program as members of a group refine shared investigative practices and come closer to realizing commonly valued purposes. But progress of this kind is possible within any community—scientific, literary, or other—that has a coherent interpretive framework based on common presuppositions and interests. If literary criticism as a whole does not progress, this is because conflict between interpretive schools prevents agreement among all members of the community about the proper goals and methods of inquiry.

Competition of this kind can, however, advance the community's interests—for example, in enhancing the preservation of literary works by demonstrating their capacity to mean in a variety of perhaps incompatible, unexpected ways. Once again, science is not fundamentally different. Paul Feyerabend argues that scientific paradigms are not as unified or free of conflict as some have suggested. He also claims that "a struggle of alternative views" in science is not a liability but an asset because it sorts out the theories fittest to survive.[30] Some kinds of disagreement may not be an obstacle to progress but may indeed contribute to the discipline's advance. Conflict between competing literary methods similarly tests their merits and weeds out the less promising approaches from the potentially more powerful ones, even if a single set of goals and procedures to unify the field never emerges from the struggle because complete agreement about what is "promising" and "powerful" cannot be attained.

"Progress" is not a simple matter in either literary criticism or science because "truth" in neither field is univocal or absolute. According to Kuhn, the historical comparison of various scientific frameworks reveals "no coherent direction of ontological development" toward a single, determinate end; indeed, he claims, Einstein's physics is in some respects more similar to Aristotle's theory of nature than to Newtonian mechanics.[31] Toulmin similarly suggests that we are not entitled to decide in advance how unifiable or pluralistic the natural world may be.[32] The image of a unified intellectual discipline gradually advancing toward a single, unchanging goal is not an accurate representation of literary criticism—but it is not much better as a depiction of the natural sciences. "Progress" is too ambiguous a notion to provide a clear line of demarcation between them.

Other Candidates for Demarcation: Causality, Language, Value

"Causality" is equally unable to mark unequivocally the boundary between the sciences and the humanities. Dilthey is once again an important source of the widespread assumption that the natural sciences search for relations of "cause and effect," whereas the humanities pursue "value, purpose, significance, and meaning." According to Dilthey, "In the historical world there is no scientific causality. . . . History only knows of the relations of striving and suffering, action and reaction."[33] The sciences explain natural causes, this view holds, whereas the humanities try to understand the motives, desires, and ambitions of people. Neither field is quite so uniform, however. Ricoeur argues, for example, that a person is a "being who belongs at the same time to the regime of causality and to that of motivation, thus of explanation and understanding."[34] Some human behavior seems caused and not freely chosen. Humanistic methods of understanding can be charted on a scale ranging from lesser to greater causality according to whether they assume that people are the agents of their destiny or that they are acted upon by sexual drives, economic forces, or semiotic codes taking the human subject as their relatively powerless object.

Similarly, not all sciences are causal. Dilthey's description of "striving and suffering, action and reaction" characterizes quite well the assumption of the ecological sciences that any environment consists of mutually interdependent, complexly interacting elements. The pioneer ecologist Darwin offered a theory of evolution that is not "causal" in the mechanical fashion of colliding billiard balls. On the contrary, "striving and suffering, action and reaction" are very much part of the "struggle for existence"—the ongoing naturalistic drama in which some variants are selected and others die off as a result of complex relations of competition and cooperation, which resist reduction to a logic of cause and effect.

The discovery of order in nature is a goal of science, but a useful scheme of categories need not be causally based. Like science, literary understanding also seeks order—the patterns of coherence that make sense of an individual work, an author's corpus, a literary period, and so forth. Indeed, the construction of consistency is a basic requirement of meaning of whatever kind.

This is one of the reasons why a scientist's use of language is not fundamentally different from linguistic practice in other fields, including literary criticism and even literary art. Cleanth Brooks states a view held by many, however, when he starkly opposes scientific and poetic language: "The poet does not use a notation at all—as the scientist may properly be said to do so. . . . The tendency of science is necessarily to stabilize terms, to freeze them into strict denotations; the poet's tendency is by contrast disruptive. The terms are continually modifying each other, and thus violating their dictionary meanings."[35] The characteristics Brooks assigns to scientific and poetic language are not unique to them, however, but are features of language in general.

Even in everyday speech, for example, a dictionary alone is not enough to tell what a word means. Most words have a range of possible meanings and are thus sensitive to context. In any sentence, a word's precise meaning is established by its interaction with other words, all of them "continually modifying" each other. If a poet uses the context to give a word a particular shade of meaning, he or she is simply employing one of the ordinary resources of language. A scientific community may agree upon conventions to limit some words to a narrower range of meanings than what generally prevails in customary usage. But this too is simply an application of one of the general characteristics of language. Linguistic conventions are established by the community that uses them, and they are always subject to alteration and modification according to its interests and purposes. Using this power, any community may narrow definitions or broaden them as it sees fit.

Poetry is not purely or even primarily disruptive but is similarly a manipulation of conventions the artist inherits from the general community of speakers and from the practice of past writers. A poet may either work within established conventions or work against them (and most great writers do both). The two sides of poetic creativity—both receptive and disruptive—are a particular illustration of how creativity in language in general can be either rule governed or rule breaking. Speakers may invent new expressions by exploiting the resources of existing conventions, or someone may attempt to upset accepted norms and set up new ones. In both cases novelty is possible only if rules exist. Poetic innovation may take either form, but neither distinguishes it from ordinary language.

Metaphors are among the most important means of creative linguistic rule breaking—disrupting the lexicon in order to extend its semantic range by using a word in an unfamiliar context or in a previously unsanctioned way.[36] Metaphor is not the peculiar property of poetry, however. Global and local metaphors play a crucial role in scientific language and conceptualization. Many regard traditional mechanistic science as purely objective, but it is metaphoric at base—seeing the universe as a "great engine" or a "giant clock."[37] Global metaphors of this kind give evidence of the constituting role of analogy in establishing a paradigm's sense of what the world presents itself *as* to the observer. Howard E. Gruber has shown, for example, that Darwin's theory of evolution has as its global figurative basis the image of a branching tree.[38] But even Darwin's particular, local terms are often metaphoric because he must disrupt conventional usage in order to express his new meaning.

The terms "struggle for existence" and "natural selection" are metaphors, for example, that violate dictionary meanings. The competition between variants for survival is not literally a "struggle" because individual plants or animals are not ceaselessly locked in actual combat with each other. The survival of a particular variant is not literally a process of "selection" precisely because it takes place "naturally," without the choice of an independent agent. However, Darwin's terms are not inaccurate. They convey his meaning very exactly—but metaphorically, as figures employing existing linguistic resources in an unprecedented, innovative way. No more than poetry does science have a language of its own, but both exploit the general characteristics of language for their own purposes.

If these various proposals for demarcating literary and scientific understanding all fail to distinguish unequivocally between them, then how can we describe their differences? The humanities and the natural sciences are obviously different enterprises—but, as I have tried to show, it is not at all obvious how to draw their boundaries. We can begin to answer this question, I think, by analyzing one remaining criterion for demarcation—not because it holds up any better than the others do but because its inadequacies point the way to a solution.

The two domains are sometimes divided by describing literary criticism as the study of human values and the sciences as the pursuit of value-free knowledge of nature. But this distinction also rests on shaky ground. The sciences are indeed laden with values, as can be seen from historical studies that show how the standards of logic, order, and proof in the physics or biology of a particular period are correlated to its philosophical assumptions or even its aesthetic tastes.[39] Contemporary science will one day be subjected to similar historical scrutiny. As George Levine argues, "Science and literature are two alternative but related expressions of a culture's values, assumptions, and intellectual frameworks."[40] If we fail to notice the implicit values and cultural biases of the sciences of our own time, this is not because they do not exist but because we are fully absorbed by the function of the sciences as cognitive instruments. When this function loses its compelling power and fascination, then the hidden cultural dimensions of a science may emerge.

To identify science with knowledge and art with value also oversimplifies the humanities. Works of art are not only embodiments of value but also ways of knowing that can challenge our habitual patterns of understanding the world. As Nelson Goodman urges, "The arts must be taken no less seriously than the sciences as modes of discovery, creation, and enlargement of knowledge."[41] Literary works take up and experiment with existing schemata for making sense of the world. When we read literary texts, we put into play our assumptions and expectations, but the surprises we encounter may persuade us to revise our interpretive frame. Novels, plays, and poems have epistemological power. Similarly, literary criticism not only is an act of appreciation but can also be a challenge to us to expand or revise our understanding of ourselves and our worlds (including nature) in light of the disclosures offered by literary works. By helping us to know literary works, literary criticism can bring us other kinds of knowledge as well. As a demonstration of the hermeneutic powers and possibilities of the presuppositions on which it is based, an interpretation of a text can offer valuable instruction about many matters not limited to the work it is analyzing.

If we do not customarily turn to science to discover human values or to literature to receive knowledge about nature, this is not because they are fundamentally different epistemological realms but because they have been assigned different functions by society—functions that can always change (hence the various shifts in what counts as "literature" and "science" over the ages). The differences between the humanities and the natural sciences are not to be found in the essential structure of understanding, truth, and expression in the two fields. They are instead different ways in which society has deployed the same basic procedures for understanding and communication in order to achieve different, ever-variable purposes.

The *Geisteswissenschaften* and the *Naturwissenschaften* are different social institutions devoted to solving different problems. I would not go to a biologist for help in understanding Wordsworth or to a literary critic for an explanation of photosynthesis. But the reason for this is not that one has better or more certain knowledge than the other does. The biologist and the literary critic employ the same fundamental operations of interpretation and validation, but they understand different things. The different interests and purposes of scientists and humanists become institutionalized in group affiliations that are recognizable through the journals they read, the meetings they attend, the academic departments they belong to, and so forth. The interpreter's community performs a variety of crucial epistemological roles—sanctioning the establishment of a framework for understanding, monitoring the validity of an investigator's decisions and results, and justifying changes in the commonly held research program. But the workings of the community in both literary criticism and science are epistemologically the same. The difference is only that the practitioners in each domain belong to different communities.

The notorious divide between the "two cultures" presents an oversimplification of the cultural map. Any society is a complex array of different ways of seeing, behaving, and speaking, which converge in some places and diverge in others. There are not just two cultures but a multitude of them. Nevertheless, the truth of the two-cultures argument is that the line of demarcation between the humanities and the natural sciences is a cultural boundary, not an epistemological schism. As I have argued, the *Geisteswissenschaften* and the *Naturwissenschaften* do not practice incommensurable methods of understanding or hold different standards of truth. Their practitioners simply belong to different cultures. The differences between the two realms are not permanent and absolute. Cultural differences never are. But they have a real felt existence to those they divide. The opposition between the sciences and the humanities is perceived by many on both sides as firm and intractable. It did not always exist in its present form, however, and it may not forever remain the same.

The Cognitive Powers of Metaphor

A variety of incommensurable methods of interpreting the world can come about only if old ways of knowing are always open to challenge by new, radically different modes of cognition. One of the most important sources of new possibilities of understanding and meaning is metaphor. The creation of novel figures renews and opens up the world by suggesting innovative, alternative arrangements of parts and wholes. In the universe envisioned by the monist, metaphor can have little purpose other than to approximate reality ever more closely or to demonstrate a preexisting truth in a different, more vivid way. For monism the purpose of new metaphor can only be to correct a false representation of the world or to decorate the truth, and figures are inherently suspect because they deliberately depart from literal, referential language. One difficulty with monistic conceptions of truth is that they leave little room for semantic innovation. By contrast, a pluralistic universe owes its life to the perpetual possibility of change and diversity that semantic innovation brings. As a primary source of such innovation, metaphor deserves special scrutiny, and this chapter is devoted to exploring its hermeneutic powers and implications. How do metaphors create new ways of understanding and meaning? How do they challenge and change our cognitive powers? If figures offer new ways of conceiving the world, how can we judge their truth?

The main achievement of the "interaction theory" of metaphor is its account of the capacity of figures to create new meaning. The thinkers responsible for this theory—primarily Max Black, Nelson Goodman, and Paul Ricoeur—contend that metaphors bring about semantic innovations by violating and extending the established rules of a language.[1] They argue that metaphor cannot be regarded as an act of substitution.[2] If a figure has indeed created a new meaning, the current lexicon will not contain an equivalent. Nor can the innovation be explained by arguing that the metaphor is based on a resemblance, because the figure typically creates a comparison that had not previously seemed possible. More often than not, a striking metaphor is powerful for the very reason that it defies our expectations. As a challenge to our customary assumptions about resemblances, the difference in a metaphor can be as important as the similarity it proposes.

A metaphor can best be understood as an interaction between a word and a context in which it seems both strange and fitting. The use of the metaphorical term may seem nonsensical according to prevailing conventions, but it becomes meaningful when we extend its customary definition by extrapolating a figurative sense that makes the word appropriate to its setting. The novel meaning of a metaphor is the product of an interaction between a surprising usage and an anomalous context we must readjust to each other in order to make them coherent. The reader discovers the metaphor's semantic innovation by responding to its challenge to create consistency where the rules show only dissonance.

Interaction theorists frequently argue that this process can change the reader's ways of thinking about the world. According to Ricoeur, for example, "the function of metaphor" is "to instruct by suddenly combining elements that have not been put together before." The result is that metaphor "adds to the ways in which we perceive" (*Rule of Metaphor*, pp. 33, 190). The editor of an influential recent anthology on the subject argues similarly that "new metaphors can alter the conceptual system in terms of which we experience and talk about our world."[3] These are important claims, and one aim of this chapter is to make them more precise.

Discussions of metaphor often become vague and inaccurate when they describe the epistemological reeducation that the reader of figurative language experiences. This is true, for example, even of Ricoeur's monumental *The Rule of Metaphor*, which is deservedly regarded in many quarters as the definitive study of metaphor's creative powers. Ricoeur's main goal is to establish how the interaction of a metaphor with the language surrounding it can institute new meaning. He acknowledges that "it is the reader, in effect, who works out the connotations of the modifier that are likely to be meaningful" (p. 95). But he does not supply the theory of reading that this observation calls for. Instead, he often seems to credit sentences with autonomous powers. He argues, for example, that "the change of meaning" brought about by metaphoric innovation "is the answer of discourse to the threat of destruction represented by semantic impertinence" (p. 152). The rediscovery of coherence, however, is the work of a reader. The discourse cannot accomplish this alone. The theory of metaphorical interaction needs the reader to fulfill the figure's promise of semantic innovation.

Metaphor can expand the limits of language because it can modify the reader's habits of understanding. How, then, are our cognitive capacities invoked when we make sense of metaphors? How can the process of construing figures modify or even overturn our customary habits of interpretation? I will try to answer these questions in three stages. I will first explain in more detail how, according to the interaction theory, metaphors make new meaning, and as I do so I will bring out the crucial role of the reader. I will then show how the semantic innovation that metaphor makes possible sets in motion interpretive processes in the reader that can have far-reaching effects on his or her ways of knowing the world. Finally, I will examine the tests by which the validity of metaphors can be assessed and will evaluate their ability to determine the truth of a figure's revelations.

The Semantics of Interaction:
How Metaphors Make New Meaning

A metaphor begins as an anomaly that refuses to fit into its context. In the words of Nelson Goodman, "Where there is metaphor, there is conflict" (*Languages of Art*, p. 69). The dissonance occurs because the meanings conventionally associated with the anomalous term are incompatible with its setting, and this incongruity is what sets the reader hunting for an extension of meaning to restore consistency and, with it, sense. Consider the following standard example:

The chairman plowed through the discussion.[4]

The term "plowed" is anomalous, obviously, because the chairman is not a farmer working his fields. Its usage is deviant, however, only if the word is taken in its literal sense. Readers take the term metaphorically by permitting themselves to change its meaning to reduce the deviation. We can alleviate the incongruity of "plowed" by expanding its meaning from a designation of agricultural labor to a description of aggressive behavior. Like someone turning up a furrow in a field, the chairman, we reason, keeps straight on his preset path and does not allow objections to alter his course. We restore coherence between the word and its context by extrapolating for "plowed" a figurative meaning that is different from but consistent with its customary usage.

Metaphor is therefore a function not of a single word but of the entire sentence. By itself, "plowed" is not metaphorical. It becomes so only because of its context—hence Max Black's argument that metaphor results from the interaction of a "focus" and a "frame" (*Models and Metaphors*, pp. 27–30). The metaphorical term is the "focus" of our attention because it is the anomaly we are trying to resolve, but it is enigmatic only because of the context that "frames" it, and we discover the meaning of the "focus" by inventing a way of fitting it into the "frame." Strictly speaking, the metaphor is neither the "focus" nor the "frame" alone but their interaction. As Ricoeur points out, "an entire statement constitutes the metaphor," even if "attention focuses on a particular word, the presence of which constitutes the grounds for considering the statement metaphorical" (*Rule of Metaphor*, p. 84).

This is another reason why a metaphor cannot be regarded as a substitute for another word that would convey its literal sense. No single word can replace the metaphor because the figure is not an isolated term but the product of an entire context of interaction. By the same token, if the interaction results in a new meaning, the "focus" term cannot be considered an ornament or a decoration—a fancy way of saying something also communicable in plain speech.[5] The paraphrase of the metaphor explains the interaction, but something is always lost in the translation. That "something" is the new meaning the reader has had to invent by fitting focus and frame together. It is the unique result of their interaction and not a substitute for an equivalent literal expression. My explanation of "plowing through a discussion" is inherently incomplete and indefinitely expandable. I could have added, for example, that the chairman acts as if the group were passive (a field to be worked over), that his tactics are cutting (the sharp edge of the implement), that his behavior may ironically seed discontent (unlike the productive farmer's labor on his land), and so on. These additions are not signs that the metaphor has a mysterious, inexpressible core of significance. They suggest, rather, that it has a unique meaning produced by an interaction that can be described but cannot be duplicated by other words in a different context.

The interaction theory of metaphor redefines the status of "literal" meaning and calls into question the notion that a figure is a deviation from the norm.[6] The "literal" is not a stable, permanent ground. Rather, as Goodman contends, "What is literal is set by present practice" (*Languages of Art*, p. 77). The standard meaning from which metaphor departs is not fixed but variable because it reflects the community's conventions and expectations. A deviant usage can come to seem normal after it has been assimilated. A widely accepted metaphor is actually more literal than figurative—what we call a "dead metaphor" because it no longer seems incongruous.

For this reason, my example of "plowing through the discussion" may seem less than the best illustration of metaphor. It is so well worn that its meaning may seem conventional. It is a good example, however, precisely because this ambiguity illustrates the instability of the normative. The uncertainty over whether to regard "plowing" as figurative or literal shows that the relation between deviation and norm does not exist absolutely but depends on the context. I was able to revivify "plowing" by stressing its incongruity in the setting in which it was employed. A dead metaphor like "plowing" can come alive again if we bring out the conflict between how one might construe it in another setting and what its current context demands. (Further evidence of the variability of deviation and norm is the presence of a second, perhaps until now unnoticed dead metaphor in my example—"chairman"— which I could have made seem anomalous, as I did with "plowing," if I had called attention to the incongruity of designating a person by a piece of furniture.) What we consider "figurative" or "literal" is a result of their interaction—the dissonance between what one expects and what one finds in a particular instance—and can vary from case to case. The search for fixed features to mark either normalcy or deviation is misguided and futile because they are variable, mutually defining terms.

An exclusive emphasis on deviation is also misleading because incongruity is only part of the story of metaphor. The purpose of anomaly is to launch a search for a new congruence. Deviation is not an end in itself but a provocation to the reader to rediscover consistency. Defying the norm cannot define metaphor because incongruity is merely the beginning of the process of innovation. A new figure is generated only when consistency has been restored.

Metaphorical interaction is a special case of the general dependence of words on their context to determine their meaning. Words typically have more than one meaning, as a quick glance at a dictionary will show. Which meaning is in force will vary according to the situation in which the word is applied. In a reciprocally defining manner that recalls the workings of the hermeneutic circle, the meaning of a sentence is built up out of the words that belong to it, but those words acquire their meaning only by virtue of their position and use in that sentence. This variability of meaning and sensitivity to context are an immense advantage to a language. As Ricoeur notes, "A language without polysemy would violate the principle of economy, for it would extend its vocabulary infinitely" (*Rule of Metaphor*, p. 115). If words could not mean several things at once, we would need a new term to convey each nuance of thought and feeling, to capture every different experience, and to report on all new objects we encounter. Polysemy allows words to be used in different, unforeseen situations. It also enables us to extend a word's meaning. Again, Ricoeur makes this point well: "Polysemy attests to the quality of openness in the texture of the word: a word is that which has several meanings and can acquire more" (*Rule of Metaphor*, p. 117).

A metaphorical use adds another meaning to a term that already has several. We do not hesitate to extend the term's meaning because we do not expect a word to be rigidly tied to a single, narrow definition. Instead, when we encounter an anomalous usage, we begin our search for coherence by exploring a word's variety of permissible, established meanings. When this fails, we then ask which of them we can extend in order to meet the demands of the context. Our license to do this is the polysemy of the word that metaphor takes off from and adds to.

Black has the multivalence of language in mind when he contends that we unravel the mystery of a metaphor by sorting through its "system of associated commonplaces" (*Models and Metaphors,* pp. 38–44). But this claim is also misleading. When we come across a statement like "Man is a wolf," Black argues, we review the set of qualities and relationships our community customarily connects with the enigmatic term. We inventory the associations our culture attaches to "wolf," and we pick out the ones relevant to "man." Black does not go far enough, however, for a metaphor must go beyond the commonplace and the accepted if it has indeed created a new meaning. "Wolf" will acquire new connotations by being compared to "man" (to the detriment of the poor wolf, most likely), just as "man" is revealed in new dimensions by disclosing his resemblance to "wolf." Metaphor can challenge us to extend the range of commonplaces affiliated with a term and to discover new associations suggested by its interaction with its context. If all we do in response to a metaphor is to recognize already established relationships, the figure has not interacted with its setting in a surprising, challenging, or innovative way.[7]

The addition of meaning that metaphor brings about should not be regarded as a hidden entity lying disguised behind or beyond the literal sense. If a metaphor results from an interaction, the meaning of the figure is not a concealed substance but a process and an event. Metaphorical meaning is not something "there," independently awaiting discovery, but is cocreated by the reader and depends on him or her to make it exist by resolving the incongruity of the figure.

A hierarchical model of meaning is, however, implicit in I. A. Richards's well-known distinction between "tenor" and "vehicle." According to Richards, "When we use a metaphor we have two thoughts of different things active together and supported by a single word, or phrase, whose meaning is a resultant of their interaction." The "vehicle" is the direct thought that carries the "tenor," "the underlying idea or principal subject."[8] Richards describes the "vehicle" and the "tenor" as relatively clear, distinct ideas that exist apart from their coming together in a metaphor. Their interaction is limited to resonating against each other. Although Richards is often considered an interaction theorist, his model misleadingly restricts the eventfulness of metaphor by limiting it to the interchange between two already permissible ideas.

The reader of figurative language attributes a "tenor" to a "vehicle," however, only after finding that the metaphorical term is anomalous and requires extension. The interaction takes place not between two ideas, each of which has an autonomous, fully adequate meaning, but between a term and a context in which it seems incongruous. The foundation of a metaphor is not a direct thought supporting an indirect one but a failure to fit that provokes a creative response from the reader. When consistency is restored, this is accomplished not by discovering the "underlying idea" beneath the literal meaning but by revising and expanding the semantic range of the figurative term. The extrapolation of meaning that creates coherence does not rest on the literal meaning as a support or a carrier but points out the limits of the term's previous stock of meaning in order to enlarge it.

A more accurate, convenient way of dividing metaphor would be to describe it as a disorientation followed by a reorientation. Ricoeur similarly characterizes metaphor as "a bringing-together of terms that first surprises" and "bewilders" before the reader "finally uncovers a relationship" to resolve "the paradox" (*Rule of Metaphor*, p. 27). The equal importance of both disorientation and reorientation is another reason why it is an oversimplification to describe metaphor as a process of establishing resemblances. Nietzsche attributes to metaphor the power of "making what is different equal [*Gleichsetzen des Nichtgleichen*]."[9] Both resemblance and opposition—like and not-like (*gleich* and *nicht gleich*)—are vital to metaphor. A metaphor must disrupt the reader's expectations in order to prompt him or her to extend its meaning in new ways. This can occur, however, only if the figurative attribution is *not* like the equivalence it proposes. Enough likeness must also remain discoverable, though, for readers to succeed in their search for a new congruence. A successful metaphor is a delicate balance of difference and similarity, disjunction and coherence, anomaly and revelation. As Goodman argues, "Metaphor requires attraction as well as resistance—indeed, an attraction that overcomes resistance" (*Languages of Art*, pp. 69–70). Even when the reader has discovered new consistency, tension from the "not-like" lingers as evidence of the labor of metaphor and the novelty it brings.

Not only is the presence of the negative a sign of the disorientation the reader has experienced; it also suggests that we identify an entity by its differences as well as by its resemblances. If metaphorical interactions create new meaning by juxtaposing dissonance and consistency, this double process parallels a crucial duality of cognition. We determine what something is by distinguishing what it is not as well as by affiliating it with others of its kind. The relation of "like" and "not-like" in a metaphor has to do not only with semantic innovation but also with cognition, and this is the issue to which we must now turn.

The Epistemology of Interaction: Understanding through Metaphors

Metaphors make new meaning by initiating basic interpretive processes in the reader. The experience of construing a novel metaphor can change the reader's habits of cognition because it manipulates fundamental aspects of understanding. The disorientation and reorientation metaphors bring about are related to the circularity of interpretation in the process of construing the meaning of a sentence. Emile Benveniste recalls the hermeneutic circle when he argues that "a sentence constitutes a whole which is not reducible to the sum of its parts."[10] This is true because we construe a sentence by discovering a pattern into which we fit its various components. Without our having a sense of their design, the features of the sentence would be meaningless; but the design in turn acquires its significance from the relations among its parts. With individual sentences as with larger textual units, we read by projecting hypotheses about the overarching patterns into which the elements we encounter combine, and we then test these guesses, modifying and refining them as necessary, by trying to align pieces into the configurations we expect to find.[11] Metaphors are disorienting because the anomaly they introduce into sentence construction disrupts the circularity of understanding. The reorientation they make possible is new knowledge about how to establish coherence.

A metaphorical term is anomalous because it defies the reader's customary habits for building consistency between part and whole. Consider, for example, Wordsworth's well-known line:

Our birth is but a sleep and a forgetting.[12]

"Sleep" is dissonant because it does not seem consistent with "birth," which might seem more like an awakening. What hypothesis can the reader discover to fit "sleep" and "birth" together? This hypothesis must furthermore make both words harmonize with "forgetting"—a complication that also furnishes a clue about the whole to which these anomalous parts might possibly belong. Perhaps "birth" is a "sleep," the reader may hypothesize, in the sense that it entails a loss of consciousness—a loss of one's memory of the state one has left. This guess about the whole meaning of the line is based on each of its elements but is necessary in turn to make sense of them. The following lines in the stanza confirm the hypothesis and allow the reader to amplify and refine it by specifying further our former state ("trailing clouds of glory do we come / From God, who is our home") and by clarifying our loss and its consequences ("Heaven lies about us in our infancy" but becomes more remote as we grow older). We give "sleep" a figurative meaning by projecting a guess about the whole of which it is part—a guess warranted by the consistency it establishes.

It is often said that there are no rules for deciphering metaphors.[13] The reason is that no pregiven instructions can tell us what hypotheses will make the elements of any state of affairs cohere. Reading figures—like all interpretation—is a process of trial and error at which one may become more adept with practice but which one never completely masters. As with Wordsworth's metaphor, comprehension is often possible only retrospectively, for later details can provide crucial clues for resolving an earlier anomaly. The whole in which the part fits can become more evident as the context expands (and the bewildering effect of some especially difficult poetry results from the frustrating of this expectation). A detail that at first surprised and confused us makes sense after we discover the pattern to which it belongs, and this backward-glancing constitution of meaning is evidence of the circularity of understanding.

Metaphor can educate the reader to new ways of understanding by refusing established practices of fitting parts together. This disruption challenges us to imagine new patterns and connections. The links and relations we discover might not previously have seemed possible to us, but we are invited to expand our cognitive apparatus by disclosing them to ourselves as we find ways of making the metaphor consistent with its setting. The surprise caused by a disorienting metaphor reveals that we approached it with expectations that it did not fulfill. These expectations reflect our customary habits of building consistency. We may have had only a vague, general sense of the predicate we expected to follow "our birth is"—but it almost certainly did not include "a sleep." The tactic of assuming that the anomalous term is a metaphor is a particular strategy for reestablishing consistency (we might have hypothesized that it was an error or a conventional usage of which we were unaware). Working from this assumption, we experiment more freely and creatively with conjectures about meaning than we otherwise might have. We loosen the bonds of conventional definitions and past habits of sense making in order to discover a new way of making the anomalous part coherent.

Our license for suspending customary limitations is that they have resulted in an incongruity. Our new guesses about the puzzling term's relation to its setting will, of course, be based on our past practice with projecting hypotheses, but they must also try to extend it for the very reason that it has not proved adequate. The circle here is that we can make sense of the unfamiliar only by grafting it onto the familiar—but that we must also change what we already know in order to account for the new and the strange.

As we try to reorient ourselves, we are free to imagine for the metaphor a variety of possible meanings that violate conventional rules, but we are constrained by the necessity of testing each hypothesis to see how well it resolves the incongruity. Both invigorating and demanding, the experience of construing novel metaphors is training in devising hypotheses to fit parts together in unaccustomed ways. Metaphors work against the tendency of repeated uses of the same sense-making hypotheses to congeal into habits. Innovative metaphors challenge us to break down our rigidity, to expand the kinds of relationships we can acknowledge, and to revive our imagination for new possibilities of combination.

Some especially ambitious metaphors may defy our expectations not only because they frustrate conventional patterns of consistency building but also because they challenge our basic assumptions about the categories and kinds that compose the world. As I have argued, our expectations about any particular phenomenon are a reflection of a general anticipatory understanding of people and things. Our presuppositions are essential aids to understanding because they give us a prior conception of the characteristics that are likely to define any state of affairs—possibilities that we actualize when we explicate its details according to the patterns we anticipate.[14] One aspect of the anomaly of finding "birth" grouped together with "sleep" and "forgetting" is that we typically do not associate them and thus lack ready hypotheses for making them cohere; another aspect is that this lack exposes a divergence between Wordsworth's vision and our own preconceptions about the matters at hand.

The disorientation of a surprising metaphor can reveal the limits of our presuppositions and challenge us to revise them. We need not permanently make Wordsworth's beliefs our own in order to interpret his metaphor, but we need to understand them. We will not be able to generate a hypothesis that can coherently join "birth" and "sleep" unless we can entertain the conviction that childhood might be a privileged spiritual state from which maturity and education unfortunately but inevitably separate us. This new assumption about the spiritual course of human development challenges the reader's preconceptions to a greater or lesser degree, which will vary from individual to individual, from culture to culture, and from one historical period to another. The extent of the challenge will be measured by our surprise at encountering a figure that associates birth with a diminution in awareness and by our relative ease or difficulty in generating hypotheses to assimilate it. After Wordsworth's attitudes have become widely known, the shock of the figure may wear off and its effectiveness diminish. Ironically, the more we understand a poem, the less we may be able to appreciate it.[15]

If the metaphor does retain its novelty for us, however, the surprise of finding our preconceptions inadequate to make sense of the incongruous term may have several different results. We may reject as alien the beliefs on which the figure is based and reconfirm our own assumptions, perhaps with a better understanding of why we prefer them than we had before alternative convictions exposed their limits. Not everyone who reads Wordsworth becomes a pantheist, but untangling his convictions can still increase our self-understanding by differentiating what we do believe from what we do not. Or the new patterns and relations to which the metaphor has introduced us may become a lasting part of our own presuppositions about the world. We may reject some assumptions that we previously held but are inconsistent with the new figure, or we may find ways of expanding our preconceptions by grafting new beliefs onto them. Or, between the poles of self-delineation and personal redefinition, we may use the otherness of the figure as a challenge to extend our ability to imagine different ways of seeing without firmly refusing or permanently adopting them. Even if we do not convert to new beliefs, the experience of experimenting with alternative hypotheses about how to establish coherence can increase our imagination for modes of vision other than our own.

There is yet another circle here—a circle joining the two levels of belief that we employ when we understand. If the hypotheses we generate to make sense of a text necessarily reflect our fundamental convictions about the world, then our experiences with projecting guesses about the meaning of texts can rebound and bring about changes in the assumptions with which we began. By challenging our imagination about possible modes of consistency, a novel metaphor also tests and questions the basic presuppositions underlying the hypotheses about coherence we typically employ. If new metaphors can change our ways of thinking about the world, this is ultimately because the demand of devising unusual, unprecedented hypotheses to make sense of them can provoke us to reconsider the basic beliefs that customarily guide our interpretations.

The two levels of belief in understanding are paralleled by two levels of figuration. The particular metaphors in any discourse embody and articulate the general figures that organize the text's overall perception of the world. Wordsworth's comparison of "birth" to "sleep," for example, is a particular metaphor based on a general figurative understanding of human development as a falling away from primal grace—an overarching, controlling trope that prompts such other metaphors as the analogy of age to a "prison-house" or of youth to "Nature's Priest." Even more obviously, the title of T. S. Eliot's poem *The Waste Land* announces his general figure for modern society's spiritual desiccation, which then finds expression in repeated images of the desert, infertility, and decay.

These two levels of figuration mutually constitute each other. The challenges to rethink the shape of consistency which are offered by individual sentences are repeated in various forms over the course of the work. The reader is thus gradually introduced to the overall configuration of the world projected by the fundamental tropes governing the discourse. The various experiences of disorientation and reorientation which a work's metaphors put the reader through are not chaotic and random but patterned. The repetition of analogous destructions and reconstructions of consistency helps the reader to understand each new metaphor he or she encounters by suggesting how it contributes to a developing design. Again circular in operation, the reader's understanding of each particular metaphor is aided by his or her sense of the whole pattern they form, just as one's knowledge of the general tropes controlling this pattern is acquired only by interpreting individual figures. At the level of both the sentence and the entire text, with particular as well as general tropes, reading figures is a process of experimenting with relations between parts and wholes.

Interpreting metaphors can change our ways of thinking and perceiving because all understanding is basically figurative. Not only when we construe a text or a trope but whenever we understand, we do so by fitting parts into wholes. Our understanding of any particular detail is figurative in that it depends on the gestalt to which we attribute it and the place to which we assign it in this structure. Our hypotheses about patterns of consistency are acts of figuration. The presuppositions on which any hypothesis is based are figurative as well because they are assumptions about the kind of entity we are dealing with and the types of relations we are likely to encounter. Goodman suggests that "a metaphor might be regarded as a calculated category-mistake" (*Languages of Art*, p. 73). It challenges our sense of the kinds and relations that make up the world by creating a linkage our ordinary groupings cannot explain. We can assimilate the innovation only by creating a new type. This process of refiguring our categories of understanding has considerable cognitive importance because the wholes by which we make sense of parts are the kinds that we assume constitute the world. Without kinds we could not understand because we would lack patterns for establishing consistency. The metaphors we have learned are a crucial source of the patterns we use as we go around the hermeneutic circle.

Metaphor is sometimes described as a process of "seeing as"—seeing something as something else to which it is analogous. But all understanding has an "as-structure," as Heidegger points out.[16] Aligning parts into wholes entails seeing them "as" components of a structure. The "as" of figuration is the design that governs the relation of part and whole. There is also another sense, however, in which understanding requires an "as." We can construe any phenomenon only by employing signs other than itself—signs that stand for it and make sense of it. An interpretation therefore has an "as"-relation to its object because it is analogous to but necessarily distinct from it. If metaphor entails "seeing as" because it describes a state of affairs that it is both like and not-like ("birth" is both like and not like "sleep" and "forgetting"), this is also what all interpretations do. Deciding the validity of an interpretation is often difficult for the very reason that any construal is not immediate truth but only a mediate presentation of a phenomenon "as" understood in a particular way. If metaphors similarly understand by deploying "as"-relations, then judging the truth-claims of figures should entail difficulties very much like those that accompany the process of validation in general.

The Validity of Metaphors: Evaluating the Truth-Claims of Figures

The truths of metaphors are many. As we try to make sense of figures, we do not encounter the same depiction of part-whole relations again and again. We find, rather, an ever-changing panoply of different configurations of consistency. Wayne Booth argues that "our stories criticize each other as expressions of how life is."[17] The same holds for our metaphors. One reason why we do not immediately and completely convert to new beliefs whenever we meet a new figure is that other stories and metaphors make competing claims for our allegiance. Bakhtin suggests one value of this competition: "Languages throw light on each other: one language can, after all, see itself only in the light of another language."[18] In their conflict metaphors illuminate each other. If we live in a world of figures, only by using figures can we recognize and criticize their limits and strengths. By contesting each other's claims to truth, competing metaphors demonstrate what their own and the other's boundaries are, what insights they offer, and what blindnesses they suffer.

The experience of construing different metaphors can have various consequences. The irreconcilability of conflicting metaphors may cause insecurity about the inadequacies of our ruling tropes or even anxiety about our inability to reach a ground beneath figuration. Or their multiplicity may seem reason to celebrate our seemingly endless possibilities for creating meaning. If the metaphors we confront do not seem to offer essential new insights, they may increase our confidence in the merits of the figures that have ably met our practical needs in the past. Or the challenge of imagining new ways of configuring the world may expose the limits of our everyday interpretive habits and compel us to change them. The result may be an invigorating expansion of our cognitive powers or a painful abandonment of cherished assumptions—or probably both, since we can build new habits only by destroying old ones.

However we respond to the novelty of metaphor, one major value of confronting a variety of figures is that they ward off hermeneutic rigidity. By testing our assumptions and our customary practices of consistency building, they keep us flexible and open to change. They prevent our sense-making hypotheses from ossifying into dogma and insist on their provisionality, being valuable insofar as they make the world cohere but expendable because others can always replace them. By presenting us with different, unexpected configurations of part and whole, new metaphors prevent our use of the hermeneutic circle from becoming closed and vicious, locked by habit into the same self-confirming patterns.

The tests we apply to judge the truth of a metaphor are no different from those we use to assess the validity of any interpretation. Noting that "difficulties in determining truth are by no means peculiar to metaphor," Goodman argues that "standards of truth are much the same whether the schema used is transferred [i.e., metaphorical] or not" (*Languages of Art*, p. 79). The three basic tests for validity—inclusiveness, efficacy, and intersubjectivity—apply as much to metaphor as to any other mode of understanding. As I have argued, these tests are capable of ruling out some interpretations as demonstrably illegitimate, although they cannot conclusively identify a single correct reading and must consequently allow genuine, irreconcilable hermeneutic conflict. Similarly, the tests for validity can judge some figures untrue; but they cannot establish either unanimity about which metaphors are eternally correct or uniformity among their claims about how the world is shaped.

If, for example, according to the test of inclusiveness, a hypothesis about the relations between parts and wholes must establish consistency among all available evidence, then some figures can be rejected on the grounds that they are internally incoherent. If our attempts to discover coherence result only in incongruity, we may reject a figure as purely disorienting and not also reorienting. We call such figures "mixed metaphors" because their juxtaposition of terms is confusing rather than illuminating. Incoherent figures create dissonance but do not allow us to generate new consistency.

This is not a conclusive test, however, because one reader's confusing mixture may be another's dynamic, productive opposition. For example, the success of Ezra Pound's classic experiment in juxtaposition, "In a Station of the Metro," is that it strains to the limit the reader's ability to hold contraries together:

> The apparition of these faces in the crowd;
> Petals on a wet, black bough.[19]

The power of this image is due in large part to the surprise of the comparison. The connection between these seemingly unrelated terms is a blank we are challenged to fill. An anonymous mass of commuters is, at first glance, not at all like leaves on a damp branch—although, on second thought, they are indeed similar enough that we can find ways of joining them that are not far-fetched (perhaps picturing featureless white and pink faces clustered together like petals on a flowering tree and imagining the day as dark and damp, as if it had just rained).

Because all metaphors require some dissonance and disruption, all are mixed to some degree. In order to make sense and claim truth as figures, they must then enable the reader to reestablish coherence—but since this depends on the reader's creativity,

not everyone will always agree about how freely we should experiment with new possible combinations before declaring a metaphor
a failure. The consistency of Pound's figure is the product of the
reader's imagination. A reader with Dr. Johnson's impatience at the
contortions of metaphysical wit might reject the figure as incoherent, however, and the only compelling evidence against this
verdict is the willingness of the majority of modern readers to
produce the connections that the figure withholds.

Even after we have made a figure consistent, we cannot judge
one metaphor the most illuminating on the grounds that it is the
most inclusive. Different metaphors offer different ways of establishing coherence between part and whole, and their qualitative
divergences prevent quantitative rankings. Pound's image suggests, for example, the anonymity and lifelessness of the urban
crowd (the faces are an "apparition," and their association seems
impersonal and accidental). By contrast, in the poem "Composed
upon Westminster Bridge," Wordsworth offers a series of figures
comparing the imposing grandeur and incipient life of the city in
the early morning ("all that mighty heart is lying still!") to the
spiritual splendor of nature.[20] The reader of Wordsworth's figure is
challenged to share his discovery of a primal sympathy uniting the
city and the country as emanations of life, whereas Pound's reader
finds an image of nature employed to reveal the urban landscape's
lack of invigorating harmony. Both figures are illuminating because
both disrupt our customary sense of relationships and challenge us
to imagine new combinations, and neither can be preferred as
more inclusive or consistent. They make different, irreconcilable
claims to truth by proposing different configurations of part and
whole. The incompatibility of equally self-consistent figures demonstrates that there can be many ways of making the world cohere,
none of which is necessarily the "truest."

The standard of efficacy is similarly able to discount some
metaphors as unworkable and not worth preserving but unable to
ascertain a single most useful way of configuring the world. Some
figures offer more effective ways of organizing entities and relationships than others do. Some of our most useful figures are the
dead metaphors that have become so deeply ingrained in everyday
discourse that we do not notice them. Dead metaphors show that
we take figures for "true" if they are effective interpretive instru-

ments. As a repository of what everyone thinks and no one questions, however, dead metaphors can be the locus of false consciousness, and this danger suggests that the hermeneutic usefulness of a figure may not be decisive proof of its truth. Figures that seem self-evidently true and no longer provocative and enigmatic have descended to the realm of platitudes and clichés. Their unquestioned obviousness can contribute to a culture's self-deceptive assurances about the necessity of its way of structuring the world—thereby disguising that this is nothing more than a product of figuration.[21] Applying the test of efficacy to metaphor reveals an important dilemma: We cannot know without employing figures, and their usefulness justifies our confidence in them, but uncritical faith in their powers is an illusion which covers over their variability and provisionality.

What counts as an effective metaphor is subject to change from generation to generation and from culture to culture. Even the metaphors that govern science are not permanent but variable. The shift from the Newtonian paradigm to Einstein's view of the universe entails, for example, a change in the global figures that scientists regard as effective models of nature. Einsteinian scientists no longer see nature as the "machine" or the "giant clock" of the Newtonian worldview. Newtonians believed that each part of the machine made the others next to it move according to the linear operations of cause and effect, and they also thought that the workings of the mechanism could be calculated with precision and certainty by an independent observer who would be limited only by the accuracy of his or her measuring instruments.

For Einsteinian scientists, however, this metaphor has reached the limits of its effectiveness; it must be replaced, they believe, by a conception of the universe as a "web" or a "field." According to this figure, the whole of the field is greater than the sum of its parts, and no element can be understood without considering its relations not just to adjacent terms but to all the other constituents of the system. The scientist can no longer assume linear causation because even a small change in any element can effect the rearrangement of the entire field. Measurement is no longer neutral, independent observation because scientists are part of the field they study and their acts will alter its shape.[22] The basic laws of physics are historical artifacts, not universal absolutes, because they rest on figures rather than reflect transparently the simple facts of nature. A shift in perspective has transformed the assumptions of science and the metaphors it currently believes in.

Newton's figures are not totally inoperative, however. They are still effective in some rudimentary situations, but they are no longer considered absolutely true. Students must still learn how to use them, but they must also know when to abandon them as unworkable. The perspective of science changed because its ruling metaphors proved powerless to account for certain crucial situations, and new figures had to be invented to explain them, but the discredited metaphors are still "true" for the problems they can solve. This ambiguity shows both the utility and the limitations of the test of efficacy. The standard of effectiveness can rule some figures false (the mechanistic view of nature is wrong), but it cannot unequivocally decide what is true (mechanistic metaphors are still useful in some situations, even though they are incorrect, because unworkable, in others).

This example also shows that "truth" is intersubjective—what the community considers valid, a judgment that can change. The invention of a metaphor is individual, but its acceptance is social. As Hazard Adams notes, "The metaphorical event is repeatable. The event's adoption in the linguistic community indicates that it has created common meaning."[23] Because the metaphor's semantic innovation requires the reader's cooperation and contribution, the ability of the community to create the new coherence it demands is the necessary prerequisite for its acceptance. In order to generate new meaning and introduce new truth, a metaphor must extend the community's imagination of possible relations beyond previously existing limits—but not so far that the community balks and refuses to go along. Successful metaphorical innovation requires social adoption. Too much acceptance, however, will rob the figure of its novelty. Complete intersubjective assimilation means the death of metaphor—its transformation from figurative to literal, from deviation to norm, from new meaning to conventional wisdom.

The test of intersubjective acceptance is socially and historically variable. The scientist who questioned the possibility of measurement under the Newtonian paradigm would be considered an impractical philosopher or an eccentric. The contemporary particle physicist who insisted on the absoluteness of measurement would not get published and promoted if, indeed, he or she had somehow managed to earn a degree. Similarly, Dr. Johnson's disapproval of metaphysical figures as forced and artificial seems quaint only because Pound and Eliot have so powerfully altered modern sensibilities. In both science and art, one community's sound, reasoned judgment may seem like prejudice and superstition to another. What will be considered an effective, coherent metaphor and what will be rejected as unworkable and inconsistent cannot be determined absolutely and invariably. As I have argued before, the standards of efficacy and inclusiveness will differ according to the norms of the community that applies them. It will accept or reject metaphors according to its criteria of legitimacy—and according to its willingness to tolerate violations of those standards and to question its own convictions. Not only the norms in force but also the degree of tolerance of their violation can change from one period or culture to another.

No community is ever totally willing to accept violations of its conventions. If it were, it would soon cease to exist. Intersubjective acceptance is consequently not only metaphor's main way of claiming truth but also a major obstacle to the new insights it offers. Jean-François Lyotard makes a similar point: "Innovation is always born of dissension. . . . The stronger the 'move,' the more likely it is to be denied the minimum consensus, precisely because it changes the rules of the game upon which consensus has been based."[24] General social recognition is inherently unlikely to be granted to daring innovations that radically challenge prevailing customs and standards. Metaphor is socially subversive to the extent that it disrupts existing norms in order to provoke us to imagine new ways of structuring the world. The community's refusal of a novel metaphor may be a sign not of the figure's incoherence or ineffectiveness but of the group's rigidity—its unwillingness to reexamine and change its categories and convictions. Without social acceptance metaphorical innovation cannot disclose new truth, but a figure's failure to win recognition may reflect the blindness of established authority rather than the falsity of its creator's vision.

Metaphorical assimilation is a political process because it is one of the ways in which a community decides what is valuable and true—or has this decision made for it. As George Lakoff and Mark Johnson observe, "People in power get to impose their metaphors."[25] The denial of an innovative figure's claim to truth may be based on a legitimate criticism of its flaws, or it may be a willful suppression of an alternative configuration of the world. A universe in which new figures ruled every day would be hopelessly unstable. Inertia in adopting proposed innovations makes possible the preservation of ways of thinking, perceiving, and acting that have a history of proven effectiveness. But a world where figures never change would be stifling and stagnant. Indiscriminate rejection of semantic innovation inhibits growth and discovery.

Metaphor is always possible, however, because it innovates by playing with existing norms. It needs no special tools or resources—just an established way of building patterns and an imagination for incongruity in order to disrupt it. There are no pregiven limits to the figurative rearrangements of part and whole that may claim validity. Any incongruity is potentially an instrument of metaphorical reeducation, provided that its disruption of our expectations is channeled to a new creation of coherence—and that we are able and willing to respond to its provocation to rethink our categories. Metaphor can be a liberating power in that it operates against the tendency of established conventions to close the world. Interpreting figures is an ongoing challenge to keep our cognitive horizons open.

History, Epistemology, and the
Example of *The Turn of the Screw*

Some contemporary critics have suggested that history offers a way out of the impasses of epistemology. In their view, the promise of epistemology has failed because theoretical reflection has not been able to devise clear, indisputable procedures for producing correct interpretations. This problem, it is thought, can be bypassed, if not resolved, by turning to history. The argument for replacing epistemological reflection with historical analysis takes several forms. If, for example, a theoretical issue like that of the relation between a writer's intention and the meaning of his work cannot be conclusively settled, then we can at least explain how this dilemma arose by analyzing the development of the concept of the author.[1] Perhaps studying the history of a problem will show us how to avoid traps others have fallen into. Or, if the inability of epistemology to legislate correctness means that different communities can regard different kinds of argumentation as persuasive, then perhaps we should study concretely the various rhetorical practices in which interpreters have engaged instead of attempting to define absolutely what a right reading must look like. This maneuver would turn epistemology into a historical issue by asking how ways of seeing are institutionalized in discursive practices.[2] Or perhaps we should abandon theoretical reflection altogether and devote ourselves to practical research, in the conviction that some problems can be solved concretely, case by case, even if they resist a global, philosophical attack.[3] For all of these arguments, historical study seems to offer a means of avoiding irreconcilable epistemological disputes.

This hope is, however, mistaken. History does not provide a neutral ground outside the theory of knowledge. "History" itself is a hermeneutic construct, and all the quarrels about validity in interpretation return in the question of how to constitute it. Instead of escaping the epistemological issues that have vexed contemporary literary theory, the move to history is destined to repeat them. Epistemology is necessarily implicated in history in a number of ways. Disinterested, unbiased description is no more possible in history than elsewhere. All historical analyses are narrations governed by a prefigurative understanding of what the relevant elements are and how they fit together in the field under study.[4] The historical narratives that different generations prefer to tell about the "same" events may change because understanding brings about a meeting of the horizons of past and present in which the meaning of the past will vary according to the different presuppositions and interests that define the standpoint of the present.[5] For this reason, the act of interpreting a literary work is itself historically variable. Indeed, individual works have histories because the epistemologies used to interpret them can and frequently do change from generation to generation. Instead of it being the case that history enables us to avoid the controversies of hermeneutic theory, we need an epistemology of interpretive multiplicity to explain why texts have histories and why historians tell different stories about the past. Epistemology is not a dispensable project which can be replaced by practical study of the past but is necessary for understanding how different interpretive enterprises work—including the many conflicting ways of studying history.

My aim in this chapter is to write a history that shows that history and epistemology cannot do without each other. Henry James's novella *The Turn of the Screw* suggests itself as an example because of the notorious interpretive disputes that have marked its reception. One of my goals is to suggest that even though historical analysis cannot transcend epistemological questions, it can shed light on them inasmuch as the hermeneutic past of literary works is an important area in which the issues of concern to contemporary theory are played out. The history of *The Turn of the Screw* provides classic evidence of why the goal of achieving a single right reading is elusive and misconceived, but it also supports my contention that debates between conflicting communities of readers are governed by various constraints and tests for validity and are not exercises in solipsism. The challenge of writing a history of the reception of James's novella will test the theory of interpretation I have been developing. After examining how *The Turn of the Screw* has been construed, I will then try to show that the epistemology of literary interpretation has essentially the same structure as historical understanding. Critics engaged in historical research related to *The Turn of the Screw* duplicate the epistemological processes involved in interpreting the work, and this is one of the reasons why different interpreters of James's text offer different versions of its reception. (My account of its reception is a case in point, for my narrative of its history reenacts my own interpretation of interpretation.) This variability in turn is evidence that history is not neutral, bias-free description but depends on the presuppositions of the interpreter.

One of the questions at stake in the debate about history and epistemology is how to understand the scope and function of the term "theory." Like all words, this term has a variety of meanings. In this chapter I am most concerned with defending the importance of two different but related senses of the term, both of which reflect my conviction that "theory" is a flexible, multifaceted enterprise.[6] The first of these definitions sees "theory" as the general activity of reflecting on the characteristics of literature and the implications of critical practice. This kind of theorizing includes inquiries into such problems as the structure of understanding, the mode of existence of a literary work, the question of value, the workings of metaphor, and so on. There are also, secondly, local "theories" about the assumptions and aims that should guide interpretation—for example, psychoanalysis, Marxism, structuralism, and the like. Because of the role of presuppositions in prefiguring understanding, all interpretation entails at least the implicit choice of a hermeneutic theory. These two definitions are related, of course, because local hermeneutic theories typically disagree about global theoretical issues.

The philosophical figure behind many critics' turn to history has been Richard Rorty, whose important book *Philosophy and the Mirror of Nature* is a convincing attack on a particular way of conceiving the discipline of epistemology. According to Rorty, "The notion of knowledge as accurate representation, made possible by special mental processes, and intelligible through a general theory of representation, needs to be abandoned."[7] As he tells it, the story of knowledge has not been a progressive improvement in the mirroring capacities of the mind as it has tried to make itself more transparent to its objects. Rather, to know has meant to participate in a series of diverse, changing conversations which have used different vocabularies to address different interests and ask different questions. Rorty argues that "the history of philosophy" is "a series, not of alternative solutions to the same problems, but of quite different sets of problems" and that "the latest vocabulary . . . may not express privileged representations of essences, but be just another of the potential infinity of vocabularies in which the world can be described" (*Mirror*, pp. xiii, 367).

If this view is correct, philosophy cannot claim foundational status as the " 'most basic' discipline" whose task it is "to establish the objectivity of the knowledge-claims made in the various empirical disciplines" (*Mirror*, pp. 132, 135). Philosophy has been made up of many kinds of discussions, which may or may not be of interest to workers in other fields and which cannot pretend to lay the ground rules by which they must abide. In a multiple world of conflicting practices of thinking and speaking, it makes no sense to try to promulgate laws for how the mind should work, because to do so would be to propose only another manner of interpreting and talking about the world, not the way to end all ways. Consequently, Rorty advises, in order to come to grips with certain perpetually vexing philosophical problems, one should not try to develop an improved model of mind but should examine the historical record to see how they arose. "Solving" these problems would entail not developing a more accurate means of representing the world but understanding how the conversations of philosophers raised them in forms that caused discussion to run into trouble or break down.

Rorty concludes from this line of reasoning that epistemology must be abandoned. By "epistemology" he understands the "project of learning more about what we could know and how we might know it better by studying how our mind worked" (*Mirror*, p. 137). This project is certainly dubious if there is no single right way of knowing, but that is grounds for redefining epistemology rather than setting it aside. Rorty's call for the demise of epistemology is self-contradictory because a theory of knowledge is implicit in his description of disciplines as diverse, changing conversations. In denying that understanding is accurate representation, he theorizes that it takes other forms—the pursuit of intersubjectively acceptable beliefs and convincing arguments. Whether or not this is a satisfactory account of knowledge is an epistemological question, and part of the answer to it requires an examination of his claim that we should "see 'justification' as a social phenomenon rather than a transaction between 'the knowing subject' and 'reality'" (*Mirror,* p. 9). Are there no "enduring constraints on what can count as knowledge" (*Mirror,* p. 9), as he argues, or are there transhistorical tests for validity? Is it sufficient to regard interpretive standards as totally internal to the community, or should we preserve some notion of otherness as the object to which interpreters are responsible and at which their various conversations aim, even if this otherness can vary radically according to how it is construed? These are some of the epistemological questions raised by Rorty's attack on epistemology.

The history of the reception of *The Turn of the Screw* suggests that, as a model for describing understanding, accurate representation is less useful than variable conversations concerned with shifting, often incommensurable problems. But it also demonstrates that there are fundamental epistemological reasons for the developments and discontinuities in the novel's reception, and we cannot understand the changes it has undergone if we stop asking theoretical questions about knowledge. The history of this work shows as well that the process of validation has certain constant forms across different communities and that validation cannot be collapsed into social agreement because it entails a responsibility to otherness.[8]

Epistemological Conflict and the Tests for Validity

The debate about the *The Turn of the Screw* supports Rorty's claim that making the mind a mirror to its object will not end hermeneutic conflict. The object's characteristics are precisely what is under dispute, and they can seem radically different to different minds. To take a classic example, for Edmund Wilson "there is never any reason for supposing that anybody but the governess sees the ghosts," and she is "self-deceived," but for Wayne Booth "the ghosts are real, the governess sees what she says she sees."[9] Attempts to mediate or resolve such conflicts by pointing to what is really there in the text extend the debate instead of stopping it. One of the earliest of such attempts is Leon Edel's claim that examining "the technique of the story-telling . . . would have made much of the dispute unnecessary." Because we are confined to the point of view of the first-person narrator, he argues, "the reader must establish for himself the credibility of the witness."[10] But that, of course, is exactly what Booth, Wilson, and many others have argued about— whether the governess's vision is to be trusted or suspected, believed or demystified. If anything, Edel shows one reason why the dispute occurred, not why it was superfluous. Appealing to the structure beneath a conflict is sometimes a useful strategy for making sense of an unresolvable controversy, but it still leaves the interpreter with the decision of how he or she will participate in the discussion—whether by choosing one of the opposing views, by trying to oscillate back and forth between them (as one does with those figures wherein one first sees a rabbit and then a duck, first an urn and then two faces), or by developing yet another alternative not yet part of the conversation.

An appeal to objective textual features is often made in an effort to stop a debate that, it is felt, has become tedious. For how long, many readers have asked, can we argue about the existence of ghosts without losing interest? Even before their reality was questioned by Wilson, however, the conversation about the novella had begun to lag. Early reviewers wondered whether so harrowing a tale about such abominable evil should ever have been written. "The story itself is distinctly repulsive," one critic complained, and another reported, "We have never read a more sickening, a more gratuitously melancholy tale."[11] Only twenty years later, however, the work's gruesome effects seem to have worn off, and Virginia Woolf found James's ghosts too domestic and worldly to be frightening. "What does it matter, then," she asked, "if we do pick up *The Turn of the Screw* an hour or so before bedtime?"[12] Wilson's hypothesis about the governess's madness—so familiar as to seem boring to readers in the 1960s and 1970s—originally had the function of revivifying interest in a text that was losing its impact.

When readers grew tired of arguing about the governess's sanity, the reason for their complaints was not that through this unresolvable controversy they had lost touch with the text itself but that suggestions for reading that had at first given new impulses to discussion had eventually become conventional and incapable of opening new interpretive possibilities. This dilemma can be resolved, not by trying to cut beneath the controversy to reach the object that gave rise to it, but only by developing new interpretive strategies to get the conversation out of its rut—by shifting suspicion to Mrs. Grose or the absent Master, for example (Eric Solomon's and John Rowe's suggestions), by introducing a new theme like interpretation as the play of differences (Shoshana Felman's way of turning the screw), or by transforming the discussion itself into the object of discussion (a tactic currently popular among many, and the strategy this chapter employs).[13]

In order to understand why interpreters of *The Turn of the Screw* have disagreed, we must ask epistemological and even metaphysical questions about their procedures and assumptions. These are consequential questions, because answering them can give us guidance about how to behave in the conversation even if it will not settle the disputes. If, as Rorty claims, different partners in a discussion may not see eye to eye because they are concerned about different problems, such divergences occur because the interpreters have conflicting beliefs about what the object is and how best to engage it. Robert Heilman claims to find fault with Wilson's Freudian reading on the grounds that it is not transparent enough in mirroring its object. He charges Wilson with making "a facile, doctrinaire application of formulae where they have no business and hence compel either an ignoring of, or a gross distortion of, the materials."[14] What lies at the bottom of Heilman's objections, however, is not so much Wilson's lack of empirical responsibility as his conception of human being. Heilman regards the governess as a heroine in a story with "the oldest of themes—the struggle of evil to possess the human soul," and he types the novella in this way because he finds in James "an almost religious sense of the duality of man."[15] Wilson's psychoanalytic view of the governess as a "thwarted Anglo-Saxon spinster" also posits a basic human doubleness—but an internal difference brought about by repression rather than the religious opposition of purity versus corruption.

His disagreement with Heilman about how to read the story is based on a metaphysical conflict about the kind of differences that constitute the origin of meaning.

Their dispute displays the interdependence of the two levels of belief that play off each other in understanding: our hypotheses about the patterns in which the elements of a text cohere, and our more enduring, fundamental presuppositions about literature and life, which we take with us from one interpretive situation to another. Heilman's hypothesis about the work's type—a religious struggle of good versus evil—gives him a sense of the whole in which he can then align the text's parts, and this conjecture about genre seems to him confirmed by the elaborate patterns of imagery that it helps him piece together in the text. But his decision about which formal relations to experiment with in reading arises out of convictions about the kinds of conflict that are most significant in human life. Different assumptions about human being attune Wilson to a different set of textual configurations because those beliefs equip him with a different range of hypotheses about how parts will likely fit together into wholes. An appeal to either interpreter to reflect the text more transparently will have no effect because what they see the work as—the typological hypothesis through which they fit its pieces together—is a consequence of convictions that do not derive from this text alone and that are incommensurable with the beliefs of the opposing camp.

This conflict is evidence once again of the inherent circularity of interpretation—the interdependence of our sense of the whole and our understanding of its various elements. After introducing the hypothesis that the governess suffers from hallucinations, Wilson declares, "When one has once got hold of the clue to this meaning of *The Turn of the Screw,* one wonders how one could ever have missed it."[16] Without his guess about the governess's pattern of self-deception, Wilson saw nothing; once equipped with this clue, however, everything fell in place to support it—even though this consistency is produced by the hypothesis it vindicates. One of the first to suspect the governess (long before Wilson did), Harold C. Goddard expressed astonishment that "what seemed the natural interpretation of the narrative was not the generally accepted one."[17] As a child, Goddard had had an insane governess, and this unusual experience predisposed him to view James's novella as a tale of mental distress. Given a particular assumption about the story's type, all the details "naturally" aligned themselves to support it, and their self-consistency gave Goddard no reason to suspect the oddity of the hypothesis that organized them.

Similarly circular confirmations abound among the governess's defenders, however, and convince them as well that their views are natural and self-evident: "Read this way [as a Hawthornian "conflict between Good and Evil"], the numerous hints throughout the story become significant and fall into the pattern"; or, "Other features of the story, if this is correct [that the ghosts are real and personify the evil of paralysis], fall into place in support of this account."[18] In each case the critic seems to himself to be a mirror to his object—things "fall" into position and are not forced—but the discovery that the pieces fit depends on the prior projection of a pattern that helps to generate the consistency justifying it.

Is the hermeneutic circle necessarily vicious, then, with no tests for validation being available to us to distinguish better from worse hypotheses? Quoting William James, Rorty describes "truth" as " 'what it is better for us to believe,' rather than as 'the accurate representation of reality' " (*Mirror*, p. 10). Interpretive conflict is indeed a contest between alternative beliefs, but this epistemological multiplicity raises the further question of how to decide which beliefs to prefer if they are mutually exclusive and to a considerable degree self-confirming. Rorty argues that "objectivity should be seen as conformity to the norms of justification . . . we find about us" (*Mirror*, p. 361). I too have contended that an important test for validity is intersubjective acceptability—the willingness of others to entertain one's assumptions and hypotheses as potentially productive or plausible. This test can vary widely in what it sanctions or discards, however, because the norms and convictions of one community may not be shared by another. Hence Rorty's assertion that "we can only come under epistemic rules"—that is, conventions for interpretation and validation— "when we have entered the community where the game governed by these rules is played" (*Mirror*, p. 187). This description of understanding as a socially closed process is epistemologically inadequate, however, because it is not sufficiently sensitive to the dangers of communal solipsism and vicious interpretive circularity. It leaves communities closed on themselves, immune to challenge from other interpreters with different assumptions and interests, and it does not take into account the adjustments that an individual interpreter must often make to a community's rules as he or she struggles to make sense of a particular text.

The conflicts over how best to understand *The Turn of the Screw* suggest that the process of validation is at least to some extent responsible to the object interpreted, even if the relation between reading and text is not an empirical bond or a mirrorlike correspondence. In addition to intersubjective acceptability, an interpretation must demonstrate internal coherence and effectiveness in meeting unexpected challenges—what I have called the tests of "inclusiveness" and "efficacy." Wilson's critics unwittingly but powerfully invoked these criteria when they thought they could prove him wrong on his facts, and their charges proved so embarrassing that he partially retracted his original reading. A. J. A. Waldock accused Wilson of ignoring "two stubborn facts of the story"—"details within the story itself that decisively negative" the hallucination theory. These "facts" are the governess's accurate, detailed description of Peter Quint and her previous ignorance of how he looked.

The language of Waldock's attack is interesting, however, because his empirical rhetoric of correct reflection alternates with images that acknowledge the circular interdependence of parts and wholes. Unless these details are "accounted for," he argues, "Mr. Wilson's whole case collapses like a house of cards."[19] These two small items can have such destructive power only if interpretation entails the projection of a pattern in which every piece depends on all the others. A single failure to fit may thus have devastating repercussions on the entire interpretive configuration, as it would not if knowing were a point-by-point process of correspondence in which the fuzziness of the mirror in one place might not impugn its transparency elsewhere. Waldock's charges posed difficulties for Wilson because they suggest anomalies that undermine the internal coherence of his reading, and they are thus a challenge to his theory's effectiveness in producing new hypotheses to assimilate new materials. Even though the dispute between Waldock and Wilson involves processes of validation that are object related and not reducible to the epistemic rules of either opposing interpretive community, their quarrel is not simply an empirical question of accurate reflection.

Wilson's response suggests that even when criteria for validity are object related, they can be satisfied in incommensurable ways. He first acknowledged the importance of these anomalies by shifting the charge of self-deception from the governess to James. If Waldock is right, then he has pointed out in the story's design flaws that suggest that James was not fully aware of the kind of narrative he was writing.[20] This is an awkward tactic, however, because instead of removing anomalies, it only shifts responsibility for them, thus converting an embarrassment for the interpreter into one for the writer. Their status as inconsistencies remains unquestioned. Several years later, however, John Silver came to the rescue and pointed out several places where the governess could have learned about Quint, including a trip to the nearby village, which she mentions in explaining why she is certain the figure on the tower was not a local resident: "I didn't tell you," she says to Mrs. Grose, "but I made sure."[21] Wilson could then proudly retract his retraction, and, as further evidence that James knew all along what he was up to, Wilson pointed to the placement of *The Turn of the Screw* in the New York Edition between two works with similarly unreliable narrators. Once again, validation is not a process of correspondence but an attempt to suggest coherent patterns—here viewing the text itself as part of a larger whole.

This crucial, well-known episode in the history of James's novella is worth telling in some detail because of its implications for the epistemology of validation. On the one hand, the dispute between Waldock and Wilson shows that interpretive communities are neither self-enclosed nor irresponsible to their objects. An antagonist in hermeneutic conflict not only has the option of questioning the opposing community's assumptions and procedures but also may attempt to create embarrassing anomalies for it by pointing to textual details that its readings have not yet accounted for. On the other hand, however, these details are not simply empirical facts, for an interpreter may defend the validity of his or her reading by assimilating anomalous evidence through ingenious hypotheses that the opponent refuses to accept. The much-discussed visit to the village has different meanings for the conflicting interpretive camps. For the governess's defenders it is an occasion where she confirms Quint's menacing strangeness. For her detractors it is a source of the information with which she browbeats Mrs. Grose into believing her wild fantasy. This interpretive disagreement suggests that an appeal to "facts in the text" cannot adjudicate correctness, because interpreters attribute different meanings to details by placing them in different overall patterns. But the way that the conflict unfolded until it reached this new deadlock calls into question Rorty's reduction of validation to a purely intracommunal exchange, because the disputants grappled with each other across epistemic boundaries by debating about the qualities of an object.

History as an Epistemological Construct

The general implication of the story I have been relating is that turning to history will not get us away from the epistemological questions about interpretive conflict that trouble contemporary theory. Rather, the history of the reception of a controversial text like *The Turn of the Screw* is one place where those questions have been most dramatically enacted. However, according to Steven Mailloux, an important advocate of abandoning epistemology for history, "The way to answer the realist/idealist question 'Is meaning created by the text or by the reader or by both?' is simply not to ask it." Instead, he argues for replacing hermeneutic theory with what he calls a "rhetorical hermeneutics," which would "provide histories of how particular theoretical and critical discourses have evolved"—a practical research project that, in his view, would make "epistemological questions . . . simply beside the point."[22] What different groups of critics have historically found persuasive is, however, an epistemological question. As I have been arguing, persuasiveness is decided by the role of belief in how we know. What is or is not persuasive to any given community at any particular moment is not simply a fact of history. It is, rather, a consequence of the way belief works in understanding—what assumptions interpreters are willing to entertain about literature and life, and how they put these convictions into practice by generating hypotheses on the basis of them about the relations between textual parts and wholes.

The dispute about *The Turn of the Screw* suggests that the "realist/idealist question" cannot be bypassed in the history of reception but turns up there again when critics with incompatible beliefs give incommensurable readings to "the facts of the text." The argument between Waldock and Wilson shows that a literary work is neither totally subordinate to nor completely autonomous of interpretation but is paradoxically both dependent and independent at once—"heteronomous," as I have called it. Wilson finds Waldock's objections troublesome because they call attention to seemingly independent features in the text which resist his hypotheses, but Wilson's solution does not satisfy the governess's defenders because they do not accept the typological pattern through which he constructs the text—a text that is self-evidently "there" only to those who share his beliefs about it. *The Turn of the Screw* is independent of either camp to the extent that both groups are pointing to and arguing about something other than themselves. But this otherness also depends for its very meaning and structure on how it is interpreted, inasmuch as each group's way of configuring the text excludes the opposing camp's. One reason why texts have histories is indeed that they are heteronomous in this manner—transcending any individual community's way of interpreting them as they are taken up again and again by different groups of readers, but varying in their shape according to the shifting patterns of coherence attributed to them.

When Mailloux writes history, the epistemological conflicts he is trying to avoid return. Like a realist, he faults other historians for "distort[ing]" the picture when "actually" and "in fact" an accurate reflection of the matter at hand would present a different image. Like an idealist, he proposes rules for interpreting the past—rules that will produce only a "version of . . . history," but one he prefers to believe.[23] This self-contradiction is inevitable, however, because history is paradoxically both real and ideal, simultaneously other to interpretation and yet dependent on how it is construed. As Collingwood notes, "The past is never a given fact which [the historian] can apprehend empirically by perception"; instead, "The historian's picture of the past is . . . in every detail an imaginary picture."[24] Collingwood does not mean to imply, of course, that historical narratives are pure products of individual fantasy. His argument, rather, is that the otherness of evidence from the past to which the historian is responsible is not given with such force and directness that it compels a single construal.

Although historians must arrange evidence in patterns that are coherent and acceptable to others, this is an imaginative act of consistency building that can be done in many different ways. As a result, according to Hayden White, "Historical explanations are bound to be based on different metahistorical presuppositions about the nature of the historical field, presuppositions that generate different conceptions of the kind of explanations that can be used in historiographical analysis."[25] This interdependence of "metahistorical presuppositions" and acceptable explanations suggests that, as in the interpretation of a literary text, there are two levels of belief at work in historical understanding—metaphysical assumptions about the being of the entities under scrutiny which then sanction a certain range of interpretive hypotheses about their relations in any particular case.

The hermeneutic circularity of historical knowledge is evident in Ricoeur's description of history as a narrative act of emplotment. According to Ricoeur, "the plots we invent" are the "means by which we reconfigure our confused . . . temporal experience." Historians achieve "the triumph of concordance over discordance" by exploiting the ability of plot to forge a "synthesis of the heterogeneous," a "congruence in the organization of events."[26] Plots give structure and direction to a sequence of actions that might otherwise seem random and incoherent. The circle here is that the plot provides a sense of the whole, which is necessary for understanding particular events, even as we can make sense of the plot only by following the individual actions that constitute it. W. B. Gallie sees in this process of "following" the foundation of the intelligibility of history. "The main job of the historian is simply to tell his story," Gallie argues, but "to tell or to follow even the simplest story is not just to assert or to accept 'one damned thing after another.'" Telling and following a story require at least "some vague appreciation of its drift or direction, a vague sense of its alternative possible outcomes," and "an appreciation of how what comes later depends upon what came earlier."[27] All of these requirements rest on the need to imagine the overall shape and design of any state of affairs in order to come to grips with its individual elements. In history as in all areas of understanding, comprehension is achieved not by sequential addition but by con-figurative combination.

What a reader can follow depends not only on the historian's skill in fitting pieces together but also on communal standards for permissible patterns. According to Ricoeur, "The probable—an ob-jective feature—must also be persuasive or credible . . . —a subjec-tive feature. The logical connection of probability cannot therefore be detached from the cultural constraints of acceptability."[28] The criterion of probability is "logical" and "objective" in the sense that it demands that the plot organize events coherently, without incon-sistencies in the pattern, and completely, without glaring gaps or unassimilated anomalies in its handling of the evidence. But what is logical and objective to one group may seem unlikely or pre-posterous to a different community with different beliefs about how parts typically fit into wholes. Because a followable coherence is a hypothetical construct that is based on the beliefs of the teller and that appeals to the willingness of the audience to share them, it is as variable and contestable as are all matters of faith. In plotting historical narratives as in interpreting literary works, the process of validation is paradoxically both responsible to the object and vari-able with the community.

I have been arguing that historical understanding and literary interpretation have the same epistemological structure. One conse-quence of this homology is that different ways of construing a text lead their adherents to write different histories of its reception. The interdependence of textual interpretation and critical history can be seen, for example, in the conflict between two recent, theoret-ically sophisticated readings of *The Turn of the Screw.* For Shoshana Felman the novella refuses to mean in a "vulgar," "literal" way that would "stop the movement constitutive of meaning" by "block[ing] and interrupt[ing] the endless process of metaphorical substitu-tion." Despite the apparent differences between Wilson and his opponents, they are thus guilty of the same kind of misreading because they try to master and reduce the text's signifying power. The text defies its readers' attempts to contain and control it by enacting a conflict of interpretations, which dramatizes, "through a clash of meanings, the very functioning of meaning as division and as conflict."[29] Where Felman finds in the text an absence of meaning that encourages play and resists mastery, John Carlos

Rowe argues that the novella masters the reader for its own ends by playing the game of absent authority. Rowe argues that the governess's employer dominates the scene by removing himself and displacing the signs of his rule onto others so as to disguise and thereby secure his power. In the history of the tale's reception, James repeats the strategy that his text dramatizes—preserving his power by pretending to give it up, withdrawing himself and handing authority over to the reader, with the result that his own name is ever resounded in the conflicts among his agents.[30] The play that Felman finds semantically liberating seems to Rowe part of a ploy to gain dominance and authority.

Felman and Rowe narrate the work's history of reception differently because they have different beliefs about the text. Configuring the text and emplotting its heritage are correlative acts. She finds in the work refusals to specify, which open up possibilities of meaning in its reception. He sees enacted in the story a strategy for winning power, which is duplicated in the author's relation to his readers. History cannot settle or bypass their dispute because writing different narratives of the work's hermeneutic past is a crucial way in which they argue about its present meaning.

Contesting the interpretation of a work may mean not only writing different histories of its reception but also suggesting different originating contexts for it. Defenders of the ghosts have expended much energy and ingenuity in tracking down parallel reports of apparitions in the nineteenth-century annals of the Society for Psychical Research.[31] They assume that the reality of the ghosts will be vindicated if it can be shown to match the behavior of supernatural beings in the historical record, which James might have known. Those who doubt the governess's sanity have been equally zealous, but their hypotheses about the text lead them to discover its sources elsewhere. They differ among themselves, too, in ways that reflect subtle but important differences about how to construe the tale. To add credence to Wilson's psychoanalytic diagnosis of the governess, Oscar Cargill suggests that William James's Continental connections and his and Henry's concern about the psychological health of their sister, Alice, could have brought to the novelist's attention an early case history from Freud's *Studies in Hysteria*, which has remarkable parallels to *The Turn of the Screw*. Mark Spilka agrees that repressed sexuality provides the necessary

clue for reading the story, but he calls the tale an appeal to the
Victorian reader's prurient interest in the erotic qualities of children. Citing pornographic literature from the time, however, Bruce
Robbins calls attention to the Victorian fascination and fear about
"love between the classes" to suggest that the sexual exploitation of
servants is the tale's original social context.[32]

In each of these instances, the historical frame of reference
proposed would serve as a larger whole in which the text would fit
as an intelligible part. Disagreements about the kind of coherence
that internally unifies the text mirror themselves in the critics' hypotheses about the type of context to which it belongs. An appeal
to origins cannot settle disputes about interpretation because in
both arenas suppositions about part-whole relations are at stake.
These are inherently contestable, as I have argued, not only because parts and wholes can be mutually confirming but also because no single belief about coherence is ever immediately self-
evident. Such a belief is only a guess—a wager about how pieces
will probably fit together and a gamble that other available hypotheses will not work better. A historical source seems self-evident to
the critic only because it corroborates his or her sense of the whole
that is the type of the story. To look for a work's source is to search
for how its history begins, and a choice about how to start a narrative is always circularly dependent on the configuration one anti-
cipates will develop as the story unfolds. Where the history of *The
Turn of the Screw* begins for any interpreter depends on where one
thinks it ends—which, at least for the moment, is with one's own
present reading of the work.

For some theorists the privileged originating context for a
work is the author's intention, and here *The Turn of the Screw* tells a
particularly interesting tale. Wilson and his critics were equally
able to find evidence in James's preface that their readings corre-
sponded with his aims. The preface calls the novella "a fairy-tale
pure and simple" designed "to rouse the dear old sacred terror."
But James also describes the work as a study "of a conceived 'tone,'
the tone of suspected and felt trouble, of an inordinate and incal-
culable sore—the tone of tragic, yet of exquisite, mystification"—
and this reference to the governess's confused emotional state
seems to some an invitation to psychological demystification. The
preface credits the tale with "a perfect homogeneity"—with "be-

ing, to the very last grain of its virtue, all of a kind."[33] But because James gives conflicting signals about what this kind is, critics with opposing hypotheses about its type could and did quote him in their defense.

When James's *Notebooks* were published in 1947, however, Wilson's antagonists thought their battle was won. In a famous entry, James gives as the germ of the work a ghost story heard from the archbishop of Canterbury, E. W. Benson.[34] The authority of this ascription was almost immediately contested, however, because Benson's sons had already declared it unlikely that their father was James's source; they had never heard the story and doubted it belonged to their father's repertoire.[35] Are they wrong, or did James's memory fail him, or is the notebook entry an attempt to send source hunters down the wrong track? James's intention seemed settled only to become unsettled again with the possibility that he might have been lying. What is curious, however, is that both sides in the dispute have accused James of planting deceptive clues. Not only does Cargill argue that James would understandably want to protect Alice by disguising the tale's connection to Freud's theory of hysteria, but also the ghost hunters mistrust the notebook entry because they believe it masks James's debt to cases, recorded by the Society for Psychical Research, which one of the group's founders, F. W. H. Myers, apparently pressed James to acknowledge as his source.[36] James seems to have anticipated this controversy in another of his prefaces, where he writes, "One's notes, as all writers remember, sometimes explicitly mention, sometimes indirectly reveal, and sometimes wholly dissimulate, such clues and such obligations."[37]

We have here a classic instance of the unreliability of documentary evidence about intention for settling interpretive disputes. Such evidence typically displaces rather than resolves arguments about the text's meaning by providing the combatants with more material to contest. Intention is never directly given but must always be construed even in such documents as notebooks and prefaces. A construal of intention is necessarily at least in part the product of the interpreter's choices, not only because he or she must decide whether to trust or suspect the evidence but also because to attribute an intention to a work is to select one of a number of possible ways of typing it. Some have argued that meaning is identical with intention because to interpret a text entails adopting a characterization of the speaker.[38] If so, then the question of what intention an utterance expresses is not merely empirical but also epistemological and theoretical because it rests on a choice about classification. Do I believe that speakers typically deceive, so that I should type the text as a lie, or do I guess that the speaker deserves credence, which would give the utterance a different kind? Here as before, the decision about how to interpret is epistemologically contestable because it is a matter of making a wager about what it is better to believe. Classifying the speaker's intention and typing the work are interdependent choices, and an appeal to one cannot justify the other.

Some advocates of the turn to history argue that it would make theoretical reflection superfluous.[39] There are at least two ways, however, in which history and theory need each other. First, hermeneutic theorizing is often a source of historical change. Psychoanalytic interpretations of *The Turn of the Screw* have not simply defended Wilson but have criticized his reading for employing Freud in a reductive, unsophisticated manner. These complaints are typically motivated by new developments in psychoanalytic theory—not neurosis but the "uncanny," for example, is Freud's central concept, or not sexual repression but Lacanian linguistic displacement defines the unconscious. As Felman argues, "The 'true Freud' is no more immediately accessible to us than the 'true James,'" since both are "equally a text, known only through the difficulties and uncertainties of the act of reading and of interpretation."[40] Reinterpreting Freud has meant rereading *The Turn of the Screw* (and to some extent the reverse has also been true). Rorty praises the capacity of human beings to generate "new descriptions" of the world because this holds out "the possibility of something new under the sun, of human life as poetic rather than merely contemplative" (*Mirror,* pp. 378, 389). Theoretical thinking can be "poetic" in this sense because creating new possibilities of interpretation by criticizing and revising past practices is one way of introducing novelty into our dealings with the world. Reflection about the assumptions and procedures of particular kinds of interpretation can be innovative and historically productive by suggesting major or minor changes in the beliefs that guide understanding.

A second way in which history and theory hang together is

that studying past interpretive practices can assist us in resolving contemporary questions about how best to understand. History can aid theory-choice. If interpretation is a matter of what it is best to believe, it always requires choices. The decisions an interpreter must make about what assumptions to entertain or what hypotheses to risk cannot always be justified as absolutely necessary and certain, because the arguments for other possibilities are frequently equally cogent. One consideration in choosing between two similarly tenable alternatives is their likely consequences. Here history can enable us "to choose our actions more wisely," as Popper argues, by "helping us to understand even the more remote consequences of possible actions."[41] Collingwood similarly describes history as an aid to self-knowledge: "Knowing yourself means knowing what you can do; and since nobody knows what he can do until he tries, the only clue to what man can do is what man has done." Collingwood's description of history as "the re-enactment of past thought in the historian's mind" is perhaps too idealistic to cover all kinds of inquiry into the past,[42] but it applies quite well to the study of the history of interpretation, where we reconstitute a work's reception by duplicating the acts of understanding through which it has existed. This exercise in imagination can increase our awareness of what different ways of knowing entail. It can also make us self-conscious about our own interpretive habits and convictions by showing us the difference between who we are and who we are not. Historical self-consciousness cannot choose for us among the various available theories about how to understand. But studying the history of interpretation can enable us to assess better the implications of our choices.

6

The Variability and Limits of Value

The validity of a piece of writing and its value are not necessarily the same, but analogous complications occur in deciding the correctness of a reading or evaluating the merits of a judgment. Whether a reading is true or false gives little indication of its worth; indeed, a demonstrably incorrect view—a myth, a fable, or a superstition, for example—can serve important purposes for a community and can therefore be deemed valuable for coherent and persuasive reasons. But the same paradox that I have analyzed in the quest for interpretive validity also characterizes the search for a secure evaluative hierarchy. Two experienced, well-regarded evaluators can give radically different, even contradictory rankings to the same literary work or critical essay, but critics of very different persuasions can still agree, and with remarkable frequency, that some poems, stories, or interpretive works are seriously deficient and not worth preserving.[1]

Disputes are commonplace and unavoidable about what to publish, what to anthologize, what to canonize, whom to award prizes to, whom to hire, whom to tenure and promote, and so on. But some decisions about such matters still meet with wide agreement across communal boundaries, and we can say with some confidence that they are probably correct (which is not to say that they will not some day be overturned). The dismissive comment "Well, everything's relative" is not always appropriate every time a referee pronounces the judgment that a collection of poems really is pretty awful or that a manuscript really does not deserve to be published. Stories also abound, however, about the novel or the essay that was rejected again and again only to become a prizewinning classic. If reasonably trustworthy evaluation were impossible, institutional decision making would be more frequently paralyzed or even more demonstrably whimsical than it is. But if incommensurable evaluations could not be defended with equal cogency, controversies about rankings and revolutions in judgment would not occur as often as they do.

As in the debate about validity in interpretation, so in the dispute about evaluation is the field of argument polarized between the equally unacceptable extremes of absolutism and relativism. Neither pole can encompass both sides of the paradox that value judgments can be reliably made and reasonably defended, even as they are also inherently contestable and variable. On the one hand, a monist like René Wellek claims that "judgment refers to an objective character that is open to inspection" and, further, that "doubts about the exact limits of literature cannot obviate the difference between art and non-art, great and bad art."[2] On the other hand, a relativist like Terry Eagleton declares that " 'value' is a transitive term: it means whatever is valued by certain people in specific situations, according to particular criteria and in the light of given purposes"—a view that leads to the conclusion, shocking to the absolutists, that "we may in the future produce a society which was unable to get anything at all out of Shakespeare."[3]

The absolutist's faith that values are lodged firmly in the object of judgment ignores the dilemma that interpreters with different beliefs about art and human being have different standards of what is good and important. These disagreements can lead to disputes about what kinds of texts are most worthy of widespread attention, serious study, and general admiration. Interpreters with different presuppositions and interests not only may prefer different sorts of things but may even see different characteristics (and, therefore, different things to approve or disparage) in the "same" work. The boundary between literature and nonliterature is consequently notoriously hard to draw, and disagreements are also common about how to rank even those works that all sides agree to value highly. But such disputes do not justify the skeptical conclusion that evaluations are simply the projections of a community's beliefs and not an engagement with a coercive otherness that may welcome or discourage some judgments more than others. Some judgments are harder to defend than others, not only to members of opposing communities but also to one's fellow believers, and this shifting coefficient of adversity suggests that evaluation is a work engaged with object-based resistance and not simply a dreamlike playing out of one's own desires and interests. We care about each other's evaluations not only because they tell us about the different assumptions we hold and the aims we variously pursue but also because they give us information about the world we share.[4]

In order to make sense of this contradictory state of affairs, I propose to invoke once again the notion of "heteronomy." In the first section of this chapter, I argue that the value of any piece of writing is "heteronomous" to its judge—both dependent on and independent of his or her interests, purposes, and beliefs. How we rank anything will vary with our assumptions and aims, but the value of a novel or an essay is not simply a reflection of our wishes and needs. Judgment is always judgment *of* something, not merely the unresisted and untested play of the evaluator's faculties. But rankings are inherently variable and unstable because they are based on beliefs about what is good and true, beliefs that are always debatable and can change. Two important corollaries of the heteronomy of value deserve attention as well, and they are the concern of the second section. First, "literature" is a shifting, internally heterogeneous category that lacks the stability absolutists desire; nevertheless, it is a functional term that carries meaning despite (or because of) its variable history, a meaning that may not be uniform but does have boundaries (not everything belongs to it). Second, preservation is the ultimate criterion of value and of literariness. Preservation is a historical activity that does not create timeless monuments, for what a community decides to regard as valuable can change, but it is also an object-related process in which the ability of a text to perform continued services and the capacity of a community's beliefs to make new sense of the tradition it inherits are constantly testing each other.

The Heteronomy of Value

The paradoxical dependence and independence of value are perhaps best illustrated by the contradictions of education. Teachers frequently find that students reject as "bad" a work like *Ulysses* or *The Waste Land* because they do not know the interpretive conventions necessary to make sense out of what consequently seems like gibberish. Their reactions are exactly analogous to the bewilderment of an early audience that disparages a revolutionary work like *Madame Bovary* because it defies their assumptions and expectations about its literary kind.[5] In both cases the interpreter does not know what sort of whole to hypothesize in order to fit the parts of a work together, and the generic patterns that he or she can invoke make the text seem either anomalous or outrageously deviant. The value of a work is not a simple given, open for inspection, but is available only to interpreters who have learned to take up particular attitudes toward it—to deploy certain assumptions about a genre that would seem wrongheaded or strange to readers with different beliefs and expectations.

If the worth of a text is not simply there but is cocreated by observers who make its value appear by projecting configurative hypotheses based on assumptions they must learn or invent, then value is a variable rather than a constant. It can change because it will be revealed differently to different communities with different conventions for reading and different beliefs about literary kinds. This is one reason why literary works have histories of appreciation, in which the ways they are valued change as new modes of understanding appear, sometimes prompted by the creation of new texts that revolutionize an audience's sense of a genre's dimensions and possibilities.

But the examples I have given also illustrate the objectlike otherness of value. They are instances in which works resist their readers or make demands to which their readers' interpretive practices are inadequate. Bewildering works can challenge the interpreter to revise his or her categories and expectations in order to reveal their values only because these values offer a resisting otherness that must educate us to meet its demands. As we struggle and play with this resistance and experiment with new hypotheses to master it, we may find ourselves forced to change ourselves—altering or extending our previous assumptions, expectations, and ways of making sense. The shock and surprise, joy and discomfort, of discovering unexpected things to appreciate or new ways of regarding art and life could not occur if judgments were merely self-projections. An interpreter may ignore the challenge of a work, and the pressures on a student or lay reader may come as much from external authorities (such as the demanding teacher or the force of educated opinion) as from the work. But texts can educate us to new modes of appreciation only because they judge us even as we judge them.

The coercive otherness of a work's worth persuades the absolutists that value must be an objective entity, which, as such, can be measured unambiguously. This, at least, is the assumption behind Yvor Winters's bold defense of the possibility of exact evaluation. Winters begins his argument by asking basic questions about evaluation and drawing the (to his mind) inescapable conclusions:

> Is it possible to say that Poem A (one of Donne's *Holy Sonnets,* or one of the poems of Jonson or of Shakespeare) is better than Poem B (Collins' *Ode to Evening*) or vice versa?
>
> If not, is it possible to say that either of these is better than Poem C (*The Cremation of Sam Magee,* or something comparable)?
>
> If the answer is no in both cases, then any poem is as good as any other. If this is true, then all poetry is worthless; but this obviously is not true, for it is contrary to all our experience.

The premise behind this reasoning is that precise rankings of comparative excellence must be determinable because, as Winters contends, the ability to identify "extreme deviation from right judgment" means that "there is such a thing as right judgment."[6]

The appearance of ruthless logical rigor in these if-then clauses disguises at least two crucial fallacies. First, the ability to recognize errors does not imply a converse ability to determine unequivocally what is right. For all of the problems with Popper's concept of "falsification," he is still correct in saying that the capacity of scientists to discover that something is wrong does not necessarily contain the promise of positive knowledge.[7] Similarly, two critics from different interpretive communities can agree that a reading fails the tests for validity—that it does not account for crucial anomalies and probably never will—but this consensus does not mean they can or will share the same "correct" interpretation. For a psychoanalyst and a New Critic to agree that *The Turn of the Screw* is not an astrological revelation of the coming apocalypse does not help them to resolve their differences about what the story does mean. By the same token, a Marxist and a phenomenologist may agree that *Hard Times* and *The Sound and the Fury* are better novels than *Love Story,* but the preference of the one critic for social verisimilitude and of the other for epistemological ambiguity may make them differ over whether to rank Dickens or Faulkner higher. The critical community at large, including all of its various camps, may decide over history that Dickens and Faulkner repay repeated attention more than Segal does, but agreement about what to exclude from the canon does not necessarily imply the possibility of a clear-cut ranking of the works that are included.

The second important fallacy is that Winters's grouping of the various examples he cites as "poems" ignores nontrivial differences in their kinds. The truth of the old saw "You can't compare apples and oranges" is that comparative rankings can be made only if prior agreement exists about the class to which the evaluated entities belong.[8] You *can* compare apples and oranges if the question is which fruit is preferable as a source of vitamin C, but if the relevant category is left unspecified, judgment can be paralyzed ("Is this apple better than this orange?" "Well, that depends what you mean"—that is, compared to what? For the purposes of the evaluation, what kind of thing are we to see them as?). Among Winters's examples, *The Cremation of Sam Magee* could be judged superior to the other poems if "popular ballad" were the class in question (just as Segal could win out over Dickens or Faulkner if "best-selling romances" were called for). Whether Donne's poem is better than Collins's depends to a large extent on whether you prefer sonnets or odes. If you reply that you are concerned with the class "poem" in general, then prior agreement about what a "poem" is must be established before comparative evaluations of the members of its class can occur. Within the class, different kinds of poems can be compared and judged only if the general definition establishes clear hierarchies among its subordinate categories (ranking sonnets above odes, for example, and both above ballads because of the aesthetic norms implicit in the definition).

Disagreement about the relevant kind that should govern comparisons is a common source of evaluative disagreement, and this in turn is a result of the indispensable role that assumptions about types play in interpretation. Just as readings of a text will disagree about its meaning if they configure its parts into different wholes (is *The Turn of the Screw* a ghost story or a tale of mental distress?), so judgments of a work will diverge if they compare it with members of different classes. One reason why critics rank a work differently is that they see it as a different kind of entity.

These disputes cannot be resolved by pointing to the objective characteristics of the work because of the interdependence of part and whole—because, that is, the identity of the elements of the work depends on the critic's assumptions about the configuration to which they belong, the governing pattern that constitutes them even as they constitute it. Critics recognize different things of value within a work when their assumptions about a text's type lead them to perceive its parts differently. The interpreter's prior understanding of a work's kind is doubly implicated in his or her evaluation. It contributes to the emergence of the qualities to be valued or disparaged, and it establishes the classification that will be the basis of the evaluative comparisons through which these qualities are judged. To see a work as a tragedy rather than a comedy, for example, is both to project an organizing hypothesis that will make a particular kind of sense of the text and at the same time to determine the type against which the work will be judged.

I have argued in earlier chapters that interpretive disagreements about how to type a work frequently go back to the critics' different presuppositions about the basic patterns and characteristics defining literature and life. By the same token, disputes about evaluation are often manifestations of opposing assumptions about the best way to organize and categorize art and the world. Interpretations of meaning and judgments of worth both rest on fundamental, inherently contestable decisions about the configurative patterns that an interpreter thinks should guide understanding because, he or she believes, they are inherent in the order of things.

The dependence of a work's value on the critic's prior decision about the kind of entity to see it as contradicts the notion, common among absolutists, that values are properties that a work possesses on the model of an object with particular, determinate qualities.[9] In this view, differences in judgments of the same work are legitimate only if they are based on different selections from its overall stock of values, and such judgments should ultimately be harmonious and mutually completing—not real, irreconcilable disagreements after all. Also, if values are only some among the many properties of an object, then it should be possible to distinguish them from its other characteristics and to demarcate which qualities carry value and which do not.[10]

This reification of value is inconsistent, however, with the part-whole dialectic that characterizes both interpretation and evaluation. Disagreements about evaluations can be based not only on different selections from the same stock of qualities but also on conflicts about how to type a work—disputes not merely about what parts to pick out of a preexisting whole but, more fundamentally, about what sort of whole to see those parts as belonging to (and "those parts" will not always be the same for different assumptions about the whole). Similarly, the relation between what is value-laden and value-neutral in a work cannot be determined once and for all but is a gestaltlike configuration of foreground and background, which will vary according to the interpreter's hypotheses about a work's overall shape. Just as foreground and background determine each other's outlines and features, so what seems to an interpreter to have value in a work will be shaped by and will help to shape his or her sense of what seems unimportant.[11] To reify values as separable, determinate properties of an object is to ignore the wholistic, configurative interdependence of part and whole in both understanding and judgment.

The variability of part-whole relations does not seem a problem to many absolutists, however, because they believe that there is a single, intuitively self-evident aesthetic attitude. Murray Krieger claims, for example, that works of art, unlike other objects, demand to be "treated as self-enclosures, as totalizations, with self-fulfillment that raises them above all non-aesthetic human fabrications."[12] Wellek argues similarly that there is an "undeniable" and "immediately evident" aesthetic experience, which constitutes the work as "a structured self-sufficient, qualitative whole" and which "yields a state of contemplation, of intransitive attention that cannot be mistaken for anything else."[13] This Kantian claim that disinterestedness is the privileged aesthetic attitude is called into question by the very existence of hermeneutic conflict. As I have repeatedly argued, the various interpretive postures available to us posit different notions of art according to their different interests and purposes. There is consequently no naturally given, intuitively self-justified aesthetic attitude. Rather, the question of how best to understand and appreciate works of art is a cultural issue that different communities of belief contest among themselves in their battle for our allegiance.

The claim that works of art are "self-sufficient wholes" may seem to echo my language about parts and wholes, but this resemblance is misleading. As I have argued before, the hermeneutic circle does not necessarily entail the ideology of organicism. There is no understanding without coherence, but there are many different ways in which consistency can be established. Although to interpret means to project hypotheses about how parts fit together in a whole, many different kinds of assumptions about totality can enable interpreters to configure works. The assumption that these wholes are self-sufficient and self-enclosed is a particular belief about the kind of entity works of art are. As such, it competes with other beliefs about the typological hypotheses that will best establish coherence. To say that parts and wholes must fit together is not to endorse any particular interpretive attitude but to describe what all modes of understanding do. Furthermore, creating patterns that unify elements in a totality is not uniquely the achievement of works of art or the defining characteristic of the aesthetic attitude but the activity all understanding engages in, regardless of its objects and aims.

The variability of judgment explains the strength and appeal of the argument that value lies in the eyes of the beholder. Although Barbara Herrnstein Smith denies that value is merely "an arbitrary projection of subjects," neither is it, in her view, "an inherent property of objects": "All value is radically contingent," she argues, because it is "the product of the dynamics of an economic system."[14] Smith's use of the metaphor of "economy" to explain value is one of the most important recent contributions to axiology, and it deserves careful attention.

The metaphor implies that any text or other object is valued or disparaged, sought after or ignored, not according to its intrinsic characteristics but according to the role it plays in various sets of relationships, or "economies." These economies can vary in scope and complexity, from an individual's system of desires and needs to the network of exchanges in which a community engages as it pursues its own particular interests and purposes. If economic relations determine value, then it is dependent on the assumptions, aims, and resources that define the relevant system. As a result of this dependence, "the most fundamental character of literary value . . . is its mutability and diversity" ("Contingencies," p. 10). Not only are "the 'properties' of the work . . . at every point the variable products of some subject's interaction with it," but "there are no functions performed by artworks that may be specified as unique to them," and the boundary between art and nonart will vary according to the desires and needs of the evaluating group (pp. 27, 14). When the value of anything seems stable and continuous, the reason is not a resisting otherness traceable to the object but a "co-incidence of contingencies" (p. 17). If several observers or different communities perceive the features of a work or of a class like "art" in the same way, they will attribute this identity to the object rather than to its true source—the convergence of their own assumptions, needs, and interests.

This economic theory of value seems to deny that judgment has any basis outside the interplay of desiring subjects. Actually, though, the metaphor of economy demands a heteronomous notion of value. It can work only if value is not "radically contingent" but an engagement with a resisting otherness, which sets limits to the possibilities open to the judge. This holds for both of the kinds of value that economists typically distinguish: "exchange-value" and "use-value."[15] Object-based resistance and variable compliance are implicit even in exchange-value, the notion that the worth of anything is determined by what it can bring in trade for something else. This is often opposed to the notion that value has its source in the inherent characteristics of the object, properties that help to define its use-value, or what its intrinsic features allow it do. But even trade is trade *of* something *for* something, and the features of the objects of exchange are not irrelevant to the parties involved—hence their concern with whether the object is in good or poor condition, whether it is authentic or a forgery, or whether or not it is able to satisfy their desires and needs as well as some other potential substitute (and here exchange-value begins to blur with use-value).

The judgment of texts is partly determined by the economics

of exchange-value. Sometimes only a limited number of texts of approximately the same usefulness can be accommodated in a system (a syllabus, a publishing list, a set of required readings for doctoral exams, or the like), and judgments must then be made about equivalences between items that are roughly equal in use-value—judgments about what one is wiiling to trade for what, assessments of the relative worth of the text in comparison with possible substitutes. Like all kinds of decisions about how to maximize one's advantages in a world of scarce commodities, these considerations are typically made not only with the desires and assumptions of the judge in mind but also on the basis of characteristics perceived to exist in the object. These will vary according to the interests and beliefs of the interpreter, and different evaluators may consequently have different understandings of the trade-offs and equivalences involved in any judgment. But decisions about exchange-value are possible only if there is a differentiated otherness to choose from—some features that make A different from not-A and thus a possible substitute for it and a competitor for the evaluator's preferences. These differences must have their origin outside the interpreter; otherwise, what we have is not an economy of trade-offs between distinct yet in some senses equivalent entities but a solipsistic projection of a subject's desires. Scarcity could not compel choices if judgments were not made in a world of resistances, and the otherness of the entities between which an evaluator must choose is what allows them to act as substitutes for each other in an economy of exchange-values.

The evidence of the heteronomy of value is even clearer in the case of use-value. Texts, works of art, and other objects have value not only according to how they are traded and substituted for each other within a system of exchange but also according to the purposes they serve. Use-value is not entirely a matter of the intrinsic characteristics of an object, because it can and will vary according to the functions that an evaluating agent deems urgent and important. But use-value is not an unlimited variable. Use implies the otherness and resistance that make work possible and that make some jobs easier and others more difficult for a particular entity to perform. A screwdriver and a hammer are both useful tools, but they are not useful in the same ways or for the same tasks. They can be substituted for each other, if necessary, but only at the cost of considerable awkwardness, which is a sign of a resisting otherness (try hammering with a screwdriver or using a hammer on a screw). Similarly, the rise and the fall of a work of art are due not only to the changing interests and purposes of the critics but also to qualities traceable to the work that make it more or less able to satisfy various aims, desires, and needs. Use-value is a measurement *of* something's ability to *do* something—of a text's capacity to perform certain valued functions. A text's usefulness will be judged differently by communities with different interests and needs for the very reason that no entity can do all things equally well, and the differential capacity of works to perform varying functions is evidence of their otherness.

Measurements of a text's usefulness also evaluate the interpretive community making the judgment. Some assumptions and aims may seem questionable if they call for devaluing or discarding a work that others over history have found useful, interesting, and important. A text that has over time shown itself able to serve a variety of useful purposes is typically presumed, and for good reason, to be worth preserving in the future. A version of the pragmatic test is at work here. It is prudent to hesitate before casting aside something that has been effective in meeting past demands, even if one cannot predict with certainty what one will need or want in the future. Our sense of an entity's usefulness is based on our reasoned guesses about its possibilities, and these possibilities are not mere figments of our imagination but have a differentiated otherness that distinguishes them from the potentialities other entities are assumed to possess. Critics with new standards or beliefs not only test works to evaluate the reality of these possibilities but find their assumptions tested in turn by their ability to disclose the as yet unrealized potentialities that past experience has led readers to expect from texts. Once again, the use-value of a text is heteronomous to any particular judge in the sense that it has a history beyond his or her assessment, even as this heritage is created by a series of acts of appreciation.

The historical variability of the canon is frequently cited as proof of the contingency of assessments, but it is better evidence of their heteronomy. Jane Tompkins states the relativist's case: "Great literature does not exert its force over and against time, but changes with the changing currents of social and political life."[16] But Smith herself notes that "the canonical work begins increasingly not merely to survive within but to shape and create the culture in which its value is produced and transmitted and, for that very reason, to perpetuate the conditions of its own flourishing."[17] A work is capable of exerting force on its culture in this way only because it is at least to some extent an independent agent. Although it is dependent on its changing judges because it would cease to exist without their continued admiration, it cannot be simply reduced to them if it can influence their decisions and promote its own endurance.

Attempts to change the canon require work against a resisting otherness of two kinds: the historical weight of community opinion, and the limits on how a work can be interpreted. Both are evidence of the heteronomy of value. Community opinion is an important vehicle of preservation—and therefore both an aid and an obstacle to changing the canon—for the very reason that literary works have an intersubjective existence originating in but also going beyond individual experiences of understanding. The challenge to the would-be changer of the canon is to influence community opinion by offering a new way of understanding a work which is persuasive both because it speaks to the group's interests, needs, and beliefs and because it passes the tests for validity.

Efforts to change the canon require grappling with otherness attributable both to the community and to the work, and Tompkins herself demonstrates as much. Her attempt to resuscitate sentimental novels like *Uncle Tom's Cabin* invokes both levels of belief in understanding—the group's presuppositions about literature and life as well as the hypotheses necessary to make coherent sense of particular texts. A prerequisite for changing an evaluation of something is to realign the type through which it is understood, and Tompkins begins by proposing that we "see the sentimental novel not as an artifice of eternity answerable to certain formal criteria, . . . but as a political enterprise . . . that both codifies and attempts to mold the values of its time."[18] Whether or not her reclassification of this novel will be persuasive depends on her ability to convince us of the effectiveness of a particular set of assumptions about literature and culture: "It is the notion of literary texts as doing work, expressing and shaping the social context that produced them, that I wish to substitute finally for the critical perspective that sees them as attempts to achieve a timeless, universal ideal of truth and formal coherence" (p. 200). The intersubjective accept-ability of this belief is subject to reasoned debate, even if the culmi-nation of the dispute will be not that logic causes the triumph of one side but that the formalists and the historicists agree to dis-agree by embracing one rather than the other set of the equally defensible assumptions offered to them.

Part of their reason for the choice they make will be the prom-ised efficacy of their preferred beliefs as a guide for making sense of particular texts, and Tompkins consequently invokes text-based evidence to support her reevaluation by trying to show that histor-icist presuppositions are more capable than formalist principles of generating inclusive hypotheses about the meaning and value of particular works. Formalist critics are unable "to appreciate the complexity and scope of a novel like Stowe's," she argues, whereas her scheme for understanding not only clarifies all of the work's apparent anomalies but also explains the inclusiveness of its vi-sion—"the impression it gives of taking every kind of detail in the world into account . . . and investing those details with a purpose and a meaning which are both immediately apprehensible and finally significant" (pp. 125, 139). Tompkins's attempt to realign the canon invokes all three tests for validity—intersubjectivity, efficacy, and inclusiveness. It asks us to adopt new presuppositions about literature and culture, but it also attempts to demonstrate that these assumptions are worthy of our collective allegiance by showing that they are better able than the alternatives of making an other-wise anomalous text cohere.

Canons change, but they usually do not change overnight. The typical slowness with which reevaluations occur is in part attributable to the conservatism of communities—their prudent re-luctance to give up beliefs and values that have worked well and to replace them with others that may seem promising but have not yet shown their efficacy. Reevaluation also takes time because consid-erable effort and ingenuity are required to reinterpret and reassess texts. Proposing a new typology is only the first step in canon reformation. This step must then be followed by the detailed labor of developing particular interpretive patterns to reconstrue and reassess individual works, particular reconfigurations that must in each case demonstrate their ability to make the parts of the text cohere without anomaly.[19] This process of revision and testing is best explained by seeing meaning and value not as absolutes or as contingencies but as heteronomous entities. Canons could not change at all (except to correct past mistakes in judgment) if values were objectively given in works, but they would not change as slowly as they do if texts posed no resistances to our attempts to revalue them.

Literature and Preservation

An important issue in the debate about value is whether or not "literature" can be defined as a determinate, internally coherent entity distinct from "nonliterature." Those who consider value stable believe absolute differences divide art from nonart. "All relativism breaks down when we are confronted with the difference between very great poetry and pretentious trash, kitsch," claims Wellek. Although he acknowledges that "literature is not a structured synchronic totality but an enormous, historically and locally diversified manifold," he still contends that "there is a common feature in all art" and "a common humanity that makes all art, however remote in time and place, accessible to us."[20] However, these arguments do not make the relativists collapse. "There is no 'essence' of literature whatsoever," Eagleton responds. "Anything can be literature, and anything which is regarded as unalterably and unquestionably literature—Shakespeare, for example—can cease to be literature." His skeptical conclusion is that "literature, in the sense of a set of works of assured and unalterable value, distinguished by certain shared inherent properties, does not exist."[21] Many of those who interpret, teach, and otherwise investigate "literature," however, worry that they will be paralyzed if they cannot give a coherent definition of their object of study. If we cannot explain what makes "literature" unique and distinct from nonliterature, they ask, how can we defend the importance of literary study to an often unsympathetic society and fight effectively for institutional support against competitors who can state clearly what they are doing and why it matters?

Both Eagleton and Wellek link two issues that are not necessarily connected—first, whether certain "common features" or "inherent properties" distinguish literary from nonliterary works, and second, whether great art can be determinately and permanently differentiated from nonart. Someone could argue that there are certain properties (for example, a playful use of language, self-referentiality, or a predominance of figuration) that mark off literature from nonliterature, but that not all instances where these properties occur are "art." The argument would be that a bungled use of these features would be "literary," but not "artistic," and the result would be "bad literature." Eagleton and Wellek both use "literature" in an honorific sense that would make "bad literature" a contradiction in terms. My argument will circumvent this problem. I will contend that we cannot locate unique properties that distinguish literary from nonliterary works (of whatever quality) because different interpretive communities can hold opposing beliefs about the characteristics of literary works. But I will also maintain that it is still possible to talk meaningfully about "art" and "literature" (or "bad art" and "bad literature") without such agreement about defining common features.

My purpose in making this argument is not to provide an exhaustive examination of all possible candidates for defining "literariness," but rather to show that my notion of the paradoxical heteronomy of value can help to answer the hotly debated question of whether "literature" is a stable, coherent entity. Here as elsewhere, it is my contention that absolutism and relativism lead to dilemmas that we can avoid only by adopting a paradoxical position between these extremes—in this case, by regarding "literature" as both variable and bounded, heterogeneous and yet limited in its meaning (some things do not belong to it, although its constituent parts are not necessarily homogeneous or definable by the same principles).

"Literature" is an inherently multifarious entity which conflicting communities define in sometimes irreconcilable ways because of their different presuppositions, interests, and purposes. Literary studies are for that reason a multifaceted enterprise, made up of a variety of more or less congenially coexisting subgroups, each with its own set of projects, procedures, and aspirations. But we are no less able to speak intelligently about "literature" and "literary studies" or to defend their importance than we are in the case of the many other polysemic words in our vocabulary. Although ambiguity can seem paralyzing, conflicts about how to define inherently contested concepts like these show not how worthless they are but how much they matter. These disputes are not a sign of incoherence, which should make literary study intellectually suspect; rather, they are evidence that vital, difficult issues are at stake which defy easy resolution because basic disagreements about what to value and believe are involved.

The internal diversity of a concept or an enterprise does not make it meaningless or boundless, impossible to distinguish from other, perhaps equally heterogeneous states of affairs. Ludwig Wittgenstein notes, for example, that it is impossible to "give a full grammatical description" of the term "God." We can "assemble a sort of collection of examples," he says, "and make some contributions to such a description"—a work of explanation that will require frequent use of qualifiers like "sometimes," "often," "usually," "nearly always," or "almost never." But, Wittgenstein claims, "No more than this is necessary."[22] Believers from different religions have different conceptions of "God," but their disagreements do not make the term meaningless or so hopelessly confused that it is useless. The semantic diversity of the term "God" does not prevent us from recognizing its difference from other terms in the lexicon, even if explanations of this difference will vary according to which definition of the term is invoked and what other terms it is opposed to. Which of the word's possible meanings is in force is usually clear from the context. Similarly, what "literature" means is ordinarily comprehensible from our sense of the assumptions and aims of the discourse in which it is used. The context typically also makes clear whether "literature" includes all examples of a particular kind of work, regardless of quality, or only excellent instances. The meaning of a word accrues to it over its history, but even words as variable as "God" or "literature" are ordinarily stable enough that it is possible to recognize their meanings across cultures or centuries (although the meanings may not be ones we are very familiar with).

The usefulness of a term is a matter of both its variability and its distinctiveness. Words can become ineffective if they tend too far in either direction, becoming either too diffuse to be recognizable or too rigid to be widely applicable. There is a wide ground between these extremes, however, on which polysemous terms function effectively. Indeed, one reason why such terms are useful is that they can be meaningfully invoked for different purposes and in a variety of senses without losing their identity.

The functional effectiveness of polysemous terms suggests that we need not worry that a term might be meaningless just because no core of uniform and unique properties defines it. This is the point that John Ellis makes by using the example "weed," a word with a different valence than "God" but an equally variable term that follows similar semantic principles. Ellis argues that "a definition need not be in terms of any common features at all." He notes that different members of the class "weeds" often share very few properties and can be very similar in structure and appearance to positively valued plants. Experienced gardeners still know which plants to pull or poison and which ones to protect and preserve. Their decisions may seem confusing to nongardeners because the favored and unfavored plants may have much in common, and in a different community a weed may be a valued plant (goldenrod is a weed in the United States, for example, but a flower in Great Britain). Such ambiguities show not that a term is senseless but that membership in a category is "what is currently agreed to be usable in this way by members of the community."[23] These uses cannot always be best explained by listing the characteristics of an entity. They are often better described by explaining the community's practices and the assumptions, interests, and aims behind them.

Because the meaning of a term like "God," "weed," or "literature" depends on its use rather than on the common properties of its members, there will be disagreements about how to define it in different communities with different beliefs, values, and practices. These disputes themselves become part of the term's meaning because they help to determine how it can be used and with what implications and consequences. Translation from one community to another may not be possible if the term has incompatible uses, purposes, and values in each group, but members of opposing interpretive schools can still understand how a term functions in the worlds of their adversaries without agreeing that those are its best uses. Disagreements about how to use a term do not make it meaningless or ineffective—just complicated, so that one employs the word carefully, especially in circumstances where one can easily be misunderstood because customs different from one's own prevail.

The heterogeneity and variability of "literature" require that analogies that do not imply a common, fixed core of properties be sought to make sense of it—hence Wolfgang Iser's suggestion that "literature," like "art," is "whatever the community decides to put in the museum."[24] The collection of a museum is typically diverse (the very term "collection" implies a loose amalgamation of assorted entities), and its boundaries are always open to change as new contenders for inclusion emerge and demand that the criteria for entry be revised to make room for them. Not all pieces in a collection are equally valuable, and even very highly regarded collections can contain pieces some critics would consider "bad art." Museums can also differ markedly from one another. Their collections typically vary in emphasis, for example, with strengths in some areas and weaknesses in others. There are also many different kinds of collections in museums, from what is almost unanimously agreed on as "art" to interesting borderline cases (does a craft museum house "art" or "folk history"?).

A problem with the analogy, however, is that "museum" has theological connotations to some. Krieger calls museums "the churches of the secular world," filled with "aesthetic idols," elite objects segregated from the everyday world for special "worship."[25] Museums are social institutions, however, whose contents and borders are the result of the decisions and conflicts of communities. Their collections can be put to quasi-theological uses by those whose interests and purposes call for valuing art in such a way, but this is an instance of the social practices that constitute museums, not evidence of their sacral qualities.

"Literature" is a social institution defined as much by the hermeneutic conflicts over how to construe it as by the agreements of readers about what it includes. Such a conclusion is not as unambiguous as the absolutists desire, nor is it as skeptical as the relativists prefer. Institutions differ in identifiable ways from each other even when they are internally diverse. "Literature" does exist and can be discussed with the assurance that it is distinct from other entities, even if its meaning is heterogeneous and variable. Although institutions have histories, continuities usually persist across the changes they go through and help to give them a semblance of stability. "Literature" has changed in many ways, but it has also remained the same in others.

Inasmuch as literature is an institution whose membership is decided by often conflicting community practices, the best way to define it is to explain how this particular institution operates—how, for example, the decisions are made about what to include within it and what to exclude. The crucial concept here is "preservation." The activity of preservation decides what goes in the museum and how its collection will be understood and valued. Those texts that readers value sufficiently to continue interpreting and reinterpreting and to urge others to pay attention to as well attain and maintain membership in the institution, and texts not accorded such regard fail to gain admission or fall out of the class (whether temporarily or permanently, only time will tell). Preservation is not unique to literature. Other kinds of texts (legal or political documents, for example) are often deemed important enough to be handled similarly. By the same token, some critics may have legitimate reasons for wanting to preserve works that they concede are "bad art" but that have value on other than aesthetic grounds. But texts that at least some influential group does not value enough to take up anew and then to hand on again cease to enjoy the status of "literature." To the extent that they continue to exist at all, such works remain in the archive (the basement of the museum) as historical documents—of interest as evidence, among other things, of how communities evaluated and interpreted in the past.

Preservation is an active and not a passive process. As Gadamer explains, it "means transmission rather than conservation"—"learning how to grasp and express the past anew"—in a manner more "equivalent to translation" than to repetition.[26] The paradox of preservation is that literary works can endure only if they allow themselves to change—that is, if they hold themselves open to new interpretations and show themselves able to perform new functions. A work that was a timeless absolute, the status some attribute to the "classics," would not be adaptable to new interests and uses and could not survive. An immutable classic might even seem boring and not worth returning to because it presented the same predictable face, with never a surprise or a variation, to every interpreter.[27]

The necessity that a work welcome new readings as a condition of its preservation leads some to suggest that plurivocity is the distinguishing feature of classic works. Frank Kermode argues, for example, that "the coexistence in a single text of a plurality of significances . . . is, empirically, a requirement and a distinguishing feature of the survivor."[28] However, attributing an intrinsic semantic multiplicity to texts that win preservation is not acceptable. Their range of possible meanings cannot be a preexisting, objectlike stock of significances because the history of reception can take courses not imaginable at the moment of creation. A conception of the work as an autonomously existing entity, even a semantically multivalent one, is not adequate to describe preservation.

History is characterized by discontinuity as well as continuity, unexpected and unpredictable change as well as endurance and similarity from one generation to the next. The history of preservation is an example of this general rule, and the shifting ratio of continuity and discontinuity as generations of readers succeed each other requires a text that can be different from itself even as it remains the same text. An autonomous text is not paradoxical enough to have a truly historical existence. Nor, however, can a work's meaning and value be seen as radically contingent on its various readings without "it" ceasing to have an identity that could have a history. The paradox of identity enduring in and through changes is not adequately accounted for by reducing the text to the flux of hermeneutic variation. Both poles of the paradox of identity maintained in and through difference are required by preservation.

The epistemology of hermeneutic belief is integral to preservation because the workings of hypotheses and presuppositions in understanding make possible the ongoing process of reinterpretation and reassessment that gives a text a history. A work's meaning and value can change because the hypotheses through which readers establish textual coherence vary with their presuppositions about literature and life. These presuppositions can and typically do change from one generation to the next as new assumptions about art, human being, and the like are proposed, win adherents, or fall out of favor and are discarded. As different presuppositions come and go, the hypotheses change through which a work is understood and assessed. But hypotheses are always guesses *about* something, and one reason why presuppositions are revised or overturned can be their persistent failure to enable interpreters to deal effectively with the otherness they are engaged with when they read. An important aspect of such otherness is the historical distance between a work's originating context and the present circumstances of interpretation—a distance that makes preservation a labor against resistances and that requires translation if transmission is to occur. A text can be transmitted only if it can be applied to new purposes and read in new ways, but this is an effort and an achievement because something other than the interpreter reaches across historical distance as a result. Once again, a heteronomous conception of meaning and value is required to understand the dynamics of preservation, and such heteronomy is implicit in the epistemology of belief.

Part of the past that endures in this process is the history of preservation itself. This history belongs to the horizon of the interpreter to the extent that past acts of reading have helped form his or her presuppositions and hermeneutic practices and have shaped his or her expectations about the particular text at hand. These assumptions and expectations belong to the interpreter's historical situation as elements of the hermeneutic past he or she has inherited. How the interpreter engages this legacy is open to wide variation—from conserving it to rebelling against it. But the interpreter's sense of what hypotheses about meaning and value are possible, including viable modes of revolt, always depends on the beliefs previous readers have experimented with and where these have led.

Just as literature is a social institution, so preservation is a social activity. The experiences of receiving, translating, and retransmitting works are inherently social. Reconfiguring works handed down from the past is a social process in which individual interpreters participate in a history that depends on each one of them for its continuation even as it goes beyond any single reader. We are always with others when we interpret—others who are part of the community of readers we have joined. But these others are also necessarily absent, not immediately there alongside us, because they are with us only across our horizons (past readers whose interpretive acts have influenced our sense of our alternatives, or contemporaries from whom we may anticipate encouragement or dissent, or future audiences to whom we may wish to convey our discoveries about how certain assumptions or configurative patterns work).

The paradoxical presence and absence of others as we read is an example of mediation, the social process by which cohesion is established across the boundaries between selves by the texts, symbols, beliefs, and values we share. As literature shows, a mediator has a heteronomous relation to those it unites. The mediator's meaning and value can be different for each of those who share it and from one generation to the next, and this mutability is indispensable for the mediator's capacity to bring a variety of selves together despite divergences in their interests, assumptions, and desires. But a mediator can establish cohesion only if it is an entity held in common by various interpreters and is not merely reducible to them. A mediator (whether a literary work or any other kind) must be other to its interpreters if it is to be the shared object of their regard, even as it must be various and changeable because this regard may value it in many different, perhaps incompatible ways.

When absolutists and relativists interpret literary works, they unwittingly demonstrate that meaning and value are heteronomous, because their arguments about how texts should be understood and judged contribute to the history of preservation. Their readings are part of the conversation through which works remain in circulation, even if that process operates according to principles different from those guiding their interpretations. For example, Cleanth Brooks asks that poems be read *"sub specie aeternitatis"*—as if they were fixed and immutable objects, eternally constant and beyond the vicissitudes of history. "Otherwise," he warns, "the poetry of the past becomes significant merely as cultural anthropology, and the poetry of the present, merely as a political, or religious, or moral instrument."[29] His discovery that paradox, irony, and contradiction molded into unity are everywhere in poetry seems to him a revelation of a universal aesthetic principle, although now, a generation later, it seems evidence of preoccupations that characterized the historical moment when New Criticism dominated the institution of interpretation.

Placing Brooks in the history of preservation does not discredit his contributions as an interpreter, however, but helps better to define them. Although he did not disclose the universal, unchanging meaning and value of Wordsworth, Donne, or Keats, he adapted their works to new purposes and thus transmitted them across historical distance. He did not end the history of interpretation by showing once and for all the right way to read but, instead, performed the more valuable service of giving a new impetus to interpretation by suggesting different presuppositions about literature that seemed promising to many and by demonstrating their implications with a skill and imagination that seemed worth emulating. Under the guise of revealing eternal truths about poetry and poems, Brooks contributed powerfully to the historical process of keeping works in circulation and helped shape the social institution of literature.

The interpretive practice of historicist critics similarly gives evidence of the heteronomy of meaning and value, even though they define literature differently. Tompkins argues, for example, that "the power of a sentimental novel [like *Uncle Tom's Cabin*] to move its audience depends upon the audience's being in possession of the conceptual categories" available to its original readers but no longer accessible to readers whose "modernist prejudices . . . consign this fiction to oblivion."[30] If she were right, however, she would have demonstrated not why such works deserve to be preserved but why they are forgotten. Instead, she shows that *Uncle Tom's Cabin* should be revived because it speaks to the concerns of two powerful contemporary movements—feminism and the new historicism—whose interests and purposes she adapts Stowe's text to serve. Tompkins makes this work seem valuable and comprehensible again not by converting us into Victorian sentimentalists but by reading Stowe's novel as a vision of the potential powers of a matriarchal community and as a demonstration of how rhetoric can act as a political instrument that shapes perceptions of reality. Like Brooks, she contributes to the general work of preservation by reconfiguring the past through hypotheses based on assumptions and interests deemed important in the present.

The absolutist and the historicist have opposing notions of textuality, but both participate in the history of a social institution, literature, which heteronomously both depends on and transcends them. The coexistence within literary studies of groups with opposing beliefs and desires makes preservation a political activity because such differences spawn conflicts over power. "Since not everyone's values are the same," Richard Ohmann notes, disagreements about which categories should guide understanding and judgment are, "among other things, a struggle for dominance."[31] Disputes are inevitable about what beliefs are most worthy of our allegiance and about how entities should be classified. Some desires and interests exclude each other, and, in a world of limited resources, conflicts necessarily ensue about what to value and what purposes to pursue.

It is accurate to call these disputes "political" not only because power is at stake (control over how things may be seen and over the allocation of scarce time, energy, and resources) but also because they are not merely personal quarrels between individual interpreters. They are, rather, battles between different groups, with different commitments and aims, within the larger community of literary inquiry. To describe a conflict as "political," however, is not to claim that it lacks epistemological substance or is purely irrational. Disputes about value are rarely bare-knuckled fights about power pure and simple but usually proceed by argument, and the reasons that the combatants can produce for preferring one set of categories, beliefs, or purposes to another can have as much of an effect on the outcome as can the sheer institutional authority at their disposal. Public debates about value are ways of adjudicating the allocation of institutional power, and force unconnected to reasons and arguments can distort such conflicts. But one value of these disputes is that they test the prevailing distribution of power and offer the community at large the chance to reassess its choices about what to hold good and true. Public arguments about what to value and disparage are influenced by the existing patterns of institutional dominance, but they can also test and challenge the rights of authority to its powers.

Power and the Politics of Interpretation

Interpretation can be regarded as a political activity for a variety of reasons and in a variety of ways. Some critics call for the act of interpretation to become political and to contribute to social change by unmasking the social determinants and ideological implications of literary works.[1] Others investigate the relation of literary criticism to different surrounding social and cultural institutions whose dominance it may reflect or contest.[2] Still others examine the political implications of different modes of interpretation by uncovering and criticizing their assumptions about such matters as history, community, power, and change.[3] The one assumption that all of these approaches to the politics of interpretation share is that power is deeply implicated in the process of understanding. Literary criticism and works of art are especially open to extra-aesthetic political involvements because they have an intrinsic political dimension—that is, because ways of understanding and representing the world are deployments of power or contestations of authority. Because power and authority are inherent in the process of interpretation itself, literary knowledge is particularly likely to be significantly enmeshed with other regions of power and authority in society.

Interpretation is an intrinsically political activity because power is present in the act of understanding in many forms. The issue of who is in charge in the relation between interpreter and text is, among other things, a question about the distribution of power. The competition of opposing interpreters for dominance and authority is also, of course, a battle for power. Michel Foucault is certainly correct when he declares that "knowledge and power are integrated with one another, and there is no point in dreaming of a time when knowledge will cease to depend on power."[4] From the perspective of a theory of hermeneutic conflict and validity, however, an important problem raised by the integral relation of what Foucault calls "power/knowledge" is whether or not force necessarily undermines interpretation. How does the role that power plays in the act of understanding and in disputes about meaning affect the validity of a reading? What are the uses and dangers of power in interpretation, and what can and should be done to enhance its productivity and to minimize its potential disturbances?

The paradox of hermeneutic power is that it requires limits on itself to be maximally effective. Power is not necessarily devious and distorting. It can also be creative and illuminating. The desire of power for uncontested hegemony is its own worst enemy, however, because the effectiveness of interpretive authority diminishes when it goes unchallenged. The reason is that unchecked power is an invitation to vicious hermeneutic circularity. The checks that individual interpreters and communities of readers need to prevent their hypotheses and presuppositions from becoming simply self-confirming would cease to operate if their will to power never ran up against resistances. The interpreter's dream of unrestrained power and unchallenged authority is an epistemological nightmare because such hermeneutic hegemony would quickly degenerate into the blindness of self-validating belief. Although nothing inherent in the drive for interpretive power guarantees that it will recognize the wisdom of curbing itself, it is in the epistemological self-interest of authority to limit its claims and to encourage its own contestation. Power would rather reign unchallenged, but an ongoing competition for dominance and control is more likely than uncontested hegemony to make interpretation productive, resilient, and trustworthy.

This chapter explores the paradox of hermeneutic power first in the act of interpretation itself and then in the embattled relations between opposing communities of readers. The hypotheses through which an interpreter seeks to configure a work according to his or her deeply held presuppositions about literature and life are an effort to assume power over the text. Interpretation is appropriation in the same way that any constructive activity is an attempt to take charge of its materials and make them serve a particular design, but appropriation breaks down if it fails to heed resistances from the object it seeks to mold to its desires and interests. Readers unmindful of resistances to their hypotheses will rigidly and monotonously replicate their presuppositions instead of refining, revising, or extending them. Letting one's will to power run rampant over a text risks a dogmatic fixation of belief. Allowing the text to test one's hypotheses and convictions may persuade one that they are ineffective and should be abandoned, but taking that chance is the necessary price of checking their powers by engaging them with resistances.

Strengthening one's powers through rigorous testing is also one of the main epistemological advantages of conflicts between interpretive communities. Such battles prevent authority from rigidifying. The habits and beliefs of even an expert interpreter lose effectiveness when they become entrenched, no longer open to revision and adaptation with changing circumstances. The veneration of an authority from within his or her interpretive community is a temptation to entrenchment, but challenges from across communal boundaries provide a tonic test of the assumptions and practices one's adherents think unquestionable. Interpretive conflicts require a vigorous defense of the beliefs and hypotheses one holds true, but mounting arguments for them is also a test of their ability to meet new challenges. The result may be useful modifications in them, or an awareness of unnoticed problems that deserve attention, or a more refined sense of what one's position does and does not enable one to do. If the narrowness and rigidity of dogmatic belief are the dangers of unchallenged authority, then contests for interpretive power are therapy against the blindness of entrenchment.

Democracy is the institutional form of life in which interpretation is most likely to flourish. The reason is that democratic conditions provide a political situation in which interpretive power and authority are, at least in principle, constantly subject to challenge and testing. Two of the main characteristics of democracy are also conditions requisite for productive hermeneutic conflict: vigorous advocacy of one's own beliefs and interests, coupled with negotiation and competition with opposing views to test one another's perspectives and to discover possible accommodations. We cannot be certain that democratically conducted conflicts will ensure that justice is done or that "truth" prevails. Precisely because democracy is a conflictual form of life, it can go wrong in many ways—entrenching advantage rather than contesting it, or squelching or ignoring marginal voices rather than giving them a full, fair hearing. Although democracy tests authority's power, there is no guarantee that a fair balance of rights and benefits will result from conflicts between different views, desires, and interests. But if hermeneutic power requires resistance and testing to maximize its effectiveness, democratic relations within and among interpretive communities are more likely to provide them than are less open, more hierarchical political arrangements. The enlightened self-interest of interpretive power calls for the effective functioning of democracy.

Power and the Act of Interpretation

A complex array of power relations can be seen in every attempt of an interpreter to make sense of a text. On the one hand, texts may seek to compel their readers to see and act in a particular way, either reconciling them to the existing state of things or inciting them to protest and resistance, and that is why politically oriented critics find it useful and important to expose the ideologies of literary works. The potential power of a text over its readers is what can make it a political force in society. Critique of textual ideology seeks to tilt the balance of power from text to reader by liberating us from unquestioned immersion in and acceptance of a work's social vision. On the other hand, the beliefs of interpreters have power over texts, and that is why political critics question the ideological implications of different ways of reading. The assumptions and habits of understanding of the interpretive community to which we belong may have power over us because they can restrict and direct our way of reading a work, and these constraints matter in turn because interpretive practices have power over texts—configuring them in one form or another to serve different visions of human life and social relations. Unmasking the ideologies of readers and literary works is useful political work only because the relation of interpreter to text is a relation of power, which can be constituted in different ways for different purposes.

It is not in the interest of a text to have unlimited control over the reader because understanding is an active process of filling in gaps and building consistent patterns. A completely subdued, dominated reader would not have the freedom and power to contribute to the work what it needs in order to take on meaning.[5] But it is also not in the interest of the interpreter to have complete, unchallenged power over a work because uncontested force can be blinding. If interpretation is circular in the sense that the meaning of any part of a work depends on one's hypotheses about its relation to the whole, then an ever-present danger is that one's understanding of both parts and whole will be self-enclosed, mutually confirming, and impregnable. Because the whole one posits as one's governing interpretive pattern gives meaning to the part even as the detail substantiates one's guess about the whole, a belief about a text's configuration can very easily become self-validating and impervious to counterevidence or dissent. Interpreters may rudely force all the details into a particular pattern without being aware that the fit is forced, if they are enthralled by beliefs that they have no way of seeing past.

The differences between a rudely forced fit and an elegantly synthesized composition are impossible to spell out clearly and definitively, but signs of this distinction are an alert, forthright awareness of possible anomalies and a readiness to admit the potential advantages of alternative hypotheses. Someone who stubbornly persists in a reading even as contrary evidence and dissenting views accumulate is very likely caught in a vicious interpretive circle, although that is not necessarily so. In such instances the very stridency of an interpreter's insistence on the power of his or her beliefs can be evidence of their weakness. The dilemma is that nothing inherent distinguishes a solvable puzzle, which will yield to persistence and ingenuity, from a falsifying anomaly, which can be removed only by discarding one's hypotheses about the entire design. Although an awareness of anomaly and a willingness to entertain opposing hypotheses suggest that an interpreter is not enthralled by his or her beliefs, tenacity in struggling against resistances in the forms both of textual evidence and of opposition from other interpretive schools is sometimes necessary to give a hypothesis a chance to vindicate itself.

A contradictory attitude is required—the assertion of the power of one's hypotheses, coupled with a sense of their limits and a consequent willingness to abandon or revise them. Hermeneutic power that refuses any checks on itself is likely to degenerate into the solipsism of self-confirming belief, but hermeneutic power that does not assert itself against obstacles, resistances, and dissent will not have the chance to demonstrate its capacities. Interpreters must be forceful in applying their beliefs and assumptions to the text even as they remember that their convictions about textual configurations are only hypotheses and are therefore provisional and open to change and refutation. As hypotheses, guesses about meaning must be held with conviction even as they must also be viewed tentatively and warily. The paradox that hermeneutic power requires limitation to be effective is a reflection of the doubleness of belief as an epistemological structure. A belief is a guess about what we do not know, and it must consequently be both embraced with faith and questioned with skeptical detachment.[6]

This contradiction is also an embodiment of democratic attitudes toward convictions—asserting one's own perspective even as one remains open to alternatives that may turn out to be preferable. To be a citizen in a democracy requires a paradoxical ethos. On the one hand, participating effectively in democratic debates demands vigorous advocacy and defense of one's own convictions against competing views. On the other hand, democratic negotiation about the future course of the community's affairs necessitates open-mindedness about the possible benefits of other perspectives and a willingness not only to tolerate but also to hear dissent, including a readiness to change one's mind if persuasive reasons for doing so emerge (and they have a chance of surfacing only if debate is vigorous and free). Stridency that refuses to consider the possible advantages of opposing beliefs is disruptive to democratic exchange. Democracy is a precarious political state both because it requires paradoxical behavior from its citizens and because it works best when the balance of power is not permanently fixed. But this very precariousness is what makes democratic conditions essential for the effective functioning of interpretive power.

Unopposed interpretive force is likely to rigidify, and that is a danger because interpretation is a matter of projecting and testing hypotheses. Force not open to resistance and opposition runs the risk of losing the flexibility necessary for responsive, innovative guessing. Hypothesis testing requires resiliency and openness to the unexpected. Interpreters must have the ability to experiment with the various possibilities made available to them by their presuppositions in order to choose those most worth actualizing. Interpreters also need a capacity to revise and extend their assumptions to meet new situations and challenges if none of the options made possible by their presuppositions seems adequate or desirable. Interpretation requires the freedom to experiment with different assumptions and configurations. Unlimited hermeneutic power is not likely to be very good at hypothesis testing because it would lack the tentativeness and flexibility characteristic of the experimental attitude. Hermeneutic power demands both openness and opposition to work effectively, in the same way that freedom requires both possibility and constraint to be meaningfully exercised.[7] The need for conditions conducive to freedom provides another reason why interpretation is most at home in democracy.

There is no structural guarantee that unconstrained hermeneutic power will ultimately fail because of its own inherent weaknesses any more than it is certain that democracy will prevail as the dominant political form. The most one can say is that hermeneutic power that is open to resistance and contestation is more likely over the long run to do useful work and, as a consequence, to be judged by future generations removed from its immediate influence to be worth preserving. There are limits to what any authority can control. Something always exceeds the grasp of any form of power. To win the positive regard of parties outside its sphere of dominance, authority needs to be concerned about the intersubjectively recognizable qualities of its products. It is possible for a dominant mode of interpretation to retain power for quite some time by controlling the institutions of education, dissemination, and advancement. Over the long term, however, choices about what to preserve and what to discard are made on the basis of recognitions of value that exceed the direct influence of the originating authority whose products are being judged.[8] As in many other things, the benefits of short-term advantages may blind interpretive authority to its best interests over the long term. But one of the main pragmatic hopes that interpretive power will recognize its enlightened self-interest and curb its claims is nothing more than that—a hope—the hope that it will regard the chance of historical preservation as more important than uncontested hegemony in the present.

Power is involved not only in the relation between interpreter and text but also in the relation between an interpreter and the rules, assumptions, and practices that define his or her discipline or hermeneutic school. Foucault has been the most forceful proponent of the argument that "truth . . . is produced only by virtue of certain forms of constraint" defining a community's " 'general politics' of truth"—that is, "the types of discourse which it accepts," "the mechanisms and instances which enable one to distinguish true and false statements," and "the techniques and procedures accorded value in the acquisition of truth."[9] Ways of understanding are forms of domination, he argues, which constrain and coerce those who practice them. As Paul Bové explains, interpreters are always "to various degrees instruments of the . . . impersonal power of the disciplines" to which they belong.[10] To become an effective, respected practitioner of any method of interpretation requires training, and that in turn demands that one subordinate one's will to the habits and techniques one wishes to acquire. Here again, however, power is not unlimited, or else it could not function. If disciplines were entirely coercive, they would leave their adherents no power to enact their epistemological possibilities. The relation of an interpreter to a method or discipline is inherently paradoxical, both bound and free.[11] Only by allowing the interpreter who submits to its constraints the freedom to explore and experiment can a set of techniques actually be used.

One of the limitations on the power of interpretive techniques is that they are conventions rather than dictatorial forces. As Edward Said notes, "the power of institutions to subjugate individuals" is not the same as "the fact that individual behavior in society is frequently a matter of following rules and conventions."[12] Following conventions typically allows choices that subjugation does not. Few conventions specify in each and every detail how they are to be actualized, and considerable innovation is consequently possible even by those who stay within their general limits. There is also usually the possibility, to a greater or lesser extent, of innovating against the rules—the possibility of creating by bending or breaking conventions (as in the invention of a metaphor), a possibility that depends on the existence of conventions but is not entirely constrained by them. Such behavior may be punished or rewarded or simply ignored, but the fact that it is possible (and that its consequences are not simply determined by the conventions themselves) suggests that disciplinary practices allow more freedom than the attribution to them of monolithic, absolute power would suggest.

Another reason why the power of an interpretive method over its adherents is inherently limited has to do with the role of belief in understanding and, in particular, with the relation between the defining presuppositions of a hermeneutic method and the textual hypotheses to which these give rise. By accepting the presuppositions about literature and life that define a particular manner of understanding, an interpreter grants these assumptions the power to restrict and guide his or her way of seeing. But accepting presuppositions is rarely simply the result of coercion. It is at least in principle a choice because there are always alternatives, even if the options are in some situations less numerous and more difficult to elect than in others.[13] In conditions of vigorous interpretive conflict, choice is more open and viable than when unanimous agreement prevails about the proper methods and aims of interpretation. But even in monolithic hermeneutic states, dissent is possible if one is willing to pay the price (taking the risk, for example, of being neglected or even persecuted in one's own time in the hope of receiving vindicating recognition from later generations). Still another reason why democracy is the preferable hermeneutic state is that it facilitates the innovation that such dissent makes possible.

Even if the dominance of a set of presuppositions and practices makes dissent difficult and unlikely, their control over the act of interpretation is never absolute and deterministic. Here again, interpretive power is inherently limited because the basic assumptions of a hermeneutic school cannot determine completely and in advance the textual hypotheses they will inspire. Which particular hypotheses an interpreter with a given set of presuppositions will come up with is open to considerable latitude: They will vary not only according to the different interpretive challenges an interpreter faces but also according to his or her creativity in responding to them. Understanding operates in the space of freedom between the basic beliefs defining an interpretive method and their particular, variable applications. If presuppositions did not allow a range of applications, they would have to be invented anew with every different text to be interpreted, and their lack of transferability would considerably diminish their usefulness. The fundamental assumptions of a hermeneutic school do not simply coerce their adherents. Their role is as much liberating as dominating. Not only do they limit the vision of those who accept them, but they also make possible the discovery and creation of an unpredictable array of interpretive hypotheses.

By submitting oneself to the rigors and constraints of a particular discipline, an interpreter not only acquires the powers of understanding it offers but may also win the right to question and revise the paradigm itself. One of the ultimate signs of interpretive authority is the power to change the beliefs and techniques that have given one authority. Challenges to an interpretive school's fundamental assumptions and practices made by those who have shown themselves expert in applying them are particularly powerful. Such authorities not only are likely to have a detailed, thorough knowledge of the weaknesses as well as strengths of their methods but also enjoy such respect and trust from within their hermeneutic communities that they can expect a hearing from other adherents even when they challenge unquestioned beliefs which outsiders would be met with hostility for criticizing. The freedom and power to challenge a paradigm are, perhaps curiously, best acquired by submitting to it. It is in the interest of a school's leading figures to avoid letting power become entrenched so that they can demonstrate their own powers by redefining the paradigm itself. Illustrating once again the paradox that interpretive power is most effective when it accepts limits to power, this way of exercising authority simultaneously gives evidence that all authority is provisional and subject to change.

Power and Interpretive Conflict

Under democratic conditions it is explicitly assumed that any authority is only temporarily and provisionally in power, and this is a considerable epistemological advantage to the extent that entrenched authority erodes the effectiveness of interpretation. An important value of interpretive conflicts is that they remind authority that its mandate is only provisional and offer the chance of dislodging it when and if its effectiveness diminishes. Bové warns that the very "figure of the masterful or leading intellectual" is an "antidemocratic structure," which, as such, is complicit with the "application of power upon the subjugated."[14] Rather than causing us to despair that subjugation is inescapable, however, such warnings should increase our vigilance against the tendency of authority to insulate itself against challenges. Said observes that all forms of authority are "contingent" because they are "constructed by humans" and are "therefore not invincible, not impervious to dismantling."[15] Democratic contestations of authority call attention to the contingency of power and facilitate the possibility of dismantling it. Interpretive conflicts both within and across the boundaries defining hermeneutic communities are a useful, even necessary counterforce to the dynastic tendencies of authority.

Even within a hermeneutic community, the position of the master interpreter or leading intellectual is rarely uncontested. As Mary Louise Pratt notes, "Consensus is never peaceful. . . . Interpretations are always jostling for space, thumping on each others' walls."[16] Competition for ascendancy does not stop just because interpreters share more or less the same set of assumptions and practices. A sense of commonality may instead lead to increased efforts to assert one's differences. Aspirants for power are usually alert for opportunities to dethrone the dominant figures. Although they may be protected by various institutional privileges, authorities must continue to demonstrate the powers that entitled them to their position of ascendancy, or else their voices will be gradually disregarded. Hermeneutic communities are both hierarchical and egalitarian structures, where certain figures enjoy special respect but where interpretations compete for recognition.

Some communities are more egalitarian than others, of course, and that may be to their epistemological advantage. Although hierarchy may usefully reinforce the sense of internal coherence necessary for group identity, internal dissension and debate offer the community the chance to sift out the strengths and weaknesses of its assumptions and techniques, to weigh different possible improvements, and to select the most promising future course of research by comparatively testing various alternatives. Radical internal conflict may split a community apart (as sometimes happens when interpretive schools divide). But if hermeneutic communities allow themselves to become rigidly hierarchical, they may become stultified and die.

When a community (even a lively one) is relatively homogeneous, some presuppositions and habits of understanding may seem so obvious to everyone that they are immune from criticism. This state of affairs is a serious limit to the ability of a community to monitor itself. The danger here is naturalization, the tyranny of what seems self-evident, unchangeable, simply "there."[17] One way of demystifying the seeming naturalness of a set of beliefs or interpretive practices is to juxtapose them against opposing conventions that organize the world according to different principles that may seem equally obvious to their adherents. As Robert Scholes points out, "The way to see one discourse is to see more than one."[18] Claiming that "knowledge is never neutral," Katherine Cummings consequently calls for "competing narratives" to expose and contest each other's claims to "ideological hegemony."[19] Strong interpretive disagreement calls into question the "naturalness" of presuppositions and practices that may seem self-evident to one group but arbitrary and extremely problematic to another. If naturalization closes off choice and change, the juxtaposition of interpretive possibilities brought about by hermeneutic conflict opens them up, and this, in turn, emphasizes the contingency of interpretive authority, the mutability and constructedness of any way of seeing, no matter how powerful.

Fredric Jameson claims that "if everything were transparent, then no ideology would be possible, and no domination either."[20] Perfect, ubiquitous transparency is an impossible dream because opacity of some kind is the necessary cost of the particular illumination any set of presuppositions offers. In the absence of universal transparency, however, the juxtaposition of different modes of blindness and insight may not only demystify the naturalness of each one but also free interpreters to choose deliberately and self-consciously the assumptions and practices they will allow authority over themselves. Escaping the dominion of some sort of hermeneutic paradigm may not be possible, but vigorous interpretive conflict increases the ability of readers to choose the constraints to which they will submit.

In the battle for ascendancy waged by conflicting interpretive methods, two extreme states that are possible and equally undesirable are tyranny and anarchy. If one way of understanding wins out over all the others, its triumph may seem like a useful, even "scientific" consolidation of inquiry around a single research program, which all investigators will then pool their resources to pursue. But such monolithic epistemological consensus runs all the risks of rigidity, self-confirmation, and naturalization against which interpretive conflict is a healthy antidote. The usefulness of variety and disagreement is a reason why the so-called hard sciences are internally more heterogeneous than outsiders frequently assume.[21] Nevertheless, even though conflict and dissent aid interpretation, the extreme disorder and violence of anarchy can undermine it. Only by joining together in relatively coherent groups with shared assumptions and goals can interpreters pursue the possibilities opened up by a particular way of understanding in a sufficiently sustained, rigorous manner to discover its strengths and expose its weaknesses. Orderly exchange within an interpretive community is necessary to facilitate the pursuit of common goals. Orderly exchange between opposing communities is necessary if they are to test one another's assumptions, aims, and results by engaging in reasoned debate about texts and problems that they prefer to address in different ways. An anarchic free-for-all is not the restrained, deliberate contest between opposing views that can make interpretive conflict a socially useful test of comparative epistemological power.

If interpretive conflict is a conversation between parties with opposing views, dialogue requires not only the genuine differences of opinion that the tyranny of consensus would suppress but also the continuity of argument and response that the disruptions of anarchy would prevent. Democracy similarly needs to avoid the extremes of stifling uniformity and perpetual discontinuity. One aim of democratic traditions and institutions is to establish a coherent, relatively continuous social framework, which facilitates open, vigorous disagreements without allowing them to disintegrate into violence and disarray. An important, inescapable contradiction of democracy is that it does not require belief in any particular creed even as it does demand from its citizens allegiance to the principle of free exchange and the promise that they will not disrupt the political structures that contain their conflicts. This contradiction is necessary to make democratic debates both free and orderly. Participants in interpretive conflict must similarly agree to a kind of implicit social contract that regulates disputes by requiring combatants to place their disagreements within a tradition of disciplinary conversation and to restrict their attacks on each other according to certain conventions of professional decorum. The notion of free and orderly conflict is self-contradictory, but it is essential if power is to be limited and made socially useful.

There is a difference between productive and unproductive conflict, and one value of democratic forms of exchange is that, at their best, they maximize the likelihood that disputes between individual parties will benefit the collectivity as a whole. It is easier to describe the difference between productive and unproductive conflict, however, than to orchestrate or control it. Unproductive conflict can take the form of force confronting force without an attempt to justify one's position with reasoned arguments, or it can take the form of differences that never result in an exchange, as when two sides fail to engage one another because each is solipsistically preoccupied with its own concerns and is unable, unwilling, or simply not inclined to hear other views. The precondition for productive conflict is reasoned engagement and exchange. Mutual respect and an agreement not to resort to force or trickery to gain advantage are necessary to make conflict productive. Agreement about essentials at some bedrock level is not necessary, but combatants must try to prevent themselves from simply talking at each other or at cross-purposes by directing their arguments at a commonly shared problem or text (even if they disagree about how to define it).

Productive conflict can have a variety of outcomes. It may result in the victory of one party and the defeat of another in a struggle for the survival of the "fittest." In combats of this kind, the disputing parties compare the ability of their assumptions and hypotheses to meet such transcommunal standards for validity as inclusiveness in accounting for potential anomalies or efficacy in meeting unexpected challenges, and the embarrassments and difficulties of one side may be greater than those of the other. The result of productive conflict need not be triumph for one party, however. Productive conflict can have the structure not of a zero-sum but of a positive-sum game—not "win/lose" but "win/win."

If neither side triumphs, both may still gain from their encounter in various ways. Interpretive disputes can lead to the discovery of unsuspected common ground, or they can culminate in an agreement to disagree made with a fuller understanding of what that means than either side had before. Confronting presuppositions radically different from one's own may lead one to become clearer about what one believes and why, or the challenge of rigorous opposition may compel adherents of an approach to refine their methods or to clarify their hypotheses with more subtlety and precision than they might have developed if they had not met resistance. Both communities gain from such increased self-understanding, as do outside observers who, if they are contemplating joining one or another of them, may see more clearly what they would gain and lose from such a declaration of allegiance. It is in the epistemological best interest of all interpreters, regardless of their assumptions and goals, to comport themselves and to structure their profession so as to make productive conflict prevail.

One of the main political responsibilities of the critic is an ethical obligation—the imperative of behaving in such a way as to facilitate productive conflict. As Wayne Booth suggests, such behavior is necessarily paradoxical: "If the first commandment . . . is 'Pursue some one chosen monism as well as you can,' the second is like unto it: 'Give your neighbor's monism a fair shake.'"[22] Because some assumptions and aims exclude others, interpreters must choose between different, incommensurable commitments, and this diversity of hermeneutic belief is what makes conflict possible and unavoidable. But even as interpreters pursue vigorously and single-mindedly the assumptions they have selected in full confidence of their "truth," they must also hold themselves open to the possibility that other, perhaps radically divergent beliefs might have equal or even greater advantages. Such openness helps to avoid dogmatic, naturalized self-enthrallment with one's beliefs by testing one's commitments against alternatives (and thereby reminding oneself that they are not inevitable but are choices). Balancing commitment against openness is also necessary to enable one to see beyond the limits of one's own perspective in order to understand what others with different assumptions and practices are saying.

One cannot make sense of the messages emitted from a position different from one's own unless one is able to enter into it imaginatively, and the failure of combatants to get temporarily outside of themselves in order to hear their foes is a frequent cause of unproductive conflict.[23] Although the presuppositions and aims of interpreters always restrict their understanding, they can escape solipsism and converse effectively with others from opposing communities only if they can actively entertain the possibility of viable other worlds. Productive hermeneutic conflict requires adversarial defense of one's own world coupled with an imaginative appreciation of the potential values of otherness.

Some institutional arrangements are more conducive than others to this paradoxical form of behavior. Mutually beneficial combat ceases, as W. J. T. Mitchell notes, when conflict disintegrates "into polemical sloganeering or, even worse, into the ominous silence which signals the continuation of the struggle by other means—the control of jobs, publication, funding, and of opportunities to practice the arts of interpretation."[24] Faculty appointments, tenure, refereed publications, research fellowships, endowed chairs—these are all signs of authority that constrain and control what is possible in the institution of interpretation. If the possessors of these advantages become locked into place and the allocation of them is not openly contested, the likelihood of vigorous, mutually beneficial conflict is diminished. The beliefs, values, and personalities that enjoy privileged institutional status are not and should not be permanent, and their liability to displacement helps keep the institution open to challenge and dissent.

In order to protect and preserve productive conflict, any profession whose business is interpretation should work to ensure that authority is regularly and publicly tested and that power in the institution is dispersed. Dismantling all legitimately earned rights and privileges that are marks of epistemological power would weaken the hermeneutic productivity of the institution, however, as would making access to them so easy that the rigor and innovation encouraged by conflict and competition are lost. But keeping authority honest and preventing the excessive consolidation of power are in the interest of any interpretive profession. Maintaining openness about the processes by which rewards are distributed is the minimal precondition for preserving accountability.

Tolerance that is a mask for indifference will not facilitate productive conflict. Richard Ohmann rightly complains, "It is easy to translate [pluralism] into the implied language of the powerful:

'You are entitled to your opinion, and it won't affect my actions one whit.' "[25] Unless openness to otherness includes the possibility that the encounter might change our mind, we are not really testing our beliefs but are merely disguising our dogmatic commitment to them. Tolerant indifference can be not merely passive but active. One of its typical tactics, as Gerald Graff points out, is to defuse conflicts not by repressing opposing voices but by making a place for them within the institution and then, in the belief that it has done its democratic duty, ignoring them: "Whenever cross-factional conflict threatens to break out, it tends to be muffled by the expedient of adding another unit to an aggregate that remains unchanged or silently adapts."[26] To have a different perspective represented in one's faculty or on one's list of courses is not enough to ensure that socially useful interpretive conflict will occur. Peaceful coexistence is not the same as lively engagement and exchange but can be a way for the institution to ward off the threat of fundamental change while it deceives itself about its vitality. In our classrooms and in our curricula as well as in our scholarly interactions, we need to create structures that make it likely that our differences will productively confront each other and not just sit inertly side by side.[27]

The beneficiaries of such conflicts are ultimately not only the interpreters themselves but also their students and their societies. Graff notes that "unresolved conflict" is "just the sort of thing a democratic educational system should thrive on."[28] As training in how to conduct productive disputes with others who hold opposing assumptions and aims, learning how to participate in the conflict of interpretations is excellent education for democracy. Helping students understand the causes and consequences of irreconcilable hermeneutic disputes is simultaneously a way of inculcating in them the responsible use of freedom and disagreement. Learning how to choose between irreconcilable but equally tenable beliefs is necessary not only for literary interpretation but also for effective citizenship in a heterogeneous, pluralistic society. Learning how to defend one's commitments vigorously even as one listens sympathetically to others and holds oneself open to changing one's views is essential not only for productive hermeneutic conflict but also for democratic political negotiations. Interpretive conflict requires democratic institutions and practices, and effective democracy requires facility in interpretive conflict.

Postscript

Any theory of interpretive conflict must answer the question of where it stands in relation to the field of disagreement it describes. Does it claim to be free of presuppositions, even though the modes of understanding it attempts to account for differ among themselves according to their assumptions? Or is it itself based on inherently contestable beliefs, in which case its ability to provide a fundamental or all-inclusive explanation of the hermeneutic field might seem questionable?

My theory of conflicting readings has its own defining assumptions, interests, and aims, but this is not an embarrassment or a deficiency. I would be in danger of self-contradiction only if I asserted for my interpretation of the activity of interpretation an absolute authority, which, as I have tried to show, no mode of understanding can claim. One of my main assumptions is that interpretive conflict occurs because there are two related levels of belief at work in understanding. Interpretation is an activity of projecting hypotheses about configurative patterns, hypotheses that in turn reflect more enduring presuppositions about the matters at hand. These presuppositions can be irreconcilably at odds with other assumptions that people of good will may choose to embrace. But I also believe that these hypotheses and presuppositions are testable responses to otherness. They are attempts to make sense of texts, people, or states of affairs that exceed their grasp, and some beliefs are more effective and persuasive than others in doing this work (although no single belief is the most effective and persuasive). My own theory of interpretive conflict is exactly that—a theory. As such, it is a set of beliefs that differs from theories other students of hermeneutics may prefer, but it is also one that I have tried to test and prove by exploring its power to deal with a variety of problems that concern contemporary critics.

My interests and aims in attempting to make a case for this theory are various. I want to deny the existence of a single logic or rationality that all right readings must heed and that could act as a decisive arbiter in instances of interpretive disagreement. One of my motives here is that my desire to believe in the possibility of human possibility makes me resist closing the door on what can count as "truth." Rather, my inclination is to celebrate epistemological innovation and diversity. But I also believe that beliefs have consequences and that they can be debated and evaluated. Although I want to avoid a univocal conception of "truth," I am also interested in finding ways of distinguishing between legitimate beliefs and solipsistic fantasies. One is free to entertain a variety of beliefs, but we are accountable for our beliefs to the world and to the community. Some beliefs work better than others do, and the price of holding certain views may be isolation from skeptical or even hostile others.

The effectiveness and persuasiveness of beliefs, including my own, are not necessarily conclusive, univocal tests of their worth, but the ability to pass such tests is a valuable sign that our beliefs are probably not mere figments or delusions. My commitment to the value of such tests reflects my interest in preserving standards of reasonableness for arguments, assumptions, and hypotheses, despite my skepticism about an all-encompassing rationality. Literary criticism, I have tried to argue, is a "rational enterprise" not because some universal logic lies at its foundation (my theory of interpretive conflict is not an attempt to provide something of this kind) but because interpreters can and do give reasons for their beliefs, reasons that others can criticize, reject, or accept (and my theory is an attempt to explain this process even as it will itself be judged by it, and that is as it should be).

My theory is not an umbrella so broad that it can claim to cover all other theories or a foundation so deep and indubitable that it provides a bedrock on which all other beliefs about interpretation must rest. What I am offering is a general explanation of why particular modes of understanding may disagree about how to construe a state of affairs, but I myself have disagreed throughout this book with other theorists about a variety of issues at what I have called the "global" (as opposed to the "local") level of hermeneutic theory—about the stability and determinacy of literary works, for example, or about the existence of transcommunal tests for validity, or about metaphor, value, history, and politics. The global level replicates many of the conflicts at the local level because each general theory of interpretation or literature is a way of construing a state of affairs and, as such, may be at odds with other possible modes of understanding it. My disputes with other general theories might in turn be analyzable at an even more general level of analysis than the one my theory operates on. There can be a theory of theories of interpretation, a theory of theories of theories of interpretation, and so on.

This state of affairs recalls the well-known story of the man who tells the philosopher that the world is supported on the back of a turtle. When the philosopher asks him what holds up the turtle, the man replies, "Another turtle." When asked what that turtle stands on, he answers with some exasperation, "Sir, it's turtles all the way down." The quest for foundations invariably leads ad infinitum to ever more foundations. Nevertheless, the possibility of such an endless regress does not diminish our ability to stand, walk, or otherwise move around on any level we happen to be on. The number of turtles supporting the world is of little consequence for my ability to do things in that world. The number of foundations that could be posited for the act of interpretation does not impair my ability to read any particular text. The value of work done at any individual level of understanding remains, regardless of the possibility that it might at some point be subsumed by a more general level of knowledge. The insights offered by a particular mode of understanding at the "local" level are still of worth despite the claim of a "global" theory like my own to offer an explanation of its powers and limits. In just the same way, a "global" account of the interpretive field like the one I am proposing can be of use even if disagreements with other possible general theories of interpretation prevent it from claiming the status of a foundation at the bottom of all foundations.

The umbrella metaphor can be read to make a similar point. Pluralists sometimes describe a theory that encompasses another theory as an "umbrella," and they then often note that no umbrella is so big that it cannot be encompassed in turn by another, more commodious umbrella.[1] This image is a little ludicrous because umbrellas are not usually used to cover other umbrellas. If we need a bigger umbrella, we do not put it over the smaller one we had previously been using but instead replace one with the other. But this absurdity is revealing because it suggests that the way to evaluate the relation of one umbrella to another is to ask not which one can enclose the other but rather which one serves our purposes best. Even though there is no such thing as the most commodious umbrella, the absence of one is immaterial for the usefulness of the umbrellas we do have. The uses of a large umbrella do not call into question or in any way impair the effectiveness of others with different attributes (and the largest umbrella is not always the one best suited to our purposes—indeed, its very size may often make it less helpful than umbrellas of smaller scope). The moral I am trying to suggest is this: My theory of interpretation should be judged (like an umbrella) not according to whether it is all-encompassing and immune from being enclosed by a still larger, more general theory but rather according to whether, at its own level of generality, it is useful for the purposes it is designed to serve.

Pluralists searching for the most commodious umbrella often desire to find a theory that would allow them to combine different, partial, incomplete modes of understanding. They hope to overcome the limits of each mode by supplementing it with the powers of others. Wayne Booth argues for "the value of a pluralism of pluralisms" on such grounds: "Each mode has yielded results of importance to me," he reports, but he also recognizes "that I cannot extend any one of them fully to incorporate the others," and yet he also insists that "my 'total' assent to any one of them does not, finally, inhibit—though it complicates—my assent to the others."[2] All of the qualifiers in this last assertion suggest Booth's awareness of the crucial issue here: Can one's "'total' assent" to a particular method of interpretation allow one's equally "total" commitment to another, conflicting mode? What should a pluralist seeking a synthesis of methods do when the presuppositions of opposing approaches contradict each other? Ellen Rooney argues that the "antipluralist stance" is marked by a recognition of "the necessity—the inevitability—of making exclusions."[3] My theory of interpretive conflict is pluralistic in the sense that it claims that different presuppositions can give rise to a variety of ways of understanding which cannot necessarily be reconciled. But this very skepticism about the possibility of overcoming interpretive disagreements through some grand epistemological synthesis makes my theory antipluralistic in its emphasis on the inevitability of exclusions.

The possibility of "strong disagreement" between presuppositions that exclude each other makes me distrust the dream of a theory of theories that would allow an interpreter to embrace all competing modes of understanding. No theory (including my own) can say in advance which modes can be productively combined with others. Such syntheses must be left for individual interpreters to try out for themselves, although they should recognize that a combination may be weaker than the methods it amalgamates for the very reason that the radical, exclusionary claims of an approach may be an important source of its powers. Because some presuppositions exclude each other, however, an eclectic pluralism can get an interpreter into trouble. Self-consistency in one's presuppositions and aims is not a good in and of itself (and is probably something none of us ever attains), but contradictions in an interpreter's operating assumptions can cause breakdowns and embarrassments of various sorts. Contrary presuppositions can lead to the production of disabling anomalies by prompting an interpreter to generate contradictory hypotheses about a state of affairs without providing a way of resolving them. Or, if a reader somehow manages to avoid self-induced impasses of this kind, the contradictions in his or her assumptions may provide an opponent with an all too easy opening for attack. If, as I have argued, interpretation is based on beliefs that are accountable for their effectiveness and their persuasiveness, then embracing contrary methods based on imperfectly compatible assumptions is not necessarily useful or advisable.

My theory of hermeneutic conflict argues that interpreters must accept on faith various inherently contestable presuppositions if they are to be able to generate hypotheses about whatever they are trying to understand, and the role of belief in understanding means that choices are inescapable at all levels and metalevels of interpretation. These choices are precisely that—choices—for the reason that the alternatives facing an interpreter invariably at some point exclude each other. My emphasis on the necessity of choice in interpretation—whether in adopting presuppositions about literature, language, and life or in selecting hypotheses about a particular text—means that my theory is not a calculus for determining right readings. Neither I nor any other theorist can provide rules for guaranteeing correct interpretations because reading always entails choices whose consequences can be assessed only after the fact. The tests for validity I have proposed do not provide rules for right reading but instead describe how the claims of opposing choices about how to understand are adjudicated, and my argument has been that these tests cannot conclusively vindicate one set of choices over another. To interpret means to accept responsibility for commitments that could always have been otherwise and whose implications one can never fully foresee.

The role of choice in understanding means that my theory does not insist deterministically on any particular interpretive approach as the necessary consequence of my own beliefs about how understanding works. My assumptions about the act of interpretation may have more affinities with the presuppositions of some critical methods than with those of others, but my theory of interpretive conflict allows all modes of understanding equal opportunity to test their powers. Because I argue that an interpreter enters the field of conflicting methods by choosing what to believe, my theory does not compel any particular set of choices about how to read.

In that sense my theory of conflicting readings has no consequences for the actual practice of reading. Anyone who accepts my theory is free to continue reading as he or she wishes. In other ways, however, my theory does have consequences, perhaps the most important of which are the political implications that my views about the necessity and desirability of productive interpretive conflict would have for preserving and enhancing democracy in the institution of literary criticism. My theory also has consequences for the practice of individual interpreters—not dictating their choices, but perhaps making it possible for such choices to be more informed. If interpretation is a matter of deciding what it is better to believe, then an important role for theory is to increase the interpreter's self-consciousness about the possible implications of various alternatives. Such self-consciousness cannot guarantee that an interpreter will make good choices, but it can help to make sure that our commitments will be ones we decide to pursue rather than ones we fall into by accident or as a result of institutional pressure. Although no theory can predict where any set of beliefs will lead, one value of studying hermeneutic conflict is that an interpreter may thereby understand more clearly the risks and powers of a particular mode by comparing it with others. If one can understand only by entertaining beliefs, then setting competing beliefs against each other is a useful way of seeing what each entails. A theory of interpretive conflict cannot promise to make us better readers. It can, however, help us to understand more fully our own commitments and to appreciate the commitments of others whose beliefs we choose not to share.

Notes

Preface

1. See my two books of practical criticism, *The Phenomenology of Henry James* (Chapel Hill: University of North Carolina Press, 1983) and *The Challenge of Bewilderment: Understanding and Representation in James, Conrad, and Ford* (Ithaca, N.Y.: Cornell University Press, 1987). As I argue in the first of these books, phenomenology is itself a heterogeneous field that replicates many of the oppositions characteristic of the conflict of interpretations at large. This is also true of many other interpretive schools, of course, which may seem homogeneous to outsiders but which have their own internal disagreements and schisms, which matter considerably to insiders. The point of this endless regress from one arena of interpretive dissension to another (from conflict between communities to conflicts within them) is that there is no escaping the need to choose presuppositions that will ally one with some interpreters and put one at odds with others.

Chapter 1

1. This view is typically associated, more or less correctly, with the Yale deconstructionists and their mentor, Jacques Derrida, but others, such as Norman Holland and Stanley Fish, hold similar positions. The Yale school includes Geoffrey Hartman, the late Paul de Man, J. Hillis Miller (no longer at Yale), and Harold Bloom; see their anthology *Deconstruction and Criticism* (New York: Continuum, 1979). Also see Norman N. Holland, *Five Readers Reading* (New Haven: Yale University Press, 1975), and Stanley E. Fish, *Is There a Text in This Class?* (Cambridge, Mass.: Harvard University Press, 1980). These critics have many crucial differences, which I cannot explicate in detail here. The deconstructionists, for example, are much

more diverse than many of their critics realize. For a helpful assessment of their similarities and differences, see Jonathan Arac, Wlad Godzich, and Wallace Martin, eds., *The Yale Critics: Deconstruction in America* (Minneapolis: University of Minnesota Press, 1983). My ultimate concern, however, is not with the distinctions between recent critical positions but with the basic epistemological question of relativism—a question with a long history before it entered the contemporary critical scene.

2. I am referring to E. D. Hirsch, Jr., René Wellek, and John Reichert: See Hirsch, *Validity in Interpretation* (New Haven: Yale University Press, 1967); Wellek, "The New Criticism: Pro and Contra," *Critical Inquiry* 4 (1978): 611–24; and Reichert, *Making Sense of Literature* (Chicago: University of Chicago Press, 1977). Reichert calls himself a pluralist (*Making Sense of Literature*, p. xi), but his allegiance to monism is made unmistakably clear in the argument of his book and in the dispute that he and Fish fought in the pages of *Critical Inquiry* 4 (1978) and 6 (1979–80).

3. Given the importance of this task, I am obviously not the first to have tackled it. Two of the most significant attempts to explain and justify a limited hermeneutic pluralism are Paul Ricoeur, *The Conflict of Interpretations*, edited by Don Ihde (Evanston, Ill.: Northwestern University Press, 1974), and Wayne Booth, *Critical Understanding: The Powers and Limits of Pluralism* (Chicago: University of Chicago Press, 1979). I explain later in this chapter how my theory is related to their views.

4. Leo Spitzer, *Linguistics and Literary History* (Princeton: Princeton University Press, 1948), pp. 7, 19.

5. Wolfgang Iser, "The Reading Process: A Phenomenological Approach," in *The Implied Reader* (Baltimore: Johns Hopkins University Press, 1974), pp. 283–90. Also see Iser, *The Act of Reading* (Baltimore: Johns Hopkins University Press, 1978), pp. 118–34.

6. Martin Heidegger, *Being and Time*, translated by John Macquarrie and Edward Robinson (New York: Harper and Row, 1962), pp. 188–95.

7. Although Heidegger's distinction between "interpretation" and "understanding" is important for my point here, it is not necessary for my argument throughout the rest of this book to maintain this distinction. For the sake of stylistic variation, I often use interchangeably terms like "interpretation," "understanding," "reading," and "construing" as long as the issue I am concerned with does not require attention to possible differences between them. When such distinctions are important to my point (as in chapter 4, where I argue that the experience of reading a metaphor can change our habits of construing the world), the context of the argument will make this clear. My justification for substituting these terms for each other is that the same epistemological structure characterizes the different aspects of understanding—from reading a text to perceiving an

object, from writing history to experimenting with scientific hypotheses. All entail projections of belief according to the dynamics of the hermeneutic circle. The differences among them have to do not with essential epistemological structures but with the particular ways in which assumptions and beliefs are deployed.

8. Rudolf Karl Bultmann, "The Problem of Hermeneutics," in *Essays Philosophical and Theological*, translated by James C. G. Greig (New York: Macmillan, 1955), p. 239; translation modified. There is an extensive literature on the role of presuppositions in interpretation. Any list of the most interesting examples would have to include—in addition to Heidegger, Bultmann, and Ricoeur—R. G. Collingwood's notion of "the logic of question and answer" in his *Autobiography* (Oxford: Oxford University Press, 1939); Hans-Georg Gadamer's defense of "prejudice" in *Truth and Method*, translated by Garrett Barden and John Cumming (New York: Seabury Press, 1975); and Thomas S. Kuhn's concept of "paradigms" in *The Structure of Scientific Revolutions*, rev. ed. (Chicago: University of Chicago Press, 1970).

9. Gerald Graff describes the New Criticism, for example, as the purveyor of "modernist assumptions about language, knowledge, and experience" (*Literature against Itself* [Chicago: University of Chicago Press, 1979], p. 5). Also see his *Poetic Statement and Critical Dogma* (Evanston, Ill.: Northwestern University Press, 1970), and Frank Lentricchia, *After the New Criticism* (Chicago: University of Chicago Press, 1980).

10. Cleanth Brooks, *The Well Wrought Urn* (New York: Harcourt, Brace, and World, 1947), p. 1.

11. T. S. Eliot, "The Metaphysical Poets" (1921), in *Selected Prose of T. S. Eliot*, edited by Frank Kermode (London: Faber and Faber, 1975), p. 61.

12. Heidegger makes a similar point in *Being and Time*, pp. 191–92.

13. My use of the terms "blindness" and "insight" may call to mind Paul de Man's well-known *Blindness and Insight*, but he and I define them somewhat differently. His argument is not that every hermeneutic insight comes at the price of a specific mode of blindness but that "critics' moments of greatest blindness with regard to their own critical assumptions are also the moments at which they achieve their greatest insight" (*Blindness and Insight* [New York: Oxford University Press, 1971], p. 109). From my point of view, these are moments of special interest and importance because in them the interpreter unwittingly criticizes his or her presuppositions by seeking to transcend their limits—even while reaffirming allegiance to them and acknowledging their necessity by refusing to recognize that they are in any way deficient.

14. Paul Ricoeur, "Existence and Hermeneutics," in *The Conflict of*

Interpretations, edited by Don Ihde (Evanston, Ill.: Northwestern University Press, 1974), pp. 21–22.

15. This paragraph refers to Claude Lévi-Strauss, "The Structural Study of Myth," in *Structural Anthropology,* translated by Claire Jacobson and Brooke Grundfest Schoepf (Garden City, N.Y.: Anchor, 1967), pp. 210–13, and to Karl Marx, "Introduction to a Critique of Political Economy," in *The German Ideology,* edited by C. J. Arthur (New York: International Publishers, 1970), pp. 149–51.

16. Ricoeur, "Existence and Hermeneutics," p. 14. Also see Ricoeur's monumental critique of psychoanalysis, *Freud and Philosophy,* translated by Denis Savage (New Haven: Yale University Press, 1970).

17. Ricoeur, "Existence and Hermeneutics," pp. 15, 19, 23, 24. For a study of Ricoeur's project, see Don Ihde, *Hermeneutic Phenomenology: The Philosophy of Paul Ricoeur* (Evanston, Ill.: Northwestern University Press, 1971).

18. Maurice Merleau-Ponty, *Phenomenology of Perception,* translated by Colin Smith (London: Routledge and Kegan Paul, 1962), p. xix.

19. John Reichert, "But That Was in Another Ballpark: A Reply to Stanley Fish," *Critical Inquiry* 6 (1979): 166.

20. The terms "heteronomous" and "concretization" derive from Roman Ingarden, *The Literary Work of Art,* translated by George G. Grabowicz (1931; reprint, Evanston, Ill.: Northwestern University Press, 1973); see particularly pp. 336–43. Here and in the next paragraph, my assertions about the mode of existence of the literary work are necessarily brief. For the moment, my purpose is only to suggest the counterarguments that can be made to the typical, seemingly conclusive appeal to the identity of the text as a constraint on interpretation. The next chapter offers a more detailed analysis of the work's ontology as implied by a pluralistic epistemology.

21. Wayne Booth, "The Limits of Pluralism," *Critical Inquiry* 3 (1977): 412–13; Booth's italics. Also see his discussion of "common knowledge" and his distinction between "understanding" and "overstanding" in *Critical Understanding,* particularly pp. 241–50.

22. A good account of this problem can be found in Mary Louise Pratt's incisive refutation of the distinction between "ordinary" and "literary" language; see her *Toward a Speech-Act Theory of Literary Discourse* (Bloomington: Indiana University Press, 1977), particularly pp. 3–78. Also see John Ellis's discussion of the impossibility of achieving a single, universal definition of literature in *The Theory of Literary Criticism: A Logical Analysis* (Berkeley: University of California Press, 1974), particularly pp. 24–53. I explore this issue more fully in chapter 6.

23. The classic formulation of the general claims of pluralism is William James, *A Pluralistic Universe* (1909; reprint, Cambridge, Mass.: Harvard University Press, 1977). An important defense of a pluralistic epistemology is Stephen C. Pepper, *World Hypotheses: A Study in Evidence* (Berkeley: University of California Press, 1942). Even though individual scientific fields are frequently characterized by a high degree of consensus, they are not always so, and it is not clear that the natural sciences can all be unified or translated into each other's terms. Chapter 3 examines in detail the argument that different scientific disciplines may not be mutually transparent and that, consequently, the natural sciences as a whole may be pluralistic rather than monistic.

24. Stephen Toulmin, *Human Understanding: The Collective Use and Evolution of Concepts* (Princeton: Princeton University Press, 1972), pp. 133–99. Literary criticism would not qualify as a "discipline," however, according to Toulmin's definition. With an atypical and unfortunate lapse into monism, he reserves this term for fields in which all (or by far most) of the investigators are committed to a single explanatory goal and to a common agenda of problems which must be overcome to attain the ideal state of knowledge.

25. Hirsch, *Validity in Interpretation*, p. 227.

26. Stanley Fish, "A Reply to John Reichert; or, How to Stop Worrying and Learn to Love Interpretation," *Critical Inquiry* 6 (1979): 178.

27. Joseph Conrad, *Lord Jim*, edited by Thomas C. Moser (1900; reprint, New York: W. W. Norton, 1968), p. ix.

28. "The Fixation of Belief," in *Collected Papers of Charles Sanders Peirce*, edited by Charles Hartshorne and Paul Weiss (1934; reprint, Cambridge, Mass.: Harvard University Press, 1965), 5:235.

29. Hans Robert Jauss, *Ästhetische Erfahrung und literarische Hermeneutik* (Munich: Wilhelm Fink, 1977), 1:50–51. In chapter 7 I explore further the uses and dangers of power in interpretation.

30. Spitzer, *Linguistics and Literary History*, p. 38. For a penetrating critique of the value of consensus, see Jean-François Lyotard, *The Postmodern Condition: A Report on Knowledge* (Minneapolis: University of Minnesota Press, 1984), especially pp. xxv, 61–67. Also see Paul Feyerabend, *Against Method* (London: Verso, 1978).

31. William James, *The Will to Believe* (1897; reprint, Cambridge, Mass.: Harvard University Press, 1979), p. 32.

32. Peirce, "The Fixation of Belief," pp. 235, 234. The references to Peirce in the next paragraphs are also from this essay, pp. 235–39.

33. See Toulmin, *Human Understanding*, pp. 261–81. The dangers and benefits of authority have recently been the subject of considerable critical debate. On one side of the question, Gadamer argues that authority is not

always wrong. He distinguishes between the blind acceptance of authority, which "obedience to a command" typically entails, and the "recognition of superior knowledge," which, as he describes it, is a freely made decision and a reasonable act of deference (*Truth and Method*, p. 248). On the other side, however, Michel Foucault and Edward Said point out that the power of authority to control how we think, speak, and write is more pervasive and insidious than we ordinarily believe. Said is certainly right when he contends, in explaining Foucault, that "a text is a place among other places (including the body) where the strategies of control in society are conducted" ("The Problem of Textuality: Two Exemplary Positions," *Critical Inquiry* 4 [1978]: 704). But it is also true that he and Foucault are the beneficiaries of the sort of authority that Gadamer defends. For a further analysis of the problem of authority, see chapter 7 below.

34. E. D. Hirsch, Jr., *The Aims of Interpretation* (Chicago: University of Chicago Press, 1976), pp. 7, 90; italics deleted. Two further problems with Hirsch's defense of the author as the norm for correct interpretation should also be mentioned, even though they are tangential to the point I make in discussing this quotation. First, as Booth rightly argues, "author" is an essentially contested concept (*Critical Understanding*, p. 8). It cannot be invoked as a criterion to resolve critical disputes because it is frequently what is under dispute. Second, although Hirsch defends authorial intention as the only standard that can make literary studies a progressive discipline, the coherent and goal-oriented program of research he desires can be achieved by any group of investigators who jointly pursue the consequences of a certain set of assumptions. But because the interpretation of literature welcomes many different kinds of presuppositions, our field has a variety of competing research programs, not a single agenda of problems to be progressively solved.

35. See Roland Barthes, "The Death of the Author," in *Image/Music/Text*, translated by Stephen Heath (New York: Hill and Wang, 1977), pp. 142–48, and Michel Foucault, "What Is an Author?" in *Textual Strategies*, edited by Josué Harari (Ithaca, N.Y.: Cornell University Press, 1979), pp. 141–60.

36. Fish, "A Reply to John Reichert," p. 175. The danger that critics who disagree about fundamental principles will not hear each other's arguments gives urgency to Booth's warning against dismissing too hastily the views of others. His description of the responsibilities of "a good citizen in the republic of criticism" is an important pragmatic guide for the successful functioning of critical exchange—the ongoing debate that provides one of the bases for our field's claim to the status of a "rational enterprise" (see Booth, *Critical Understanding*, pp. 1–34, 351–52).

37. Graff, *Literature against Itself*, p. 38; Graff's italics. In his more recent

work, Graff accepts the inevitability and even desirability of interpretive conflict: See his "What Should We Be Teaching—When There's No 'We'?" *Yale Journal of Criticism* 1 (1987): 189–211, and his *Professing Literature: An Institutional History* (Chicago: University of Chicago Press, 1987).

Chapter 2

1. Fish claims, for example, that "interpretation is not the art of construing but the art of constructing. Interpreters do not decode poems; they make them" (*Is There a Text in This Class?* p. 327).

2. Two classic statements of this position are Roland Barthes, *S/Z*, translated by Richard Miller (New York: Hill and Wang, 1974), especially pp. 3–16, and Foucault, "What Is an Author?"

3. For example, see René Wellek, *The Attack on Literature* (Chapel Hill: University of North Carolina Press, 1982).

4. As I mentioned earlier (see chap. 1, n. 20), I borrow the term "heteronomy" from Roman Ingarden. I give it a different application, however. He argues, for example, that a literary work is heteronomous to the creative acts of its author in that it paradoxically both depends on them for its existence and yet also outlives them. A character in a literary work is similarly heteronomous to the sentences that are its foundations: A character can be discussed, imagined, and analyzed independently of those sentences even though it would not exist without them (see Ingarden, *The Literary Work of Art*, especially pp. 95–160). Ingarden's notion of the literary work is monistic rather than pluralistic, however, inasmuch as he claims that a self-identical "artistic object" underlies the many "aesthetic objects" that readings of it produce.

This technical use of "heteronomy" to signify a paradoxical condition of simultaneous dependence and autonomy is in line with one of the standard definitions of the term but not with another. The *OED* defines "heteronomous" as a condition of being "subject to different laws, involving different principles." A secondary definition it gives is "subject to an external law." The first definition fits Ingarden's examples inasmuch as a literary work or a fictional character can be seen as accountable to "different laws" or "principles" because their foundations are outside themselves even as they are also to a considerable degree self-contained entities. The second definition is less appropriate, however. Texts or characters are "subject to an external law" in the sense that they depend on various authorial acts or sentences that establish them, but they are also a "law" unto themselves in the sense that they are not reducible to their founding conditions. My notion of textual heteronomy is similarly more in line with the first than with the second of these definitions. It implies the coexistence of "different principles" of explaining the relative "subjection" of an entity, inasmuch as I argue that texts depend on the varying acts of interpretation through which they exist even as they transcend any individual construal. But this degree of relative independence makes a heteronomous text not simply answerable to rules, norms, or conditions outside itself.

5. For example, see Fish, *Is There a Text in This Class?* p. 306.

6. I am concerned here with the rules for reading that characterize a particular method of understanding. In the next section I will consider the argument that texts supply rules or norms to direct our interpretation. One of the best arguments for regarding rules for reading as constitutive of texts is Steven Mailloux, *Interpretive Conventions: The Reader in the Study of American Fiction* (Ithaca, N.Y.: Cornell University Press, 1982).

7. Lévi-Strauss argues, for example, that a game in which every move is predetermined is actually not a game but a ritual (*The Savage Mind* [Chicago: University of Chicago Press, 1966], pp. 30–33). My argument about games and rules is indebted to Ludwig Wittgenstein's well-known analysis in *Philosophical Investigations,* translated by G. E. M. Anscombe, 3d ed. (New York: Macmillan, 1953), pp. 31–43.

8. See Toulmin, *Human Understanding,* pp. 41–130.

9. Fish, *Is There a Text in This Class?* pp. 365, 68; Fish's italics.

10. William James, *A Pluralistic Universe,* p. 50; James's italics. Also see Peirce, "The Fixation of Belief."

11. See Collingwood, *Autobiography,* pp. 29–43. Collingwood's claim that "you cannot tell what a proposition means unless you know what question it is meant to answer" (p. 33) may be applied to literary criticism in two converse but complementary ways. On the one hand, every analysis of a literary work is an answer to questions that reflect the presuppositions, interests, and purposes of the interpreter's hermeneutic school. Just as, as Collingwood argues, "no two propositions . . . can contradict one another unless they are answers to the same question" (p. 33), so two interpretations offered by opposing methods do not necessarily refute each other if they are responses to different inquiries. The presuppositions behind them may be mutually exclusive, but the interpretations need not "contradict" each other in the sense that one must be wrong if the other is right. On the other hand, every literary work may be seen as an answer to an implicit question that the interpreter must explicate in order to make sense of the text (this is Gadamer's interpretation of Collingwood in *Truth and Method,* pp. 333–41). But conflicting hermeneutics will disagree here as well, because they assume that texts answer different kinds of questions.

12. Norman N. Holland, "Unity Identity Text Self," in *Reader-Response Criticism: From Formalism to Post-Structuralism,* edited by Jane P. Tompkins (Baltimore: Johns Hopkins University Press, 1980), p. 124.

13. Gadamer, *Truth and Method*, p. 319.

14. See my book, *The Challenge of Bewilderment*.

15. Henry James, *Partial Portraits* (1888; reprint, Ann Arbor: University of Michigan Press, 1970), pp. 227–28.

16. Merleau-Ponty, *Phenomenology of Perception*, pp. 358, 364, 359.

17. My thinking about interpretation, self-consciousness, and intersubjectivity owes much to Iser, *The Implied Reader*, pp. 290–94, and *The Act of Reading*, pp. 180–231.

18. Hirsch, *Validity in Interpretation*, p. 142.

19. The classic and still extremely influential statement of the text's autonomy is René Wellek, "The Mode of Existence of a Literary Work of Art," in *Theory of Literature*, coauthored with Austin Warren, 3d ed. (New York: Harcourt Brace Jovanovich, 1956), pp. 142–57. The preface assigns primary responsibility for this chapter to Wellek, and an early version of the chapter appeared under his name in the *Southern Review* 7 (1941–42): 735–54. He claims that the literary work "must be conceived as a structure of norms, realized only partially in the actual experience of its many readers. Every single experience (reading, reciting, and so forth) is only an attempt—more or less successful and complete—to grasp this set of norms or standards" (p. 150). For evidence that Wellek's argument continues to command authority in many quarters, see the essays, under the heading "The Newer Criticism," by O. B. Hardison, Jr., Douglas Paschall, and David H. Hirsch in the *Sewanee Review* 91 (1983): 397–425. Also see Adele Davidson's critique of my pluralistic epistemology and my response in *PMLA* 99 (1984): 242–44. When I quote Wellek in the following paragraphs, my aim is not to offer a commentary on *Theory of Literature* but to use his arguments about textual independence as an example of views shared by many.

20. Wellek, "Mode of Existence," p. 152.

21. Merleau-Ponty, *Phenomenology of Perception*, p. xix.

22. Wellek, "Mode of Existence," p. 156.

23. See Ingarden, *The Literary Work of Art*, pp. 369–72.

24. Victor Shklovsky, "Art as Technique" (1917), in *Russian Formalist Criticism: Four Essays*, translated by Lee T. Lemon and Marion J. Reis (Lincoln: University of Nebraska Press, 1965), p. 12.

25. See Mark Schorer, Introduction to *The Good Soldier: A Tale of Passion*, by Ford Madox Ford (1915; reprint, New York: Vintage, 1951), and Samuel Hynes, "The Epistemology of *The Good Soldier*," *Sewanee Review* 69 (1961): 225–35. Thomas C. Moser notes, "Careful readers of good will, in utter disagreement as to the reliability of its narrator, seem not to be discussing the same book" ("Towards *The Good Soldier*: Discovery of a Sexual Theme," *Daedalus* 92 [1963]: 312).

26. Booth, *Critical Understanding*, pp. 241, 247. He borrows these terms from Pepper, *World Hypotheses*, pp. 48–50.

27. Booth, *Critical Understanding*, pp. 243, 236.

28. Edmund Husserl, *The Phenomenology of Internal Time-Consciousness*, translated by James S. Churchill (Bloomington: Indiana University Press, 1973), pp. 52–57. Also see Merleau-Ponty's chapter titled "Temporality" in *Phenomenology of Perception*, pp. 410–33.

29. Hans Robert Jauss, *Toward an Aesthetic of Reception*, translated by Timothy Bahti (Minneapolis: University of Minnesota Press, 1982), p. 30; my italics. The original text refers to "die sukzessive Entfaltung eines *im Werke angelegten*, in seinen historischen Rezeptionsstufen aktualisierten Sinnpotentials" (Jauss, *Literaturgeschichte als Provokation* [Frankfurt: Suhrkamp, 1970], p. 186; my italics). This talk of "steps" in a sequence of "successive unfolding" further makes meaning-potential seem like a pre-given essence awaiting realization rather than an open-ended, unpredictable process.

30. Gadamer, *Truth and Method*, p. 264. I explore the historicity of understanding further in chapter 5.

31. Hirsch, *Validity in Interpretation*, p. 123. Hirsch's more recent statements suggest that he might now accept the argument I make in this paragraph. He now recognizes that literary texts are often "authored with intentions directed towards futurity. With such texts, meaning-then is not a complete account even of historical meaning intentions, since those past intentions were also directed towards the future" ("Past Intentions and Present Meanings," *Essays in Criticism* 33 [1983]: 83). Hirsch does not realize, though, how damaging this concession is. If authors can intend that the meanings of their texts vary beyond what they can foresee, then intention cannot perform the regulative function Hirsch assigns to it as a control on validity.

32. Hirsch, *Validity in Interpretation*, p. 45. Also see Hirsch, *The Aims of Interpretation*, p. 6.

33. Iser, *The Act of Reading*, pp. 59, 29; Iser's italics. Iser has recently come under attack from some quarters for arguing that the text itself "prestructures the role to be assumed by each recipient" (*The Act of Reading*, p. 34) and thus does not take on fundamentally different shapes according to the reader's interpretive schemes: See Stanley Fish, "Why No One's Afraid of Wolfgang Iser," *Diacritics* 11 (1981): 2–13, and Iser's reply, "Talk like Whales," *Diacritics* 11 (1981): 82–87. A close analysis of *The Act of Reading* suggests, however, that Iser is gradually but steadily moving away from the assumption, which he inherited from Ingarden, that "the artistic pole" (the author's text) is fixed and "the aesthetic pole" (the reader's response) is variable. The notion of an objective prestructure is called into question, for

example, by Iser's own arguments against "the classical norm of interpretation," which holds that meaning is a "thing" hidden in the text rather than an activity and an event (see pp. 3–19). Indeed, he criticizes Ingarden for "referring to a one-way incline from text to reader and not to a two-way relationship" (p. 173). Iser describes "the relation between text and reader as a kind of self-regulating system" (p. 67)—a metaphor that implies that changes at the reader's end can and will bring about transformations in the work itself. Iser seems very close to my notion of heteronomy when he argues, "Nor can the control be understood as a tangible entity occurring independently of the process of communication. Although exercised *by* the text, it is not *in* the text" (p. 168; Iser's italics).

34. Fish, *Is There a Text in This Class?* p. 173.

35. Hirsch, *Validity in Interpretation,* p. 249.

36. Ibid., p. 114. For a more extensive elaboration of this position, see Alastair Fowler, *Kinds of Literature* (Cambridge, Mass.: Harvard University Press, 1982).

Chapter 3

1. Stephen Toulmin has recently argued that "the older, absolute division between human and natural sciences has dismantled itself" ("The Construal of Reality: Criticism in Modern and Postmodern Science," *Critical Inquiry* 9 [1982]: 106). Also see the important volume edited by George Levine, *One Culture: Science and Literature* (Madison: University of Wisconsin Press, 1987). For evidence that the divide still exists, however, see Hans Eichner, "The Rise of Modern Science and the Genesis of Romanticism," *PMLA* 97 (1982): 8–30, especially p. 25, and George Slusser and George Guffey, "Literature and Science," in *Interrelations of Literature,* edited by Jean-Pierre Barricelli and Joseph Gibaldi (New York: Modern Language Association, 1982), pp. 176–204. The most influential modern description of this division was given, of course, by C. P. Snow: See "The Two Cultures and the Scientific Revolution" and "The Two Cultures: A Second Look," in *Public Affairs* (New York: Scribner's, 1971), pp. 13–79.

2. Wilhelm Dilthey, *Selected Writings,* edited and translated by H. P. Rickman (Cambridge: Cambridge University Press, 1976), pp. 262–63, 89, 228, 181, 208.

3. Francis Bacon, *Novum Organum,* edited by J. Spedling et al. (1620; reprint, New York: Hurd and Houghton, 1878), pp. 76–77. For an important recent commentary on these issues, see Richard Rorty, *Philosophy and the Mirror of Nature* (Princeton: Princeton University Press, 1979), especially pp. 284–305. I examine Rorty's theory at some length in chapter 5.

4. Isaac Newton, *Mathematical Principles of Natural Philosophy,* translated by A. Motte (1687; reprint, Berkeley: University of California Press, 1934), pp. 546–47.

5. Karl Popper, "Normal Science and Its Dangers," in *Criticism and the Growth of Knowledge,* edited by Imre Lakatos and Alan Musgrave (Cambridge: Cambridge University Press, 1970), pp. 56, 52.

6. Karl Popper, *Conjectures and Refutations* (New York: Basic Books, 1962), pp. 46–47; Popper's italics.

7. Spitzer, *Linguistics and Literary History,* pp. 28–29, 19.

8. Ibid., p. 34.

9. Popper, *Conjectures and Refutations,* pp. 36–37. Also see Karl Popper, *The Logic of Scientific Discovery* (New York: Basic Books, 1959), especially pp. 78–92, 251–81. The discussion of Marxism, psychoanalysis, and Einstein in the remainder of this paragraph is based on *Conjectures and Refutations,* pp. 35–36.

10. Barbara Von Eckardt, "The Scientific Status of Psychoanalysis," in *Introducing Psychoanalytic Theory,* edited by Sander L. Gilman (New York: Brunner/Mazel, 1982), p. 145.

11. For a clear, useful discussion of these possibilities, see the editorial commentary entitled "The Utility of Confirmation and Disconfirmation," in *On Scientific Thinking,* edited by Ryan D. Tweney, Michael E. Doherty, and Clifford R. Mynatt (New York: Columbia University Press, 1981), pp. 123–28.

12. Kuhn, *Structure of Scientific Revolutions,* p. 146.

13. Gerald Holton, "Mach, Einstein, and the Search for Reality," in *The Twentieth-Century Sciences,* edited by Holton (New York: W. W. Norton, 1972), p. 361; Holton's italics. Einstein is not displaying unusual stubbornness here. As Imre Lakatos points out, "Scientists have thick skins. They do not abandon a theory merely because facts contradict it. They normally either invent some rescue hypothesis to explain what they call a mere anomaly or, if they cannot explain the anomaly, they ignore it, and direct their attention to other problems" (*The Methodology of Scientific Research Programmes* [Cambridge: Cambridge University Press, 1978], p. 4).

14. For interesting examples of early opposition to Darwin from distinguished Victorian scientists, see the selections by Adam Sedgwick and Sir Richard Owen in the Norton Critical Edition of *Darwin,* edited by Philip Appleman (New York: W. W. Norton, 1979), pp. 220–26.

15. Popper, "Normal Science and Its Dangers," p. 55.

16. Max Planck, *A Scientific Autobiography,* translated by Frank Gaynor (New York: Philosophical Library, 1949), p. 46.

17. See Kuhn, *Structure of Scientific Revolutions,* pp. 10–11. For a critique of Kuhn's ambiguities, see Margaret Masterman, "The Nature of a

Paradigm," in *Criticism and the Growth of Knowledge,* edited by Imre Lakatos and Alan Musgrave (Cambridge: Cambridge University Press, 1970), pp. 59–89.

18. Kuhn, *Structure of Scientific Revolutions,* p. 111.

19. Ibid., p. 169. Kuhn compares a paradigm shift to a "conversion" or a gestalt switch on pp. 111–35 and 150–52.

20. Larry Laudan, *Progress and Its Problems* (Berkeley: University of California Press, 1977), p. 53.

21. Popper, "Normal Science and Its Dangers," p. 56.

22. Kuhn, *Structure of Scientific Revolutions,* pp. 155–59.

23. See Paul Ricoeur, "Structure, Word, Event," and "Creativity in Language," in *The Philosophy of Paul Ricoeur,* edited by Charles E. Reagan and David Stewart (Boston: Beacon, 1978), pp. 109–33.

24. Popper, "Normal Science and Its Dangers," p. 56.

25. Thomas S. Kuhn, "Reflections on My Critics," in *Criticism and the Growth of Knowledge,* edited by Imre Lakatos and Alan Musgrave (Cambridge: Cambridge University Press, 1970), pp. 266, 268. Of the many philosophers of language who have made similar arguments, see especially Ernst Cassirer, *Language and Myth,* translated by Susanne Langer (New York: Dover, 1953); Nelson Goodman, *Ways of Worldmaking* (Indianapolis: Hackett, 1978); and Benjamin Lee Whorf, *Language, Thought, and Reality,* edited by John B. Carroll (New York: John Wiley, 1956).

26. See Kenneth Burke, "Terministic Screens," in *Language as Symbolic Action* (Berkeley: University of California Press, 1966), pp. 44–62. The next chapter explores in a more general way the relation between understanding and figuration.

27. "For the chemist the atom of helium was a molecule because it behaved like one with respect to the kinetic theory of gases. For the physicist, on the other hand, the helium atom was not a molecule because it displayed no molecular spectrum" (Kuhn, *Structure of Scientific Revolutions,* p. 50).

28. Rorty, *Mirror,* pp. 348–49.

29. Toulmin argues similarly that "the displacement of one system of concepts by another is itself something that happens for perfectly good reasons, even though these particular 'reasons' cannot themselves be formalized into still broader concepts, or still more general axioms" ("Does the Distinction between Normal and Revolutionary Science Hold Water?" in *Criticism and the Growth of Knowledge,* edited by Imre Lakatos and Alan Musgrave [Cambridge: Cambridge University Press, 1970], p. 44). Also see Toulmin, *Human Understanding,* especially pp. 41–130.

30. Paul Feyerabend, "Consolations for the Specialist," in *Criticism and the Growth of Knowledge,* edited by Imre Lakatos and Alan Musgrave

(Cambridge: Cambridge University Press, 1970), p. 211. Also see Feyera-bend, *Against Method*, especially pp. 17–46.

31. Kuhn, *Structure of Scientific Revolutions*, pp. 206–7.

32. Toulmin, "Construal of Reality," p. 103.

33. Dilthey, *Selected Writings*, pp. 214, 212.

34. Paul Ricoeur, "Explanation and Understanding," in *The Philosophy of Paul Ricoeur*, edited by Charles E. Reagan and David Stewart (Boston: Beacon, 1978), p. 158.

35. Brooks, *The Well Wrought Urn*, p. 9. For similar pronouncements, see Slusser and Guffey, "Literature and Science," p. 180, and I. A. Rich-ards, "The Two Uses of Language," in *Principles of Literary Criticism* (New York: Harcourt Brace, 1947), pp. 261–71. A strict parallelism might rule out this comparison. Brooks could be accused of a category mistake in compar-ing an object of inquiry from one field (poetry, the object of literary analy-sis) to the methods of another (science, the investigation of nature). Strictly speaking, it might be argued, literary criticism is to literature as science is to nature. This ratio is a little too neat, though, inasmuch as literature (like science) is a way of knowing the world. Even if we were to maintain strict parallels, however, Brooks's argument deserves to be taken seriously be-cause any method carries with it a host of assumptions about its object. The linguistic practices of a literary method will vary according to its assump-tions about the language of poetry, just as the linguistic practices of science will depend on its presuppositions about what nature is and how best to approach it. We should consequently ask whether, as Brooks claims, a great linguistic divide separates the literary and scientific worlds—or whether both employ similar features of language for different purposes.

36. See Paul Ricoeur, *The Rule of Metaphor*, translated by Robert Czerny (Toronto: University of Toronto Press, 1975). Also see Ricoeur, "Metaphor and the Main Problem of Hermeneutics," *New Literary History* 6 (1974): 95–110. My concern here is with the role of metaphor in poetic and scientific language; chapter 4 offers a more general analysis of how meta-phor can create and multiply meaning.

37. See Eichner, "Rise of Modern Science," especially pp. 15–17. Eich-ner points out the metaphors that control mechanistic science, but, curi-ously, he still maintains that scientific truth is ahistorical and purely refer-ential (pp. 21–25).

38. Howard E. Gruber, "Darwin's 'Tree of Nature' and Other Images of Wide Scope," in *On Aesthetics in Science*, edited by Judith Wechsler (Cambridge, Mass.: MIT Press, 1978), pp. 121–40. For other discussions of the role of metaphor in science, see Arthur I. Miller, "Visualization Lost and Regained: The Genesis of the Quantum Theory in the Period 1913–27," in *On Aesthetics in Science*, edited by Judith Wechsler (Cambridge,

Mass.: MIT Press, 1978), pp. 73–102; Mary B. Hesse, *Models and Analogies in Science* (South Bend, Ind.: University of Notre Dame Press, 1966); and Max Black, *Models and Metaphors* (Ithaca, N.Y.: Cornell University Press, 1962). On the general issue of reference and representation in literary and scientific language, see E. Fred Carlisle, "Literature, Science, and Language: A Study of Similarity and Difference," *Pre/Text* 1, nos. 1–2 (Spring–Fall 1980): 39–72.

39. For a particularly illuminating analysis of the relations between Newton's notion of logic and seventeenth-century assumptions about order, see M. M. Slaughter, *Universal Languages and Scientific Taxonomy in the Seventeenth Century* (Cambridge: Cambridge University Press, 1982), pp. 1–11. Also see Robert M. Markley, "Objectivity as Ideology: Boyle, Newton, and the Languages of Science," *Genre* 16 (1983): 355–72. On the deep structural similarities governing the epistemologies of the different disciplines in a period, also see Michel Foucault, *The Order of Things* (New York: Vintage, 1973).

40. Levine, *One Culture*, p. vii.

41. Goodman, *Ways of Worldmaking*, p. 102.

Chapter 4

1. See Black, *Models and Metaphors*; Nelson Goodman, *Languages of Art*, 2d ed. (Indianapolis: Hackett Publishing Co., 1976); Ricoeur, *Rule of Metaphor*. These are the central texts of interaction theory, and subsequent references to them will be given parenthetically.

2. An influential theory of metaphor as substitution is Roman Jakobson, "Two Aspects of Language and Two Types of Aphasic Disturbances," in Jakobson, *Selected Writings* (The Hague: Mouton, 1971), 2:239–59.

3. Mark Johnson, "Introduction: Metaphor in the Philosophical Tradition," in *Philosophical Perspectives on Metaphor*, edited by Johnson (Minneapolis: University of Minnesota Press, 1981), p. 33.

4. This is the first of seven examples that Black lists in his classic essay, "Metaphor," in *Models and Metaphors*, p. 26. However, the analysis of it, which follows, is my own. The workings of metaphor are essentially the same in all the realms of language—everyday discourse (as in this case), science, and literature. During the course of my argument, I will consider examples from each of these areas.

5. For a short history of the decorative view of metaphor, see Terence Hawkes, *Metaphor* (London: Methuen, 1972), pp. 24–33.

6. For example, see Jan Mukarovsky, "Standard Language and Poetic Language," in *A Prague School Reader*, translated by Paul L. Garvin (Wash-

ington, D.C.: Georgetown University Press, 1964), pp. 17–30. Also see Ricoeur's discussion of deviation theories in *Rule of Metaphor*, pp. 134–57.

7. Black recognizes this problem and amends his theory accordingly: "Metaphors can be supported by specially constructed systems of implications, as well as by accepted commonplaces; they can be made to measure and need not be reach-me-downs" (*Models and Metaphors*, p. 43). This does not explain, though, how the relevant "system of implications" is constructed; it only concedes that "commonplaces" cannot account for truly novel metaphors. Ricoeur makes a similar objection in *Rule of Metaphor*, p. 88.

8. I. A. Richards, *The Philosophy of Rhetoric* (London: Oxford University Press, 1936), pp. 93, 97.

9. Friedrich Nietzsche, "Über Wahrheit und Lüge im aussermoralischen Sinn," in *Werke in Drei Bänden*, edited by Karl Schlechta (Munich: Hanser, 1977), 3:313. Also see Paul de Man's discussion of this phrase in "The Epistemology of Metaphor," in *On Metaphor*, edited by Sheldon Sacks (Chicago: University of Chicago Press, 1979), pp. 20–21.

10. Emile Benveniste, *Problems in General Linguistics*, translated by Mary Elizabeth Meek (Coral Gables, Fla.: University of Miami Press, 1971), p. 105.

11. This hermeneutic description of the reading process is an extrapolation of Wolfgang Iser's argument that we read by "building consistency"; see Iser, *The Act of Reading*, especially pp. 16–18 and 118–34. My model of reading extends Iser's by emphasizing the relation between the process of construing a text and the circularity of understanding in general.

12. William Wordsworth, "Ode: Intimations of Immortality from Recollections of Early Childhood" (1807), in *An Oxford Anthology of English Poetry*, edited by Howard E. Lowry and Willard Thorp (Great Neck, N.Y.: Granger Book Co., 1979), 1:651.

13. For example, see Ted Cohen, "Metaphor and the Cultivation of Intimacy," in *On Metaphor*, edited by Sheldon Sacks (Chicago: University of Chicago Press, 1979), p. 9; Ricoeur, "Metaphor and the Main Problem of Hermeneutics," p. 104.

14. See Heidegger, *Being and Time*, pp. 188–95.

15. Hans Robert Jauss makes a similar point in *Toward an Aesthetic of Reception*, pp. 25–26.

16. Heidegger, *Being and Time*, pp. 189–93. On metaphor as a process of "seeing as," see Ricoeur, *Rule of Metaphor*, pp. 213–14.

17. Wayne Booth, "Metaphor as Rhetoric: The Problem of Evaluation," in *On Metaphor*, edited by Sheldon Sacks (Chicago: University of Chicago Press, 1979), p. 69.

18. M. M. Bakhtin, *The Dialogic Imagination*, edited by Michael Hol-

quist, translated by Caryl Emerson (Austin: University of Texas Press, 1981), p. 12.

19. Ezra Pound, "In a Station of the Metro" (1916), in *Personae: The Collected Shorter Works of Ezra Pound* (1926; reprint, New York: New Directions, 1971), p. 109.

20. William Wordsworth, "Composed upon Westminster Bridge, September 3, 1802," in *An Oxford Anthology of English Poetry,* edited by Howard E. Lowry and Willard Thorp (Great Neck, N.Y.: Granger Book Co., 1979), 1:645.

21. On the role of metaphor in everyday understanding, see George Lakoff and Mark Johnson, *Metaphors We Live By* (Chicago: University of Chicago Press, 1980). For a classic demystification of the naturalization of the figures through which everyday life presents itself to us, see Roland Barthes, *Mythologies,* translated by Annette Lavers (New York: Hill and Wang, 1972).

22. On the ruling of metaphors of the Newtonian worldview, see Eichner, "Rise of Modern Science," pp. 9–12. On the figurative bases of Einsteinian science, see N. Katherine Hayles, *The Cosmic Web* (Ithaca, N.Y.: Cornell University Press, 1985); Hayles corrects Eichner's erroneous belief that the metaphors of classical mechanism are absolutely true. Also see Hesse, *Models and Analogies in Science.*

23. Hazard Adams, *Philosophy of the Literary Symbolic* (Tallahassee: Florida State University Press, 1983), p. 379.

24. Lyotard, *The Postmodern Condition,* pp. xxv, 63.

25. Lakoff and Johnson, *Metaphors We Live By,* p. 157. On the political implications of metaphor, see David Edge, "Technological Metaphor and Social Control," *New Literary History* 6 (1974): 135–47.

Chapter 5

1. See Martha Woodmansee, "The Genius and the Copyright: Economic and Legal Conditions of the Emergence of the 'Author,'" *Eighteenth-Century Studies* 17 (1984): 425–48.

2. See Steven Mailloux, "Rhetorical Hermeneutics," *Critical Inquiry* 11 (1985): 620–41. There are similar implications in Stanley Fish's turn from epistemological to sociological questions: Compare *Is There a Text in This Class?* and "Anti-Professionalism," *New Literary History* 17 (1985): 89–108. Another sign of contemporary interest in the relation between institutions, discourse, and knowledge is the widespread influence of Michel Foucault: See Hubert L. Dreyfus and Paul Rabinow, *Michel Foucault: Beyond Structuralism and Hermeneutics* (Berkeley: University of California Press, 1983).

One of the most impressive applications of Foucault's theory of power to literary history is Stephen Greenblatt, *Renaissance Self-Fashioning: From More to Shakespeare* (Chicago: University of Chicago Press, 1980). For a useful analysis and critique of the assumptions of the new historical critics, see Edward Pechter, "The New Historicism and Its Discontents: Politicizing Renaissance Drama," *PMLA* 102 (1987): 292–303.

3. This is one of the implications of Steven Knapp and Walter Benn Michaels, "Against Theory," *Critical Inquiry* 8 (1982): 723–42.

4. See Paul Ricoeur, *Time and Narrative*, translated by Kathleen McLaughlin and David Pellauer (Chicago: University of Chicago Press, 1984), vol. 1.

5. See Gadamer, *Truth and Method*, and Jauss, "Literary History as a Challenge to Literary Theory," in Jauss, *Toward an Aesthetic of Reception*, pp. 3–45. Some of the so-called new historicists recognize the impossibility of the historicist's dream of unmediated, absolute knowledge of the past. For example, after calling for a "poetics of culture" that investigates "both the social presence to the world of the literary text and the social presence of the world in the literary text," Greenblatt counsels "acceptance of the impossibility of fully reconstructing and reentering the culture of the six-teenth century, of leaving behind one's own situation" (*Renaissance Self-Fashioning*, p. 5). As Pechter points out, however, "Other new historicists usually do not make such acknowledgments (and . . . Greenblatt himself frequently writes as if he has forgotten them)" ("The New Historicism," p. 298).

6. Also see my explanation, in chapter 1, of the distinction between "global" and "local" theories. For a cogent defense of defining theory broadly, see Jonathan Culler, *On Deconstruction: Theory and Criticism after Structuralism* (London: Routledge and Kegan Paul, 1983), pp. 7–12.

7. Rorty, *Mirror*, p. 6. Subsequent quotations will be given paren-thetically in the text.

8. I am contesting Dieter Freundlieb's skeptical claim that the contro-versies surrounding James's novella show questions about interpretive cor-rectness to be unanswerable and irrelevant; see Freundlieb, "Explaining Interpretation: The Case of Henry James's *The Turn of the Screw*," *Poetics Today* 5 (1984): 79–95.

9. Edmund Wilson, "The Ambiguity of Henry James" (1938; rev. 1948, 1959), in *A Casebook on Henry James's "The Turn of the Screw,"* edited by Gerald Willen, 2d ed. (New York: Thomas Y. Cromwell, 1969), pp. 117, 147; Wayne Booth, *The Rhetoric of Fiction* (Chicago: University of Chicago Press, 1961), p. 314.

10. Leon Edel, "The Point of View" (1955), in the Norton Critical Edition of Henry James, *The Turn of the Screw*, edited by Robert Kimbrough

(New York: W. W. Norton, 1966), pp. 228, 233. The Norton Critical Edition of James's *Turn of the Screw* will hereafter be cited as Norton.

11. Reviews from *The Outlook* (October 29, 1898) and *The Bookman* (November 1898) in Norton, pp. 172, 173.

12. Virginia Woolf, "Henry James's Ghost Stories" (1921), in Norton, p. 179.

13. See Eric Solomon, "The Return of the Screw" (1964), in Norton, pp. 237–45; John Carlos Rowe, *The Theoretical Dimensions of Henry James* (Madison: University of Wisconsin Press, 1984), pp. 119–46; Shoshana Felman, "Turning the Screw of Interpretation," in *Literature and Psychoanalysis: The Question of Reading: Otherwise,* edited by Felman (Baltimore: Johns Hopkins University Press, 1982), pp. 94–207.

14. Robert Heilman, "The Freudian Reading of *The Turn of the Screw,*" *Modern Language Notes* 62 (1947): 443.

15. Robert Heilman, *"The Turn of the Screw* as Poem" (1948), in Norton, pp. 215, 221.

16. Wilson, "Ambiguity of Henry James," p. 120.

17. Harold C. Goddard, "A Pre-Freudian Reading of *The Turn of the Screw"* (originally written ca. 1920; first published 1957), in Norton, p. 184.

18. Nathan Bryllion Fagin, "Another Reading of *The Turn of the Screw"* (1941), in *A Casebook on Henry James's "The Turn of the Screw,"* edited by Gerald Willen, 2d ed. (New York: Thomas Y. Cromwell, 1969), p. 157; David S. Miall, "Designed Horror: James's Vision of Evil in *The Turn of the Screw,"* *Nineteenth-Century Fiction* 39 (1984): 326.

19. A. J. A. Waldock, "Mr. Wilson and *The Turn of the Screw"* (1947), in *A Casebook on Henry James's "The Turn of the Screw,"* edited by Gerald Willen, 2d ed. (New York: Thomas Y. Cromwell, 1969), pp. 171–72.

20. See Wilson's 1948 postscript to "Ambiguity of Henry James," pp. 145–53.

21. John Silver, "A Note on the Freudian Reading of *The Turn of the Screw"* (1957), in *A Casebook on Henry James's "The Turn of the Screw,"* edited by Gerald Willen, 2d ed. (New York: Thomas Y. Cromwell, 1969), p. 243.

22. Mailloux, "Rhetorical Hermeneutics," pp. 628, 631.

23. Ibid., pp. 632, 633.

24. R. G. Collingwood, *The Idea of History* (Oxford: Oxford University Press, 1946), pp. 282, 245.

25. Hayden White, *Metahistory: The Historical Imagination in Nineteenth-Century Europe* (Baltimore: Johns Hopkins University Press, 1973), p. 13.

26. Ricoeur, *Time and Narrative* 1:xi, 31, ix.

27. W. B. Gallie, "Explanations in History and the Genetic Sciences," in *Theories of History,* edited by Patrick Gardiner (Glencoe, Ill.: Free Press,

1959), p. 395. On the role of narrative in history, also see Arthur C. Danto, *Analytical Philosophy of History* (Cambridge: Cambridge University Press, 1965), pp. 233–56.

28. Ricoeur, *Time and Narrative* 1:47.

29. Felman, "Turning the Screw," pp. 107, 112.

30. Rowe, *Theoretical Dimensions of James,* pp. 123–28, 135, 145–46.

31. See Francis X. Roellinger, "Psychical Research and *The Turn of the Screw*" (1949), in Norton, pp. 132–42, and Miall, "Designed Horror," pp. 308–22. Also see Martha Banta, *Henry James and the Occult* (Bloomington: Indiana University Press, 1972), pp. 9–36, 116–21.

32. Oscar Cargill, "*The Turn of the Screw* and Alice James" (1963), in Norton, pp. 145–65; Mark Spilka, "Turning the Freudian Screw: How Not to Do It" (1963), in Norton, pp. 245–53; Bruce Robbins, "Shooting Off James's Blanks: Theory, Politics, and *The Turn of the Screw,*" *Henry James Review* 5 (1984): 192–99.

33. Henry James, Preface to *The Turn of the Screw* (1908), in Norton, pp. 119, 118, 120, 117.

34. The notebook entry, dated "Saturday, January 12th, 1895," can be found in Norton, pp. 106–7.

35. James alludes to Benson in his preface and wrote to one of the brothers, A. C. Benson, as early as 1898 to credit their father with the tale. These references, and not the notebook entry, prompted their denials (see A. C. Benson, *Memories and Friends* [New York: G. P. Putnam's Sons, 1924], pp. 216–17, and E. F. Benson, *As We Were: A Victorian Peep Show* [London: Longmans, Green, and Co., 1930], p. 278). The publication of James's notebooks did not refute these denials but instead called attention to them and made them even more interesting.

36. See Cargill, "*The Turn of the Screw* and Alice James," pp. 148, 164–65; Roellinger, "Psychical Research," pp. 132–34.

37. Preface to "The Altar of the Dead," in Henry James, *The Art of the Novel,* edited by R. P. Blackmur (New York: Scribner's, 1934), p. 258.

38. See Knapp and Michaels, "Against Theory," pp. 725–26, 729.

39. Ibid., p. 742; Mailloux, "Rhetorical Hermeneutics," p. 637.

40. Felman, "Turning the Screw," p. 116.

41. Karl Popper, "Prediction and Prophecy in the Social Sciences," in *Theories of History,* edited by Patrick Gardiner (Glencoe, Ill.: Free Press, 1959), p. 283.

42. Collingwood, *Idea of History,* pp. 10, 228.

Chapter 6

1. My remarks about evaluation pertain to all kinds of discourse—

analytical as well as imaginative writing, critical essays as well as novels, stories, and poems. Although I later address the specific problem of defining the category "literature," the vicissitudes of judgment are identical in all realms. The processes entailed in testing and validating an evaluation are the same regardless of the object of judgment, as are the limits to the certainty such judgments can claim. Just as my arguments about interpretation are not confined to literary understanding, so my assertions about judgment and value are not limited to literary works.

2. Wellek, *Attack on Literature*, pp. 51, 17. Similar arguments are offered by Murray Krieger, *Arts on the Level: The Fall of the Elite Object* (Knoxville: University of Tennessee Press, 1981), and Roman Ingarden, *Erlebnis, Kunstwerk und Wert* (Tübingen: Max Niemeyer, 1969).

3. Terry Eagleton, *Literary Theory: An Introduction* (Minneapolis: University of Minnesota Press, 1983), p. 11. Also see Barbara Herrnstein Smith, "Contingencies of Value," *Critical Inquiry* 10 (1983): 1–35, and Jane Tompkins, *Sensational Designs: The Cultural Work of American Fiction, 1790–1860* (New York: Oxford University Press, 1985).

4. The standoff between the absolutists and the relativists helps to explain why Barbara Herrnstein Smith warns that "the obsessive debates over the cognitive substance, logical status, and 'truth-value' of aesthetic judgments are not only unresolvable" but "pointless." Nevertheless, she also observes that, "for a responsive creature, to exist is to evaluate," and "any evaluation . . . is 'cognitively substantial' in the sense of being potentially informative about *something*" ("Contingencies," pp. 22, 19, 20). Someone else's evaluations matter to us both because they tell us about him or her and because they tell us about entities and states of affairs (including texts of all kinds) with which we also have to deal.

5. On this point in general and the example of *Madame Bovary* in particular, see Jauss, "Literary History as a Challenge to Literary Theory," especially pp. 25–36.

6. Yvor Winters, "Preliminary Problems," from *The Anatomy of Nonsense* (1943), collected in *In Defense of Reason* (Denver: University of Denver Press, 1947), pp. 361, 371.

7. See Popper, *Conjectures and Refutations*, pp. 35–37, and *The Logic of Scientific Discovery*, pp. 78–92, 251–81. Also see my critique of Popper's theory of "falsification" in chapter 3.

8. For a similar argument, see E. D. Hirsch, Jr., "Privileged Criteria in Literary Evaluation," in *Problems of Literary Evaluation*, edited by Joseph Strelka (University Park: Pennsylvania State University Press, 1969), pp. 22–34.

9. Ingarden argues, for example, that an artistic value is "something which appears in the work of art itself" and "has the basis of its existence in

the qualities" of the work (*Erlebnis, Kunstwerk und Wert*, pp. 164, 163; my translation). The positions that I criticize in this paragraph are articulated by Ingarden in especially rigorous and interesting form, although they are shared by many other absolutists (the admiration of Wellek for Ingarden, for example, is well known).

10. On both of these points, see Ingarden, *Erlebnis, Kunstwerk und Wert*, pp. 11–12, 167–68.

11. This is the reason why the attempt of stylistics to determine objectively the "marked" and "unmarked" features of a poem's language is doomed to failure. On the issues involved here, see the well-known debate between Roman Jakobson and Michael Riffaterre about poetic structure: Roman Jakobson, "Linguistics and Poetics," and Jakobson and Claude Lévi-Strauss, "Charles Baudelaire's '*Les Chats,*'" both in *The Structuralists from Marx to Lévi-Strauss*, edited by Richard T. and Fernande M. DeGeorge (Garden City, N.Y.: Doubleday, 1972), pp. 85–122, 124–46, and Michael Riffaterre, "Describing Poetic Structures: Two Approaches to Baudelaire's '*Les Chats,*'" in *Structuralism*, edited by Jacques Ehrmann (Garden City, N.Y.: Anchor, 1970), pp. 188–230. Also see Stanley Fish, "What Is Stylistics and Why Are They Saying Such Terrible Things About It?" in Fish, *Is There a Text in This Class?* pp. 68–96.

12. Krieger, *Arts on the Level,* p. 13.

13. Wellek, *Attack on Literature,* pp. 61, 31. Also see Ingarden, *Erlebnis, Kunstwerk und Wert,* p. 6.

14. Smith, "Contingencies," p. 11. Subsequent references will be given parenthetically in the text. Also see Barbara Herrnstein Smith, "Fixed Marks and Variable Constancies: A Parable of Literary Value," *Poetics Today* 1 (1979): 7–31, and Smith, "Value without Truth-Value" (paper delivered at symposium, Representation and Value: Literature, Philosophy, Science, Georgia Institute of Technology, February 21, 1986).

15. The classic discussion of these terms is the famous chapter "Commodities" in Karl Marx, *Capital*, translated by Samuel Moore and Edward Aveling (New York: International Publishers, 1967), 1:35–83. Also see Smith, "Contingencies," pp. 11–12. Smith acknowledges in places that value is heteronomous rather than radically contingent. She concedes, for example, that "the value of a work—that is, its effectiveness in performing desired/able functions for some set of subjects—is not independent of authorial design, labor, and skill" (pp. 26–27). She notes too that "entities also produce the needs and interests they satisfy and evoke the purposes they implement" (p. 13), as they could not do unless their value were somehow quasi-independent and not radically contingent. My desire is not to quibble with Smith's extremely important contribution to the theory of value but to show that a heteronomous notion of value is implicit in the

very metaphor of economy and to suggest that this makes value a more complicated, paradoxical state of affairs than the concept of contingency alone can explain.

16. Tompkins, *Sensational Designs,* p. 192.

17. Smith, "Contingencies," pp. 28–29.

18. Tompkins, *Sensational Designs,* p. 126. Subsequent references will be given parenthetically in the text.

19. An excellent example of this process is Cleanth Brooks, *The Well Wrought Urn.* His reconfiguration of the canon according to New Critical categories is most interesting when the texts he treats are most resistant to his readings, and his argument is constructed in a way that recognizes that these interpretations are therefore also the most persuasive evidence of the efficacy of the new assumptions about poetry he is proposing. In order to prove that poetry works by paradox and indirectness, he first deals not with his favorite, Donne, but with Wordsworth—a harder and therefore (he hopes) more convincing test of his assumptions because the romantic emphasis on expressive subjectivity would seem the antithesis of the detached, ironical play with oppositions he prefers (see pp. 3–10). Wordsworth's meaning and value are malleable because he can be read as a poet of ironic contradictions (as Brooks masterfully shows), but romantic poetry is a test for Brooks only because it offers an otherness that resists him. Also see the chapters on Keats and Tennyson in *The Well Wrought Urn,* pp. 151–77. On Brooks's reformulation of the canon, see Krieger, *Arts on the Level,* pp. 37–40.

20. Wellek, *Attack on Literature,* pp. 62, 82, 63. A useful sample of approaches to the problem of defining literature can be found in *What Is Literature?* edited by Paul Hernadi (Bloomington: Indiana University Press, 1978).

21. Eagleton, *Literary Theory,* pp. 9, 10, 11.

22. Ludwig Wittgenstein, *Culture and Value,* edited by G. H. von Wright and translated by Peter Winch (Chicago: University of Chicago Press, 1984), p. 82.

23. Ellis, *The Theory of Literary Criticism,* pp. 36, 46.

24. Wolfgang Iser, comment in Seminar on Literary Theory, University of Konstanz, Spring 1982.

25. Krieger, *Arts on the Level,* p. 14.

26. Hans-Georg Gadamer, *The Relevance of the Beautiful,* translated by Nicholas Walker and edited by Robert Bernasconi (Cambridge: Cambridge University Press, 1986), p. 49. Also see Gadamer, *Truth and Method,* especially pp. 357–58.

27. See Jauss, "Literary History as a Challenge to Literary Theory," p. 25.

28. Frank Kermode, *The Classic: Literary Images of Permanence and Change* (Cambridge, Mass.: Harvard University Press, 1983), p. 133.

29. Brooks, *The Well Wrought Urn*, pp. x–xi.

30. Tompkins, *Sensational Designs*, pp. 126–27.

31. Richard Ohmann, "The Shaping of a Canon: U.S. Fiction, 1960–1975," *Critical Inquiry* 10 (1983): 199.

Chapter 7

1. See Fredric Jameson, *The Political Unconscious* (Ithaca, N.Y.: Cornell University Press, 1981); Terry Eagleton, *Criticism and Ideology* (1976; reprint, London: Verso, 1986); Frank Lentricchia, *Criticism and Social Change* (Chicago: University of Chicago Press, 1983); Jim Merod, *The Political Responsibility of the Critic* (Ithaca, N.Y.: Cornell University Press, 1987).

2. See Richard Ohmann, *English in America* (New York: Oxford University Press, 1976); Peter Uwe Hohendahl, *The Institution of Criticism* (Ithaca, N.Y.: Cornell University Press, 1982); Paul A. Bové, *Intellectuals in Power: A Genealogy of Critical Humanism* (New York: Columbia University Press, 1986); Peter J. Rabinowitz, *Before Reading: Narrative Conventions and the Politics of Interpretation* (Ithaca, N.Y.: Cornell University Press, 1987).

3. For example, see John Fekete, *The Critical Twilight: Explorations in the Ideology of Anglo-American Literary Theory from Eliot to McLuhan* (London: Routledge and Kegan Paul, 1977). Two interesting skeptical analyses of this kind of inquiry are Gerald Graff, "The Pseudo-Politics of Interpretation," in *The Politics of Interpretation*, edited by W. J. T. Mitchell (Chicago: University of Chicago Press, 1983), pp. 145–58, and Oscar Kenshur, "Demystifying the Demystifiers: Metaphysical Snares of Ideological Criticism," *Critical Inquiry* 14 (1988): 335–53.

4. Michel Foucault, *Power/Knowledge,* edited by Colin Gordon (New York: Pantheon, 1980), p. 52.

5. See Sartre, *What Is Literature?* and Iser, *The Act of Reading.* Also see Roman Ingarden, *The Cognition of the Literary Work,* translated by Ruth Ann Crowley and Kenneth R. Olson (1937; reprint, Evanston, Ill.: Northwestern University Press, 1973).

6. On the contradictory attitudes required by convictions, see Peirce, "The Fixation of Belief." I am arguing against Walter Benn Michaels's dangerous notion that belief is necessarily dogmatic. "The whole point of being convinced is that we cannot help believing whatever it is we are convinced of," he argues; it is consequently erroneous to think we can "freely choose" beliefs, for we are their captives ("Is There a Politics of Interpretation?" in *The Politics of Interpretation*, edited by W. J. T. Mitchell

[Chicago: University of Chicago Press, 1983], p. 336). To believe—even to be strongly convinced about something—is, however, *not* to know for certain. Otherwise, one would not have to settle for simply believing. Because an absence of certainty is inherent in the structure of convictions, belief is (or should be) always doubled by a greater or lesser degree of doubt. Dogmatic conviction is self-deceptive because it has forgotten the necessary doubleness of belief and has translated a guess or an assumption into a certainty. The inability to know something with certainty is what makes it possible and even necessary to choose one or another set of beliefs about it. Belief does not exclude choice; quite to the contrary, it requires it. For similar arguments, see William James, *The Will to Believe* (1897; reprint, New York: Dover, 1956), and Søren Kierkegaard, *Concluding Unscientific Postscript*, translated by David F. Swenson and Walter Lowrie (Princeton: Princeton University Press, 1968), especially pp. 169–224.

7. Of the many analyses of the paradoxical interdependence of freedom and limitation, see especially Merleau-Ponty's chapter on freedom in *Phenomenology of Perception*, pp. 434–56; Paul Ricoeur, *Freedom and Nature: The Voluntary and the Involuntary*, translated by Erazim V. Kohák (Evanston, Ill.: Northwestern University Press, 1966); Calvin O. Schrag, *Existence and Freedom: Towards an Ontology of Human Finitude* (Evanston, Ill.: Northwestern University Press, 1961).

8. A complicating factor is that a text or a mode of interpretation that is preserved continues, by virtue of its survival, to exert influence over future choices about what to value. Consequently, as Barbara Herrnstein Smith notes, "Nothing endures like endurance" ("Contingencies," p. 29). Over longer and longer periods of time, however, the originating authority preserved in this process is less and less directly in control over how it is valued and transmitted—hence Smith's argument that a work's adaptability to new purposes, desires, and interests aids its chances of preservation (see pp. 27–28). This need to be adaptable to unforeseeable, not entirely controllable changes supports my point that an originating authority cannot completely determine its own historical destiny.

9. Foucault, *Power/Knowledge*, p. 131.

10. Bové, *Intellectuals in Power*, p. 77.

11. This paradox is a version of what Ricoeur calls "the paradox of the servile will." Only because we are free can we be bound, he argues, just as we can be free only if we are bound—that is, freedom is what makes it possible for us to consent to various constraints, which in turn are necessary if we are to engage and actualize specific possibilities (see Ricoeur, *The Symbolism of Evil*, translated by Emerson Buchanan [Boston: Beacon, 1969], pp. 151–57). Wayne Booth makes a similar point by invoking the classic distinction between "freedom from" and "freedom to": "All the

freedom from in the world will not free me *to* make an intellectual discovery or to paint a picture unless I have somehow freed myself *to* perform certain tasks. Such freedoms are gained only by those who surrender to disciplines and codes invented by others, giving up certain *freedoms from"* ("Freedom of Interpretation: Bakhtin and the Challenge of Feminist Criticism," in *The Politics of Interpretation*, edited by W. J. T. Mitchell [Chicago: University of Chicago Press, 1983], p. 53; Booth's italics).

12. Edward W. Said, "Foucault and the Imagination of Power," in *Foucault: A Critical Reader*, edited by David Couzens Hoy (Oxford: Basil Blackwell, 1986), p. 151. Also in this volume, see the very useful essays by Michael Walzer, "The Politics of Michel Foucault," pp. 51–68, and Charles Taylor, "Foucault on Freedom and Truth," pp. 69–102.

13. Although not directly concerned with the role of belief in understanding, Raymond Williams makes a similar argument about coercion and possibility: "However dominant a social system may be, the very meaning of its domination involves a limitation or selection of the activities it covers, so that by definition it cannot exhaust all social experience, which therefore always potentially contains space for alternative acts and alternative intentions which are not yet articulated as a social institution or even project" (*Politics and Letters: Interviews with "New Left Review"* [London: New Left Books, 1979], p. 252).

14. Bové, *Intellectuals in Power*, pp. 2, 24.

15. Said, "Foucault and the Imagination of Power," p. 154.

16. Mary Louise Pratt, "Interpretive Strategies/Strategic Interpretations: On Anglo-American Reader-Response Criticism," in *Postmodernism and Politics*, edited by Jonathan Arac (Minneapolis: University of Minnesota Press, 1986), p. 52.

17. Another name for naturalized beliefs and habits of understanding is "ideology." Gayatri Chakravorty Spivak defines "ideology," for example, as "what a group takes to be natural and self-evident, that of which the group, as a group, must deny any historical sedimentation" ("The Politics of Interpretations," in *The Politics of Interpretation*, edited by W. J. T. Mitchell [Chicago: University of Chicago Press, 1983], p. 347).

18. Robert Scholes, *Textual Power: Literary Theory and the Teaching of English* (New Haven: Yale University Press, 1985), p. 144.

19. Katherine Cummings, "Cultural Literacy or Hegemony: A Response to E. D. Hirsch" (paper prepared for English Coalition Conference, Wye Woods, Maryland, July 1987). Also see my essay "Pluralistic Literacy," *Profession 88* (1988): 29–32.

20. Jameson, *The Political Unconscious*, p. 61.

21. The radical philosopher of science, Paul Feyerabend, defends the advantages of heterogeneity and dissent in *Against Method*. He is not,

however, sufficiently concerned about the epistemological dangers of anarchy.

22. Wayne Booth, " 'Preserving the Exemplar': or, How Not to Dig Our Own Graves," *Critical Inquiry* 3 (1977): 423.

23. The importance of making imaginative leaps if one is to appreciate fully the opposition's standpoint lies behind a maxim that Peter Elbow proposes: "You may not reject a reading till you have succeeded in believing it" (*Embracing Contraries: Explorations in Learning and Teaching* [New York: Oxford University Press, 1986], p. 261).

24. W. J. T. Mitchell, Introduction to *The Politics of Interpretation*, edited by Mitchell (Chicago: University of Chicago Press, 1983), p. 3.

25. Ohmann, *English in America*, p. 88.

26. Graff, *Professing Literature*, p. 250. Also see Gary F. Waller, "A Powerful Silence: 'Theory' in the English Major," *ADE Bulletin*, no. 85 (1986): 31–35.

27. For practical suggestions about how to implement such curricula in language-arts instruction from elementary school through college, see the report of the English Coalition Conference (Wye Woods, Maryland, July 1987), entitled *The English Coalition Conference: Democracy through Language*, edited by Richard Lloyd-Jones and Andrea Lunsford (Urbana, Ill.: National Council of Teachers of English, 1989). For suggestions about how to construct a graduate curriculum on similar principles, see my essay "Replacing Coverage with Theory: Toward a Heterogeneous Field Model of Graduate Study," in *The Future of Doctoral Studies in English*, edited by Andrea Lunsford, Helene Moglen, and James Slevin (New York: Modern Language Association, 1989).

28. Graff, *Professing Literature*, p. 6.

Postscript

1. For example, see Booth, *Critical Understanding*, pp. 28–34.

2. Ibid., pp. 344–45.

3. Ellen Rooney, "Who's Left Out? A Rose by Any Other Name Is Still Red; or, the Politics of Pluralism," *Critical Inquiry* 12 (1986): 562.

Index

Absolutism, xiii, 2, 20; in science, 53, 56–57; in aesthetic judgment, 110, 113, 115–16, 124, 127, 131–32

Act of Reading, The (Iser), 6

Aesthetic attitude, 116–17

Analogy, 58–59, 64, 80–81. *See also* Metaphor

Anarchy, 146, 184 (n. 21)

Anomaly, 3, 13, 98, 138; as sign of textual otherness, 25–27, 31, 38, 42, 98–99; and interpretive conflict, 31–33; in science, 50–52; in metaphor, 69–70, 72, 74–77

Anticipatory understanding. *See* Expectations

"A priori method," 17–18

Arbitrariness, 18

Archaeological interpretation, 7–8, 53

Aristotle, 61

Art: distinguishing features of, 11, 116; different definitions of, 33–34; versus nonart, 118, 123–24

Authorial intention, 18, 39, 89, 105–7, 163 (n. 34), 167 (n. 31)

Authority, xii, 52, 113, 133–34, 140, 182 (n. 8); method of, 16–17; institutional and intellectual, 17, 143–44; dangers of, 136, 143–44, 149; uses of, 143–44, 149; contingency of, 144–45, 149

Autonomy of text, x, 20–21, 23, 30–31, 101; and interpretive conflict, 11, 31, 34, 36, 94; and historical preservation, 128–29

Bacon, Francis, 46–47

Bakhtin, M. M., 81

Being and Time (Heidegger), 3

Belief: and interpretive conflict, ix, xii–xiii, 18–19, 95–97, 103–5, 133, 151–52; and hermeneutic circle, 2–3, 12, 25–27, 139; kinds of interpretation, 4–5, 18, 148; intersubjectivity, 14, 93, 97; and validity, 16–17, 97, 100, 151–52; dogmatism, 16–18, 26–27, 139, 148–49, 181–82 (n. 6); choice of, 18–19, 78–79, 108, 142, 148, 155–57, 181–82 (n. 6); and metaphor, 78–79; role in evaluation, 111, 121; role in preservation, 129–30; and politics, 133, 137–39, 148–49. *See also* Hypotheses; Presuppositions

Benson, A. C., 177 (n. 35)

Benson, E. W. (archbishop of Canterbury), 106, 177 (n. 35)

Benveniste, Emile, 75

Bewilderment, 28, 74, 76, 112

Black, Max, 67, 70, 73, 173 (n. 7)